A012465ZN9

쿠폰사용자는 해당쿠폰을 www.vocapod.com에서 회원가입과 함께
①→② 입력 후 사용합니다.

① 쿠폰 등록(회원정보입력창, 아이디 쿠폰/포인트, 마이페이지 쿠폰내역)
② 쿠폰 사용 및 학습(구매하기 결제 신청창)

귀가 트이는

보카팟 ABC 단어장

★ ★ ★ ★ ★ ★ ★ ★ ★ ★ ★ ★ ★

BASIC 동사편

북스힐

교재의 구성과 특징

보카팟 ABC 단어장 카드 콘텐츠

① 단어

Basic 동사 520 단어를 기준으로 구성되었으며, 단어의 학습 순서는 예문에 사용된 단어 수를 기준으로 배열하였습니다.

② 영영 설명

영어 단어의 의미를 짧고 간단하게 영어로 설명하였습니다. 듣기, 말하기, 영어 문장 만드는 능력을 자연스럽게 몸에 배게 하는 학습이 가능합니다.

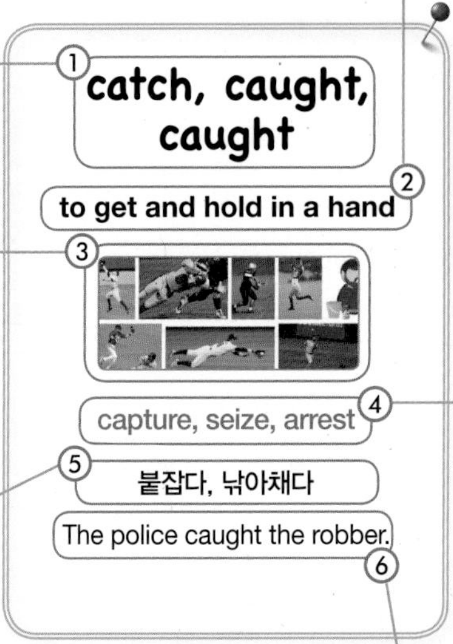

③ 이미지

여러 이미지를 동시에 보여줌으로써 소리단어의 기억 효과를 극대화하였습니다.

④ 동의어

동의어를 3개씩 함께 제시하여 1500 단어를 학습하도록 하였습니다.

⑤ 단어 뜻

우리말로 된 이미지입니다. 우리말 글자에 얽매이지 마세요.

⑥ 예문

동사 단어를 포함하는 문장으로, 짧은 문장(2개의 단어로 된 문장)에서 긴 문장(20개의 단어로 된 문장)으로 구성하였습니다.

보카팟 ABC 단어장 테스트

Test 1: Connecting Exercise

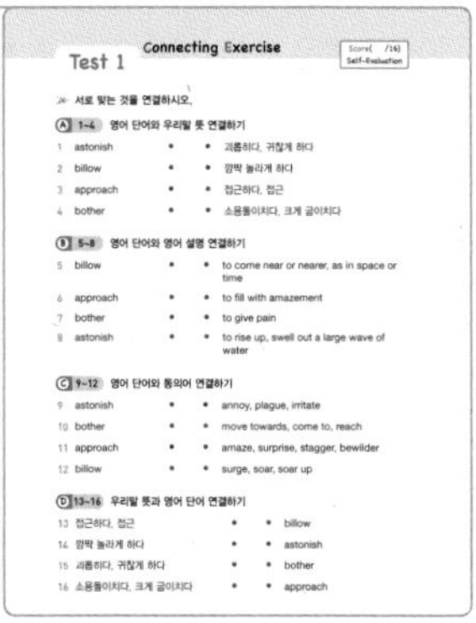
Test 1 Connecting Exercise
Score(/16) Self-Evaluation

서로 맞는 것을 연결하시오.

A 1~4 영어 단어와 우리말 뜻 연결하기

1 astonish	괴롭히다, 귀찮게 하다
2 billow	깜짝 놀라게 하다
3 approach	접근하다, 접근
4 bother	소용돌이치다, 크게 굽이치다

B 5~8 영어 단어와 영어 설명 연결하기

5 billow	to come near or nearer, as in space or time
6 approach	to fill with amazement
7 bother	to give pain
8 astonish	to rise up, swell out a large wave of water

C 9~12 영어 단어와 동의어 연결하기

9 astonish	annoy, plague, irritate
10 bother	move towards, come to, reach
11 approach	amaze, surprise, stagger, bewilder
12 billow	surge, soar, soar up

D 13~16 우리말 뜻과 영어 단어 연결하기

13 접근하다, 접근	billow
14 깜짝 놀라게 하다	astonish
15 괴롭히다, 귀찮게 하다	bother
16 소용돌이치다, 크게 굽이치다	approach

- 문제 A에서는 영어 단어와 우리말 뜻을 연결합니다.
- 문제 B에서는 영어 단어와 영어 설명을 연결합니다.
- 문제 C에서는 영어 단어와 동의어를 연결합니다.
- 문제 D에서는 우리말 뜻과 영어 단어를 연결합니다.
- 연결하기를 마친 후에는 카드 콘텐츠를 보며 스스로 점수를 평가해 봅니다.

Test 2: Writing Exercise

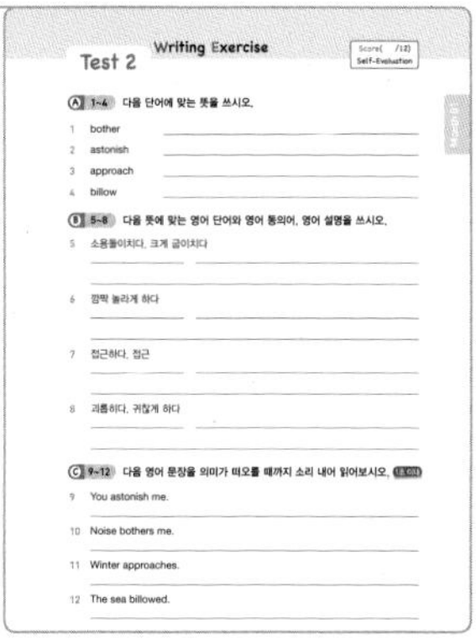
Test 2 Writing Exercise
Score(/12) Self-Evaluation

A 1~4 다음 단어에 맞는 뜻을 쓰시오.

1 bother
2 astonish
3 approach
4 billow

B 5~8 다음 뜻에 맞는 영어 단어와 영어 동의어, 영어 설명을 쓰시오.

5 소용돌이치다, 크게 굽이치다
6 깜짝 놀라게 하다
7 접근하다, 접근
8 괴롭히다, 귀찮게 하다

C 9~12 다음 영어 문장을 의미가 떠오를 때까지 소리 내어 읽어보시오.

9 You astonish me.
10 Noise bothers me.
11 Winter approaches.
12 The sea billowed.

- 문제 A에서는 영어 단어에 맞는 우리말 뜻을 적어봅니다.
- 문제 B에서는 우리말 뜻에 맞는 영어 단어와 영어 동의어, 영어 설명을 적어봅니다.
- 문제 C에서는 주어진 시간 내 주어진 문장을 읽을 수 있을 때까지 소리 내어 읽습니다. 이때 의미가 마음속에 떠올라야 합니다. 이 두 가지를 모두 할 수 있게 되었다면 소리 듣고 따라하기 학습이 제대로 된 것입니다.

Test 3: Imaging Exercise

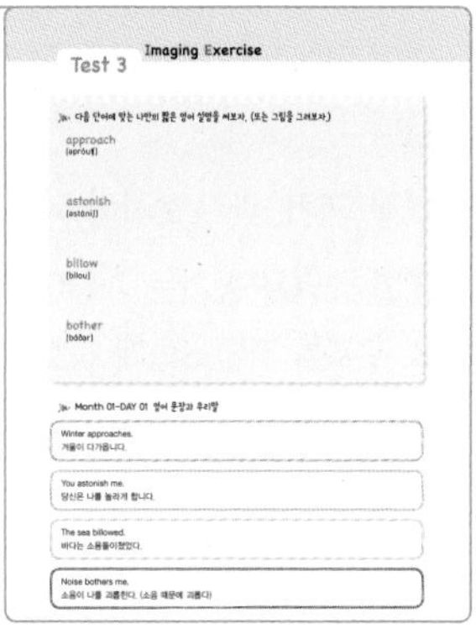
Test 3 Imaging Exercise

다음 단어에 맞는 나만의 짧은 영어 설명을 써보자. (또는 그림을 그려보자.)

approach
astonish
billow
bother

Month 01-DAY 01 영어 문장과 우리말

Winter approaches.
겨울이 다가옵니다.

You astonish me.
당신은 나를 놀라게 합니다.

The sea billowed.
바다는 소용돌이쳤었다.

Noise bothers me.
소음이 나를 괴롭힌다. (소음 때문에 괴롭다)

- 영어 단어의 이미지를 나만의 짧은 영어로 설명하여 써보거나 그림으로 표현해 보는 곳입니다. 카드 콘텐츠를 활용해도 좋고, 나만의 설명을 써봐도 좋습니다. 나만의 이미지 그림이 카드 콘텐츠의 이미지보다 훨씬 더 그 단어를 잘 표현할 수도 있습니다. Test 3의 영어 문장과 우리말 번역은 참고 용도입니다.

보카팟 ABC 단어장 학습 음원

기본학습

원어민 예문 + 우리말 예문 + 원어민 영어 단어 + 우리말 단어 + 원어민 예문 + 우리말 예문

고급학습

원어민 영어 단어 + 우리말 단어 + 원어민 영영 설명 + 원어민 동의어 + 원어민 예문 + 우리말 예문

보카팟 ABC 단어장의 **기본학습**과 **고급학습** 음원을 보카팟닷컴에서 다운로드할 수 있습니다. 또한 원어민 동영상 강의와 학습 게임으로 공부할 수 있습니다.

유튜브 채널 〈**vocapod ABC**〉에서 원어민의 단어 강의 영상을 시청학습할 수 있습니다.

보카팟 ABC 단어장 Basic 동사편

- Basic 과정은 동사편, 명사편, 꾸밈사편(동사, 명사 외편)으로 구성되었습니다.
- 영어 단어에서 동사가 가장 중요합니다. 문장에서 동사를 이해하면 문장의 반을 이해한 것과 같습니다.
- 현재, 과거, 과거 분사가 다른 불규칙 동사는 한 번에 암기할 수 있도록 함께 나열하였습니다.
- 영영 설명은 동사는 7 단어 미만으로 짧게, 명사는 동사보다 길게 설명하여, 영영 설명으로 영어의 구조를 자연스럽게 익힐 수 있습니다.

보카팟 ABC는

- **〈브레인–마우스 동기화 운동 학습 이론〉**과 **〈300시간 브레인–마우스 운동 법칙〉**으로 개발된 영어 소리 운동 학습 프로그램입니다.
- 인지과학과 IT 기술의 결합으로 개발되었으며, 〈보카팟 ABC 앱〉으로 배우고 〈보카팟 ABC 단어장〉으로 학습효과를 높일 수 있습니다.

Advanced(고급 과정)

2000 단어 + 이미지 + 동의어 5개씩 + 긴 영어 설명 + 단어가 각각 다른 뜻으로 사용되는 여러 문장

Basic 과정

2200 단어 + 이미지 + 동의어 3개씩 + 짧은 영어 설명 + 2개의 단어~20개의 단어로 만들어진 하나의 문장

Children(기초 과정)

800 단어 + 이미지 + Q & A로 된 기본 유형 550 문장

보카팟 ABC의 원리

브레인-마우스 동기화 운동

카드 콘텐츠를 통해 원어민의 음원을 들으면서 원어민의 빠르기로 소리를 냅니다. 빠르기와 정확도가 중요하므로 빠르고 정확하게 따라해야 합니다. 소리를 안 낼 때는 입만이라도 소리의 빠르기에 맞춰 움직여야 합니다. 다양한 목소리의 음원을 들으면서, 원어민의 자연스러운 빠르기를 따라 입으로 소리 내는 운동도 같이 함으로써 소리를 통해 영어를 몸에 기억시킵니다. 언어는 뇌에만 기억시켜서는 사용할 수 없습니다.

300시간 운동 법칙

언어는 뇌와 몸이 함께 하는 운동입니다. 영어를 자유롭게 말하고 못하고는 머리가 좋고 나쁘고, 열심히 공부했고 안 했고, 영어권 나라에 살았고 안 살았고의 문제가 아닙니다. 브레인–마우스 운동시간이 총 300시간을 넘었느냐 못 넘었느냐의 문제일 뿐입니다. 300시간의 브레인–마우스 운동시간을 넘기면 누구에게나 예외 없이 영어의 문이 열립니다. 보카팟 ABC 단어장으로 300시간의 브레인–마우스 운동을 시작합니다.

차례

Month 01

Month 02

Month 03

Month 04

Month 05

Month 06

Month **01** Verbs

Day 01	approach, astonish, billow, bother
Day 02	cheer, declare, erase, fail
Day 03	forgive, remember, resent, skate
Day 04	absorb, acknowledge, act, admit
Day 05	agree, amaze, applaud, beg
Day 06	blow, boil, build, carve
Day 07	change, chew, collapse, dawn
Day 08	decrease, deserve, determine, exclaim
Day 09	explore, fake, fight, frighten
Day 10	hate, hug, improve, lock
Day 11	melt, misplace, miss, pack
Day 12	pray, renew, require, sigh
Day 13	treat, accept, address, arrest
Day 14	ban, bathe, behave, bow
Day 15	breathe, bring, burn, burrow
Day 16	calculate, catch, charm, chase
Day 17	chuckle, churn, cling, comfort
Day 18	complain, conduct, confuse, connect
Day 19	consume, creep, destroy, discuss
Day 20	dive, drink, earn, enrage

➢ 음원을 들으면서 소리를 무조건 따라해 보시오. (빠르기&정확도/브레인+마우스 운동)

approach

to come near or nearer, as in space or time

move towards, come to, reach

접근하다, 접근

Winter approaches.

astonish

to fill with amazement

amaze, surprise, stagger, bewilder

깜짝 놀라게 하다

You astonish me.

billow

to rise up, swell out a large wave of water

surge, soar, soar up

소용돌이치다, 크게 굽이치다

The sea billowed.

bother

to give pain

annoy, plague, irritate

괴롭히다, 귀찮게 하다

Noise bothers me.

* 이미지는 구글에서 찾은 것으로, 단어와 이미지가 다를 수 있습니다. 'Test 3'에서 나만의 이미지를 그려볼 수 있습니다.

Test 1 Connecting Exercise

Score(/16)
Self-Evaluation

➢ 서로 맞는 것을 연결하시오.

A 1~4 영어 단어와 우리말 뜻 연결하기

1	astonish	●	● 괴롭히다, 귀찮게 하다
2	billow	●	● 깜짝 놀라게 하다
3	approach	●	● 접근하다, 접근
4	bother	●	● 소용돌이치다, 크게 굽이치다

B 5~8 영어 단어와 영어 설명 연결하기

5	billow	●	● to come near or nearer, as in space or time
6	approach	●	● to fill with amazement
7	bother	●	● to give pain
8	astonish	●	● to rise up, swell out a large wave of water

C 9~12 영어 단어와 동의어 연결하기

9	astonish	●	● annoy, plague, irritate
10	bother	●	● move towards, come to, reach
11	approach	●	● amaze, surprise, stagger, bewilder
12	billow	●	● surge, soar, soar up

D 13~16 우리말 뜻과 영어 단어 연결하기

13	접근하다, 접근	●	● billow
14	깜짝 놀라게 하다	●	● astonish
15	괴롭히다, 귀찮게 하다	●	● bother
16	소용돌이치다, 크게 굽이치다	●	● approach

Test 2 Writing Exercise

Score(/12)
Self-Evaluation

A 1~4 다음 단어에 맞는 뜻을 쓰시오.

1 bother ______

2 astonish ______

3 approach ______

4 billow ______

B 5~8 다음 뜻에 맞는 영어 단어와 영어 동의어, 영어 설명을 쓰시오.

5 소용돌이치다, 크게 굽이치다

______ ______

______

6 깜짝 놀라게 하다

______ ______

______

7 접근하다, 접근

______ ______

______

8 괴롭히다, 귀찮게 하다

______ ______

______

C 9~12 다음 영어 문장을 의미가 떠오를 때까지 소리 내어 읽어보시오. 1초 이내

9 You astonish me.

______

10 Noise bothers me.

______

11 Winter approaches.

______

12 The sea billowed.

______

Test 3 Imaging Exercise

➢ 다음 단어에 맞는 나만의 짧은 영어 설명을 써보자. (또는 그림을 그려보자.)

approach
[əpróutʃ]

astonish
[əstániʃ]

billow
[bílou]

bother
[báðər]

➢ Month 01-DAY 01 영어 문장과 우리말

Winter approaches.
겨울이 다가옵니다.

You astonish me.
당신은 나를 놀라게 합니다.

The sea billowed.
바다는 소용돌이쳤었다.

Noise bothers me.
소음이 나를 괴롭힌다. (소음 때문에 괴롭다)

DAY 02 Vocabulary

➢ **음원을 들으면서 소리를 무조건 따라해 보시오.** (빠르기&정확도/브레인+마우스 운동)

cheer

to applaud with shouts

applaud, acclaim, hurrah

환호하다, 응원

The fans cheered.

declare

to make known formally or officially

proclaim, announce

선언하다, 선포하다, 분명하게 공식적으로 알리다

War was declared.

erase

to remove (something written, for example) by rubbing or wiping

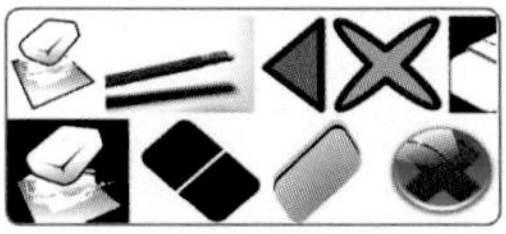

delete, eliminate, remove, eradicate

지우다

Time erases grief.

fail

to fall short of success or achievement in something expected

be unsuccessful

실패하다

The experiment failed.

* 이미지는 구글에서 찾은 것으로, 단어와 이미지가 다를 수 있습니다. 'Test 3'에서 나만의 이미지를 그려볼 수 있습니다.

Test 1 Connecting Exercise

Score(/16)
Self-Evaluation

➢ 서로 맞는 것을 연결하시오.

Ⓐ 1~4 영어 단어와 우리말 뜻 연결하기

1 fail	•	• 선언하다, 선포하다, 분명하게 공식적으로 알리다
2 cheer	•	• 환호하다, 응원
3 erase	•	• 실패하다
4 declare	•	• 지우다

Ⓑ 5~8 영어 단어와 영어 설명 연결하기

5 cheer	•	• to remove (something written, for example) by rubbing or wiping
6 declare	•	• to fall short of success or achievement in something expected
7 fail	•	• to make known formally or officially
8 erase	•	• to applaud with shouts

Ⓒ 9~12 영어 단어와 동의어 연결하기

9 cheer	•	• applaud, acclaim, hurrah
10 fail	•	• delete, eliminate, remove, eradicate
11 declare	•	• be unsuccessful
12 erase	•	• proclaim, announce

Ⓓ 13~16 우리말 뜻과 영어 단어 연결하기

13 선언하다, 선포하다, 분명하게 공식적으로 알리다	•	• fail
14 환호하다, 응원	•	• erase
15 실패하다	•	• cheer
16 지우다	•	• declare

Test 2 Writing Exercise

Score(/12)
Self-Evaluation

Month 01

A 1~4 다음 단어에 맞는 뜻을 쓰시오.

1 cheer ____________________

2 declare ____________________

3 fail ____________________

4 erase ____________________

B 5~8 다음 뜻에 맞는 영어 단어와 영어 동의어, 영어 설명을 쓰시오.

5 선언하다, 선포하다, 분명하게 공식적으로 알리다

__________ ____________________

____

6 실패하다

__________ ____________________

____

7 지우다

__________ ____________________

____

8 환호하다, 응원

__________ ____________________

____

C 9~12 다음 영어 문장을 의미가 떠오를 때까지 소리 내어 읽어보시오. 1초 이내

9 The experiment failed.

____

10 War was declared.

____

11 The fans cheered.

____

12 Time erases grief.

____

Test 3 Imaging Exercise

➢ 다음 단어에 맞는 나만의 짧은 영어 설명을 써보자. (또는 그림을 그려보자.)

cheer
[ʧiər]

declare
[dikléər]

erase
[iréis]

fail
[feil]

➢ Month 01-DAY 02 영어 문장과 우리말

The fans cheered.
팬들은 환호했습니다.

War was declared.
전쟁이 선포되었습니다.

Time erases grief.
시간이 슬픔을 지워줍니다.

The experiment failed.
실험은 실패했습니다.

DAY 03 Vocabulary

➢ 음원을 들으면서 소리를 무조건 따라해 보시오. (빠르기&정확도/브레인+마우스 운동)

forgive, forgave, forgiven

to grant pardon for, or to cease to blame against

pardon, excuse, condone

용서하다

I forgive you.

remember

to retain in the memory

memorize, not forget, keep in mind

기억하다, 기억시키다

I remember you.

resent

to feel bitter or indignant

dislike, grudge, begrudge

(싫어하거나 불쾌함으로) 분개하다, 불쾌하게 여기다

I resent that.

skate

to glide or move along on skates

ice skate, roller skate, inline skate

스케이트, 스케이트를 타다

She skates beautifully.

* 이미지는 구글에서 찾은 것으로, 단어와 이미지가 다를 수 있습니다. 'Test 3'에서 나만의 이미지를 그려볼 수 있습니다.

Test 1 Connecting Exercise

Score(　　/16)
Self-Evaluation

➢ 서로 맞는 것을 연결하시오.

Ⓐ 1~4 영어 단어와 우리말 뜻 연결하기

1	resent	• • 용서하다
2	forgive, forgave, forgiven	• • (싫어하거나 불쾌함으로) 분개하다, 불쾌하게 여기다
3	remember	• • 기억하다, 기억시키다
4	skate	• • 스케이트, 스케이트를 타다

Ⓑ 5~8 영어 단어와 영어 설명 연결하기

5	remember	• • to feel bitter or indignant
6	skate	• • to glide or move along on skates
7	forgive, forgave, forgiven	• • to retain in the memory
8	resent	• • to grant pardon for, or to cease to blame against

Ⓒ 9~12 영어 단어와 동의어 연결하기

9	skate	• • dislike, grudge, begrudge
10	resent	• • ice skate, roller skate, inline skate
11	forgive, forgave, forgiven	• • pardon, excuse, condone
12	remember	• • memorize, not forget, keep in mind

Ⓓ 13~16 우리말 뜻과 영어 단어 연결하기

13	(싫어하거나 불쾌함으로) 분개하다, 불쾌하게 여기다	• • remember
14	용서하다	• • forgive, forgave, forgiven
15	스케이트, 스케이트를 타다	• • skate
16	기억하다, 기억시키다	• • resent

Test 2 Writing Exercise

Score(　　/12)
Self-Evaluation

Ⓐ 1~4 다음 단어에 맞는 뜻을 쓰시오.

1 resent ______________________

2 forgive, forgave, forgiven ______________________

3 skate ______________________

4 remember ______________________

Ⓑ 5~8 다음 뜻에 맞는 영어 단어와 영어 동의어, 영어 설명을 쓰시오.

5 용서하다

______________ ______________________

____

6 (싫어하거나 불쾌함으로) 분개하다, 불쾌하게 여기다

______________ ______________________

____

7 스케이트, 스케이트를 타다

______________ ______________________

____

8 기억하다, 기억시키다

______________ ______________________

____

Ⓒ 9~12 다음 영어 문장을 의미가 떠오를 때까지 소리 내어 읽어보시오. 1초 이내

9 I forgive you.

____

10 She skates beautifully.

____

11 I remember you.

____

12 I resent that.

____

Test 3 Imaging Exercise

➢ 다음 단어에 맞는 나만의 짧은 영어 설명을 써보자. (또는 그림을 그려보자.)

forgive, forgave, forgiven
[fərgív, fərgéiv, fərgívən]

remember
[rimémbər]

resent
[rizént]

skate
[skeit]

➢ Month 01-DAY 03 영어 문장과 우리말

I forgive you.
내가 당신을 용서하겠습니다.

I remember you.
나는 당신을 기억하고 있습니다.

I resent that.
나는 그것에 분개합니다.

She skates beautifully.
그녀는 스케이트를 아름답게 탑니다.

Vocabulary

➢ 음원을 들으면서 소리를 무조건 따라해 보시오. (빠르기&정확도/브레인+마우스 운동)

absorb

to take something in through

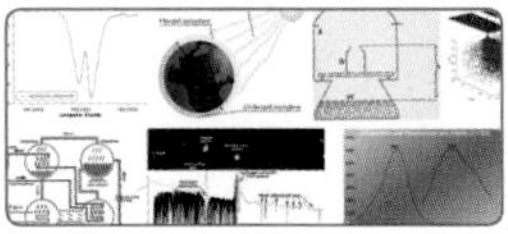

soak up, drink in, suck up

흡수하다, 빼앗다

A sponge absorbs water.

acknowledge

to recognize

admit, allow, accept

인정하다, 시인하다, 승인하다

They acknowledged their faults.

act

to carry out an action or to play the part of

do something, perform, move

행동하다, 연기하다, 행동, 행위

Don't act the fool.

admit

to permit or allow

agree, accept, acknowledge

인정하다, 시인하다, 허가하다, 승인하다

He admitted his guilt.

* 이미지는 구글에서 찾은 것으로, 단어와 이미지가 다를 수 있습니다. 'Test 3'에서 나만의 이미지를 그려볼 수 있습니다.

Test 1 Connecting Exercise

Score(　　/16)
Self-Evaluation

➢ 서로 맞는 것을 연결하시오.

Ⓐ 1~4 영어 단어와 우리말 뜻 연결하기

1 absorb •	• 흡수하다, 빼앗다
2 acknowledge •	• 인정하다, 시인하다, 승인하다
3 act •	• 인정하다, 시인하다, 허가하다, 승인하다
4 admit •	• 행동하다, 연기하다, 행동, 행위

Ⓑ 5~8 영어 단어와 영어 설명 연결하기

5 absorb •	• to permit or allow
6 act •	• to recognize
7 admit •	• to take something in through
8 acknowledge •	• to carry out an action or to play the part of

Ⓒ 9~12 영어 단어와 동의어 연결하기

9 acknowledge •	• admit, allow, accept
10 admit •	• agree, accept, acknowledge
11 absorb •	• soak up, drink in, suck up
12 act •	• do something, perform, move

Ⓓ 13~16 우리말 뜻과 영어 단어 연결하기

13 행동하다, 연기하다, 행동, 행위 •	• admit
14 흡수하다, 빼앗다 •	• act
15 인정하다, 시인하다, 허가하다, 승인하다 •	• absorb
16 인정하다, 시인하다, 승인하다 •	• acknowledge

Test 2 Writing Exercise

Score(　/12)
Self-Evaluation

A 1~4 다음 단어에 맞는 뜻을 쓰시오.

1 absorb ____________________

2 acknowledge ____________________

3 act ____________________

4 admit ____________________

B 5~8 다음 뜻에 맞는 영어 단어와 영어 동의어, 영어 설명을 쓰시오.

5 인정하다, 시인하다, 승인하다

__________ ____________________

____

6 인정하다, 시인하다, 허가하다, 승인하다

__________ ____________________

____

7 행동하다, 연기하다, 행동, 행위

__________ ____________________

____

8 흡수하다, 빼앗다

__________ ____________________

____

C 9~12 다음 영어 문장을 의미가 떠오를 때까지 소리 내어 읽어보시오. 1초 이내

9 Don't act the fool.

____

10 They acknowledged their faults.

____

11 A sponge absorbs water.

____

12 He admitted his guilt.

____

Test 3 Imaging Exercise

➢ 다음 단어에 맞는 나만의 짧은 영어 설명을 써보자. (또는 그림을 그려보자.)

absorb
[æbsɔ́ːrb]

acknowledge
[æknálidʒ]

act
[ækt]

admit
[ædmít]

➢ Month 01-DAY 04 영어 문장과 우리말

A sponge absorbs water.
스펀지는 물을 흡수한다.

They acknowledged their faults.
그들은 그들의 실수를 인정했다.

Don't act the fool.
바보같이 굴지 마라.

He admitted his guilt.
그는 그의 죄를 시인하였다.

DAY 05

Vocabulary

➢ 음원을 들으면서 소리를 무조건 따라해 보시오. (빠르기&정확도/브레인+마우스 운동)

agree

to be of one mind

accede, assent, consent

동의하다

I agree with you.

amaze

to surprise

astonish, alarm, startle, bewilder

놀라게 하다

It was amazing news.

applaud

to express approval, especially by clapping the hands

clap, encourage, praise, cheer

박수를 보내다, 칭찬하다

I applaud your decision.

beg

to ask for something, (especially money or food from strangers in a humble manner)

cadge, beseech, implore, plead

구걸하다, 빌다

I beg your forgiveness.

* 이미지는 구글에서 찾은 것으로, 단어와 이미지가 다를 수 있습니다. 'Test 3'에서 나만의 이미지를 그려볼 수 있습니다.

Test 1 Connecting Exercise

Score(　　/16)
Self-Evaluation

➢ 서로 맞는 것을 연결하시오.

Ⓐ 1~4 영어 단어와 우리말 뜻 연결하기

1	beg	박수를 보내다, 칭찬하다
2	applaud	놀라게 하다
3	agree	구걸하다, 빌다
4	amaze	동의하다

Ⓑ 5~8 영어 단어와 영어 설명 연결하기

5	applaud	to express approval, especially by clapping the hands
6	agree	to be of one mind
7	beg	to ask for something, (especially money or food from strangers in a humble manner)
8	amaze	to surprise

Ⓒ 9~12 영어 단어와 동의어 연결하기

9	amaze	cadge, beseech, implore, plead
10	agree	astonish, alarm, startle, bewilder
11	applaud	clap, encourage, praise, cheer
12	beg	accede, assent, consent

Ⓓ 13~16 우리말 뜻과 영어 단어 연결하기

13	구걸하다, 빌다	beg
14	박수를 보내다, 칭찬하다	applaud
15	놀라게 하다	agree
16	동의하다	amaze

Test 2 Writing Exercise

Score(　　/12)
Self-Evaluation

A 1~4 다음 단어에 맞는 뜻을 쓰시오.

1 applaud ____________________

2 beg ____________________

3 agree ____________________

4 amaze ____________________

B 5~8 다음 뜻에 맞는 영어 단어와 영어 동의어, 영어 설명을 쓰시오.

5 놀라게 하다

__________ ____________________

____

6 구걸하다, 빌다

__________ ____________________

____

7 박수를 보내다, 칭찬하다

__________ ____________________

____

8 동의하다

__________ ____________________

____

C 9~12 다음 영어 문장을 의미가 떠오를 때까지 소리 내어 읽어보시오. 1초 이내

9 I applaud your decision.

____

10 It was amazing news.

____

11 I beg your forgiveness.

____

12 I agree with you.

____

Test 3 Imaging Exercise

➢ 다음 단어에 맞는 나만의 짧은 영어 설명을 써보자. (또는 그림을 그려보자.)

agree
[əgríː]

amaze
[əméiz]

applaud
[əplɔ́ːd]

beg
[beg]

➢ Month 01-DAY 05 영어 문장과 우리말

I agree with you.
나는 당신에게 동의합니다.

It was amazing news.
그것은 놀라운 뉴스였다.

I applaud your decision.
나는 당신의 결정에 박수를 보냅니다.

I beg your forgiveness.
당신의 용서를 구합니다.

Vocabulary

➢ 음원을 들으면서 소리를 무조건 따라해 보시오. (빠르기&정확도/브레인+마우스 운동)

blow, blew, blown

to move along or be carried by the wind

gust, blast, exhale

바람 불다, 바람에 날리다, 입김을 불어대다

Her hat blew away.

boil

to vaporize by the application of heat

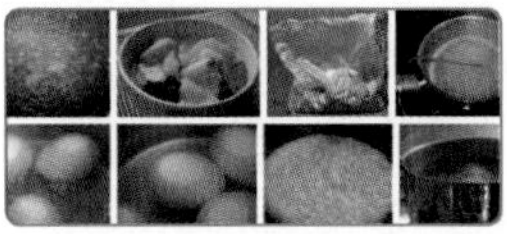

simmer, seethe, stew

끓이다

The water is boiling.

build, built, built

to make or form by joining parts or materials

construct, make, assemble, fabricate

만들다, 세우다, 건설하다

They built a building.

carve

to cut into a desired shape by cutting

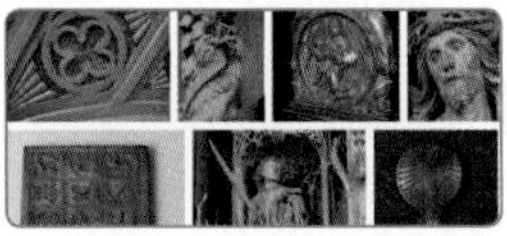

sculpt, sculpture, shape, form

조각하다, 새기다

He carved his name.

* 이미지는 구글에서 찾은 것으로, 단어와 이미지가 다를 수 있습니다. 'Test 3'에서 나만의 이미지를 그려볼 수 있습니다.

Test 1 Connecting Exercise

Score(/16)
Self-Evaluation

➢ 서로 맞는 것을 연결하시오.

Ⓐ 1~4 영어 단어와 우리말 뜻 연결하기

1	carve	•	• 끓이다
2	boil	•	• 만들다, 세우다, 건설하다
3	blow, blew, blown	•	• 바람 불다, 바람에 날리다, 입김을 불어대다
4	build, built, built	•	• 조각하다, 새기다

Ⓑ 5~8 영어 단어와 영어 설명 연결하기

5	boil	•	• to make or form by joining parts or materials
6	blow, blew, blown	•	• to cut into a desired shape by cutting
7	build, built, built	•	• to vaporize by the application of heat
8	carve	•	• to move along or be carried by the wind

Ⓒ 9~12 영어 단어와 동의어 연결하기

9	build, built, built	•	• construct, make, assemble, fabricate
10	carve	•	• sculpt, sculpture, shape, form
11	blow, blew, blown	•	• gust, blast, exhale
12	boil	•	• simmer, seethe, stew

Ⓓ 13~16 우리말 뜻과 영어 단어 연결하기

13	조각하다, 새기다	•	• blow, blew, blown
14	바람 불다, 바람에 날리다, 입김을 불어대다	•	• boil
15	만들다, 세우다, 건설하다	•	• carve
16	끓이다	•	• build, built, built

Test 2 Writing Exercise

Score(/12)
Self-Evaluation

A 1~4 다음 단어에 맞는 뜻을 쓰시오.

1 build, built, built ______

2 carve ______

3 boil ______

4 blow, blew, blown ______

B 5~8 다음 뜻에 맞는 영어 단어와 영어 동의어, 영어 설명을 쓰시오.

5 바람 불다, 바람에 날리다, 입김을 불어대다

______ ______

______

6 끓이다

______ ______

______

7 만들다, 세우다, 건설하다

______ ______

______

8 조각하다, 새기다

______ ______

______

C 9~12 다음 영어 문장을 의미가 떠오를 때까지 소리 내어 읽어보시오. 1초 이내

9 Her hat blew away.

______

10 They built a building.

______

11 The water is boiling.

______

12 He carved his name.

______

Test 3 Imaging Exercise

➢ 다음 단어에 맞는 나만의 짧은 영어 설명을 써보자. (또는 그림을 그려보자.)

blow, blew, blown
[blou, bluː, bloun]

boil
[boil]

build, built, built
[build, bilt, bilt]

carve
[kaːrv]

➢ Month 01-DAY 06 영어 문장과 우리말

Her hat blew away.
그녀의 모자가 바람에 날아갔다.

The water is boiling.
물이 끓고 있다.

They built a building.
그들은 건물을 지었다.

He carved his name.
그는 그의 이름을 새겼다.

➢ 음원을 들으면서 소리를 무조건 따라해 보시오. (빠르기&정확도/브레인+마우스 운동)

change

to make or become different

alter, switch, shift, vary

바꾸다, 변하다

I changed my mind.

chew

to bite and grind with the teeth

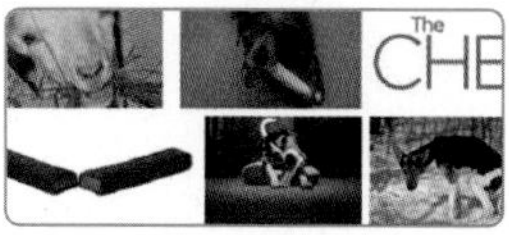

bite, crunch, masticate

씹다, 갉다, 갉아먹다

Chew your food well.

collapse

to fall down or break down suddenly

fall down, break down, crumple

무너지다, 붕괴하다, 붕괴

The whole building collapsed.

dawn

to begin to grow light in the morning

daybreak, sunrise

날이 새다, 새벽이 되다, 새벽

The day dawned cloudless.

* 이미지는 구글에서 찾은 것으로, 단어와 이미지가 다를 수 있습니다. 'Test 3'에서 나만의 이미지를 그려볼 수 있습니다.

Test 1 Connecting Exercise

Score(　　/16)
Self-Evaluation

➢ 서로 맞는 것을 연결하시오.

Ⓐ 1~4 영어 단어와 우리말 뜻 연결하기

1 dawn	•	• 씹다, 갉다, 갉아먹다
2 chew	•	• 바꾸다, 변하다
3 collapse	•	• 무너지다, 붕괴하다, 붕괴
4 change	•	• 날이 새다, 새벽이 되다, 새벽

Ⓑ 5~8 영어 단어와 영어 설명 연결하기

5 change	•	• to begin to grow light in the morning
6 chew	•	• to make or become different
7 collapse	•	• to bite and grind with the teeth
8 dawn	•	• to fall down or break down suddenly

Ⓒ 9~12 영어 단어와 동의어 연결하기

9 chew	•	• alter, switch, shift, vary
10 collapse	•	• bite, crunch, masticate
11 dawn	•	• fall down, break down, crumple
12 change	•	• daybreak, sunrise

Ⓓ 13~16 우리말 뜻과 영어 단어 연결하기

13 바꾸다, 변하다	•	• dawn
14 무너지다, 붕괴하다, 붕괴	•	• chew
15 씹다, 갉다, 갉아먹다	•	• change
16 날이 새다, 새벽이 되다, 새벽	•	• collapse

Test 2 Writing Exercise

Score(/12)
Self-Evaluation

Ⓐ 1~4 다음 단어에 맞는 뜻을 쓰시오.

1 collapse ______________________

2 dawn ______________________

3 change ______________________

4 chew ______________________

Ⓑ 5~8 다음 뜻에 맞는 영어 단어와 영어 동의어, 영어 설명을 쓰시오.

5 날이 새다, 새벽이 되다, 새벽

______________ ______________________

____

6 무너지다, 붕괴하다, 붕괴

______________ ______________________

____

7 바꾸다, 변하다

______________ ______________________

____

8 씹다, 갉다, 갉아먹다

______________ ______________________

____

Ⓒ 9~12 다음 영어 문장을 의미가 떠오를 때까지 소리 내어 읽어보시오. 1초 이내

9 Chew your food well.

____

10 I changed my mind.

____

11 The whole building collapsed.

____

12 The day dawned cloudless.

____

Test 3 Imaging Exercise

➢ 다음 단어에 맞는 나만의 짧은 영어 설명을 써보자. (또는 그림을 그려보자.)

change
[ʧeindʒ]

chew
[ʧuː]

collapse
[kəlǽps]

dawn
[dɔːn]

➢ Month 01-DAY 07 영어 문장과 우리말

I changed my mind.
나는 마음이 바뀌었습니다(마음을 바꿨다).

Chew your food well.
음식물을 잘 씹으십시오.

The whole building collapsed.
빌딩 전체가 무너져 내렸습니다.

The day dawned cloudless.
구름 한 점 없이 날이 밝았다.

DAY 08 Vocabulary

➢ 음원을 들으면서 소리를 무조건 따라해 보시오. (빠르기&정확도/브레인+마우스 운동)

decrease

to become less or smaller

reduce, diminish, contract

감소하다, 줄이다, 감소

Our sales are decreasing.

deserve

to be worthy of

merit, qualify for

할 자격이 있다, 할 가치가 있다

She deserves a promotion.

determine

to settle or decide conclusively

decide, establish, ascertain

결정하다, 결심하다

Demand usually determines supply.

exclaim

to cry out or speak suddenly

outcry, shout, yell, utter

소리치다, 외치다

She exclaimed in astonishment.

* 이미지는 구글에서 찾은 것으로, 단어와 이미지가 다를 수 있습니다. 'Test 3'에서 나만의 이미지를 그려볼 수 있습니다.

Test 1 Connecting Exercise

Score(/16)
Self-Evaluation

➢ 서로 맞는 것을 연결하시오.

Ⓐ 1~4 영어 단어와 우리말 뜻 연결하기

1	exclaim	•	• 결정하다, 결심하다
2	determine	•	• 할 자격이 있다, 할 가치가 있다
3	decrease	•	• 소리치다, 외치다
4	deserve	•	• 감소하다, 줄이다, 감소

Ⓑ 5~8 영어 단어와 영어 설명 연결하기

5	determine	•	• to be worthy of
6	exclaim	•	• to settle or decide conclusively
7	deserve	•	• to become less or smaller
8	decrease	•	• to cry out or speak suddenly

Ⓒ 9~12 영어 단어와 동의어 연결하기

9	decrease	•	• outcry, shout, yell, utter
10	determine	•	• merit, qualify for
11	deserve	•	• reduce, diminish, contract
12	exclaim	•	• decide, establish, ascertain

Ⓓ 13~16 우리말 뜻과 영어 단어 연결하기

13	감소하다, 줄이다, 감소	•	• decrease
14	할 자격이 있다, 할 가치가 있다	•	• exclaim
15	소리치다, 외치다	•	• deserve
16	결정하다, 결심하다	•	• determine

Test 2 Writing Exercise

Score(/12)
Self-Evaluation

A 1~4 다음 단어에 맞는 뜻을 쓰시오.

1 deserve ______

2 determine ______

3 decrease ______

4 exclaim ______

B 5~8 다음 뜻에 맞는 영어 단어와 영어 동의어, 영어 설명을 쓰시오.

5 할 자격이 있다, 할 가치가 있다

______ ______

______

6 소리치다, 외치다

______ ______

______

7 감소하다, 줄이다, 감소

______ ______

______

8 결정하다, 결심하다

______ ______

______

C 9~12 다음 영어 문장을 의미가 떠오를 때까지 소리 내어 읽어보시오. 1초 이내

9 She deserves a promotion.

______

10 She exclaimed in astonishment.

______

11 Demand usually determines supply.

______

12 Our sales are decreasing.

______

Test 3 Imaging Exercise

➢ 다음 단어에 맞는 나만의 짧은 영어 설명을 써보자. (또는 그림을 그려보자.)

decrease
[dikríːs]

deserve
[dizə́ːrv]

determine
[ditə́ːrmin]

exclaim
[ikskléim]

➢ Month 01-DAY 08 영어 문장과 우리말

Our sales are decreasing.
매출이 감소하고 있습니다.

She deserves a promotion.
그녀는 승진할 자격이 있습니다.

Demand usually determines supply.
수요가 보통 공급을 결정합니다.

She exclaimed in astonishment.
그녀는 놀라서 소리쳤습니다.

Vocabulary

≫ **음원을 들으면서 소리를 무조건 따라해 보시오.** (빠르기&정확도/브레인+마우스 운동)

explore

to investigate systematically

investigate, survey, examine, inspect

조사하다, 탐험하다

We explored every possibility.

fake

to create or render so as to mislead, deceive, or defraud others

counterfeit, pretend

위조하다, 날조하다, 속이다, 가짜의

He faked my signature.

fight, fought, fought

to battle or struggle against

strive, struggle, battle, contend

싸우다, 다투다, 다툼, 싸움

They fought for freedom.

frighten

to fill with fear

alarm, scare, terrify, terrorize

놀라게 하다, 두렵게 하다, 무섭게 하다

A stranger frightens me.

* 이미지는 구글에서 찾은 것으로, 단어와 이미지가 다를 수 있습니다. 'Test 3'에서 나만의 이미지를 그려볼 수 있습니다.

Test 1 Connecting Exercise

Score(　　/16)
Self-Evaluation

➢ 서로 맞는 것을 연결하시오.

Ⓐ 1~4 영어 단어와 우리말 뜻 연결하기

1 explore	•	• 놀라게 하다, 두렵게 하다, 무섭게 하다
2 frighten	•	• 조사하다, 탐험하다
3 fake	•	• 위조하다, 날조하다, 속이다, 가짜의
4 fight, fought, fought	•	• 싸우다, 다투다, 다툼, 싸움

Ⓑ 5~8 영어 단어와 영어 설명 연결하기

5 fight, fought, fought	•	• to battle or struggle against
6 fake	•	• to fill with fear
7 frighten	•	• to create or render so as to mislead, deceive, or defraud others
8 explore	•	• to investigate systematically

Ⓒ 9~12 영어 단어와 동의어 연결하기

9 fake	•	• strive, struggle, battle, contend
10 fight, fought, fought	•	• investigate, survey, examine, inspect
11 explore	•	• counterfeit, pretend
12 frighten	•	• alarm, scare, terrify, terrorize

Ⓓ 13~16 우리말 뜻과 영어 단어 연결하기

13 놀라게 하다, 두렵게 하다, 무섭게 하다	•	• explore
14 싸우다, 다투다, 다툼, 싸움	•	• fake
15 위조하다, 날조하다, 속이다, 가짜의	•	• frighten
16 조사하다, 탐험하다	•	• fight, fought, fought

Test 2 Writing Exercise

Score(/12)
Self-Evaluation

Ⓐ 1~4 다음 단어에 맞는 뜻을 쓰시오.

1 frighten ______

2 explore ______

3 fight, fought, fought ______

4 fake ______

Ⓑ 5~8 다음 뜻에 맞는 영어 단어와 영어 동의어, 영어 설명을 쓰시오.

5 싸우다, 다투다, 다툼, 싸움

______ ______

______

6 위조하다, 날조하다, 속이다, 가짜의

______ ______

______

7 조사하다, 탐험하다

______ ______

______

8 놀라게 하다, 두렵게 하다, 무섭게 하다

______ ______

______

Ⓒ 9~12 다음 영어 문장을 의미가 떠오를 때까지 소리 내어 읽어보시오. 1초 이내

9 A stranger frightens me.

______

10 They fought for freedom.

______

11 He faked my signature.

______

12 We explored every possibility.

______

Test 3 Imaging Exercise

➢ 다음 단어에 맞는 나만의 짧은 영어 설명을 써보자. (또는 그림을 그려보자.)

explore
[ikspl5ːr]

fake
[feik]

fight, fought, fought
[fait, fɔːt, fɔːt]

frighten
[fráitn]

➢ Month 01-DAY 09 영어 문장과 우리말

We explored every possibility.
우리는 모든 가능성을 조사하였습니다.

He faked my signature.
그는 나의 서명을 위조했습니다.

They fought for freedom.
그들은 자유를 위해 싸웠습니다.

A stranger frightens me.
낯선 사람이 나를 두렵게 합니다.

Vocabulary

➢ 음원을 들으면서 소리를 무조건 따라해 보시오. (빠르기&정확도/브레인+마우스 운동)

hate

to feel strong dislike for

dislike, detest, loathe, despise

미워하다, 싫어하다, 증오하다

I hate washing dishes.

hug

to clasp tightly in the arms, esp. with affection

embrace, bosom

(정겹게) 껴안다, 포옹하다, 포옹

They hugged each other.

improve

to make or become better in quality

ameliorate, meliorate, amend, enhance

향상시키다, 개선하다,
나아지다, 개선되다

Economic conditions are improving.

lock

to fasten the lock of

fasten, close, secure, confine

(자물쇠로) 잠그다, 가두다, 자물쇠

This door doesn't lock.

* 이미지는 구글에서 찾은 것으로, 단어와 이미지가 다를 수 있습니다. 'Test 3'에서 나만의 이미지를 그려볼 수 있습니다.

Test 1 Connecting Exercise

Score(　/16)
Self-Evaluation

➢ 서로 맞는 것을 연결하시오.

Ⓐ 1~4 영어 단어와 우리말 뜻 연결하기

1 lock	•	•	향상시키다, 개선하다, 나아지다, 개선되다
2 hate	•	•	미워하다, 싫어하다, 증오하다
3 hug	•	•	(자물쇠로) 잠그다, 가두다, 자물쇠
4 improve	•	•	(정겹게) 껴안다, 포옹하다, 포옹

Ⓑ 5~8 영어 단어와 영어 설명 연결하기

5 lock	•	•	to make or become better in quality
6 hate	•	•	to feel strong dislike for
7 improve	•	•	to clasp tightly in the arms, esp. with affection
8 hug	•	•	to fasten the lock of

Ⓒ 9~12 영어 단어와 동의어 연결하기

9 hug	•	•	embrace, bosom
10 improve	•	•	ameliorate, meliorate, amend, enhance
11 hate	•	•	fasten, close, secure, confine
12 lock	•	•	dislike, detest, loathe, despise

Ⓓ 13~16 우리말 뜻과 영어 단어 연결하기

13 미워하다, 싫어하다, 증오하다	•	•	improve
14 향상시키다, 개선하다, 나아지다, 개선되다	•	•	lock
15 (정겹게) 껴안다, 포옹하다, 포옹	•	•	hate
16 (자물쇠로) 잠그다, 가두다, 자물쇠	•	•	hug

Test 2 Writing Exercise

Score(/12)
Self-Evaluation

Ⓐ 1~4 다음 단어에 맞는 뜻을 쓰시오.

1 hate ____________________

2 improve ____________________

3 lock ____________________

4 hug ____________________

Ⓑ 5~8 다음 뜻에 맞는 영어 단어와 영어 동의어, 영어 설명을 쓰시오.

5 (자물쇠로) 잠그다, 가두다, 자물쇠

__________ ____________________

____

6 향상시키다, 개선하다, 나아지다, 개선되다

__________ ____________________

____

7 미워하다, 싫어하다, 증오하다

__________ ____________________

____

8 (정겹게) 껴안다, 포옹하다, 포옹

__________ ____________________

____

Ⓒ 9~12 다음 영어 문장을 의미가 떠오를 때까지 소리 내어 읽어보시오. 1초 이내

9 Economic conditions are improving.

____

10 This door doesn't lock.

____

11 They hugged each other.

____

12 I hate washing dishes.

____

Test 3 Imaging Exercise

➢ 다음 단어에 맞는 나만의 짧은 영어 설명을 써보자. (또는 그림을 그려보자.)

hate
[heit]

hug
[hʌg]

improve
[imprúːv]

lock
[lak]

➢ Month 01-DAY 10 영어 문장과 우리말

I hate washing dishes.
나는 설거지하기를 싫어합니다.

They hugged each other.
그들은 서로 포옹했습니다.

Economic conditions are improving.
경제 여건이 개선되고 있습니다.

This door doesn't lock.
이 문은 잠기지 않습니다.

Vocabulary

➢ 음원을 들으면서 소리를 무조건 따라해 보시오. (빠르기&정확도/브레인+마우스 운동)

melt

to be changed from a solid to a liquid state

liquefy, unfreeze, dissolve

녹다, 녹이다, 용해하다

Sugar melts in water.

misplace

to put into a wrong place

mislay, lose

잘못 놓다, 잘못 두다,
어디에 잘못 두고 잃어버리다

I misplaced my wallet.

miss

to fail to catch, reach, hit, or to feel the lack or loss of

lose, fail

놓치다, 그리워하다

She missed her train.

pack

to make into a pack or bundle

package, load, parcel, wrap

꾸리다, 짐, 꾸러미

I packed my luggage.

* 이미지는 구글에서 찾은 것으로, 단어와 이미지가 다를 수 있습니다. 'Test 3'에서 나만의 이미지를 그려볼 수 있습니다.

Test 1 Connecting Exercise

Score(/16)
Self-Evaluation

➢ 서로 맞는 것을 연결하시오.

Ⓐ 1~4 영어 단어와 우리말 뜻 연결하기

1 misplace	•	• 녹다, 녹이다, 용해하다
2 miss	•	• 놓치다, 그리워하다
3 melt	•	• 잘못 놓다, 잘못 두다, 어디에 잘못 두고 잃어버리다
4 pack	•	• 꾸리다, 짐, 꾸러미

Ⓑ 5~8 영어 단어와 영어 설명 연결하기

5 miss	•	• to put into a wrong place
6 pack	•	• to be changed from a solid to a liquid state
7 misplace	•	• to fail to catch, reach, hit, or to feel the lack or loss of
8 melt	•	• to make into a pack or bundle

Ⓒ 9~12 영어 단어와 동의어 연결하기

9 melt	•	• mislay, lose
10 pack	•	• liquefy, unfreeze, dissolve
11 miss	•	• package, load, parcel, wrap
12 misplace	•	• lose, fail

Ⓓ 13~16 우리말 뜻과 영어 단어 연결하기

13 잘못 놓다, 잘못 두다, 어디에 잘못 두고 잃어버리다	•	• miss
14 꾸리다, 짐, 꾸러미	•	• melt
15 놓치다, 그리워하다	•	• pack
16 녹다, 녹이다, 용해하다	•	• misplace

Test 2 Writing Exercise

Score(/12)
Self-Evaluation

Ⓐ 1~4 다음 단어에 맞는 뜻을 쓰시오.

1 misplace ______

2 pack ______

3 melt ______

4 miss ______

Ⓑ 5~8 다음 뜻에 맞는 영어 단어와 영어 동의어, 영어 설명을 쓰시오.

5 잘못 놓다, 잘못 두다, 어디에 잘못 두고 잃어버리다

______ ______

______

6 녹다, 녹이다, 용해하다

______ ______

______

7 놓치다, 그리워하다

______ ______

______

8 꾸리다, 짐, 꾸러미

______ ______

______

Ⓒ 9~12 다음 영어 문장을 의미가 떠오를 때까지 소리 내어 읽어보시오. 1초 이내

9 Sugar melts in water.

______

10 She missed her train.

______

11 I packed my luggage.

______

12 I misplaced my wallet.

______

Test 3 Imaging Exercise

➢ 다음 단어에 맞는 나만의 짧은 영어 설명을 써보자. (또는 그림을 그려보자.)

melt
[melt]

misplace
[misplei's]

miss
[mis]

pack
[pæk]

➢ Month 01-DAY 11 영어 문장과 우리말

Sugar melts in water.
설탕은 물에 녹습니다.

I misplaced my wallet.
나는 지갑을 잃어버렸습니다.

She missed her train.
그녀는 기차를 놓쳤습니다.

I packed my luggage.
나는 짐을 꾸렸습니다.

DAY 12

Vocabulary

➢ 음원을 들으면서 소리를 무조건 따라해 보시오. (빠르기 & 정확도/브레인 + 마우스 운동)

pray

to utter or address a prayer or prayers

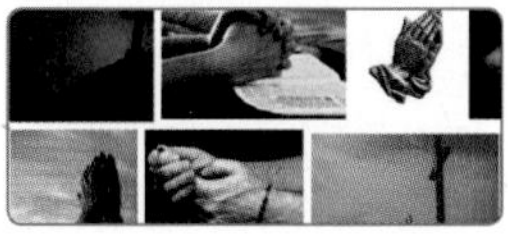

supplicate, appeal, beg

기도하다, 기원하다, 바라다

I prayed to God.

renew

to make new

replace, refresh, resume

갱신하다, 새롭게 하다

Cells are constantly renewed.

require

to have need of

need, demand, ask, call for

필요하다, 요구하다

He requires medical care.

sigh

to let out one's breath audibly, as from sorrow, weariness, or relief

suspire, respire

한숨 쉬다, 탄식하다

She sighed with sorrow.

* 이미지는 구글에서 찾은 것으로, 단어와 이미지가 다를 수 있습니다. 'Test 3'에서 나만의 이미지를 그려볼 수 있습니다.

Test 1 Connecting Exercise

Score(/16)
Self-Evaluation

➢ 서로 맞는 것을 연결하시오.

Ⓐ 1~4 영어 단어와 우리말 뜻 연결하기

1	require	•	• 한숨 쉬다, 탄식하다
2	pray	•	• 필요하다, 요구하다
3	sigh	•	• 갱신하다, 새롭게 하다
4	renew	•	• 기도하다, 기원하다, 바라다

Ⓑ 5~8 영어 단어와 영어 설명 연결하기

5	renew	•	• to let out one's breath audibly, as from sorrow, weariness, or relief
6	require	•	• to make new
7	sigh	•	• to have need of
8	pray	•	• to utter or address a prayer or prayers

Ⓒ 9~12 영어 단어와 동의어 연결하기

9	sigh	•	• need, demand, ask, call for
10	pray	•	• supplicate, appeal, beg
11	require	•	• suspire, respire
12	renew	•	• replace, refresh, resume

Ⓓ 13~16 우리말 뜻과 영어 단어 연결하기

13	갱신하다, 새롭게 하다	•	• renew
14	기도하다, 기원하다, 바라다	•	• sigh
15	한숨 쉬다, 탄식하다	•	• require
16	필요하다, 요구하다	•	• pray

Test 2 Writing Exercise

Score(/12)
Self-Evaluation

A 1~4 다음 단어에 맞는 뜻을 쓰시오.

1 pray ______

2 require ______

3 sigh ______

4 renew ______

B 5~8 다음 뜻에 맞는 영어 단어와 영어 동의어, 영어 설명을 쓰시오.

5 갱신하다, 새롭게 하다

______ ______

______

6 기도하다, 기원하다, 바라다

______ ______

______

7 한숨 쉬다, 탄식하다

______ ______

______

8 필요하다, 요구하다

______ ______

______

C 9~12 다음 영어 문장을 의미가 떠오를 때까지 소리 내어 읽어보시오. 1초 이내

9 He requires medical care.

______

10 I prayed to God.

______

11 She sighed with sorrow.

______

12 Cells are constantly renewed.

______

Test 3

➢ 다음 단어에 맞는 나만의 짧은 영어 설명을 써보자. (또는 그림을 그려보자.)

pray
[prei]

renew
[rinjúː]

require
[rikwáiər]

sigh
[sai]

➢ Month 01-DAY 12 영어 문장과 우리말

I prayed to God.
나는 신에게 기도했습니다.

Cells are constantly renewed.
세포는 끊임없이 재생됩니다.

He requires medical care.
그는 병원 치료가 필요합니다.

She sighed with sorrow.
그녀는 슬픔에 한숨을 쉬었습니다.

DAY 13 Vocabulary

➢ 음원을 들으면서 소리를 무조건 따라해 보시오. (빠르기&정확도/브레인+마우스 운동)

treat

to deal with or regard in a certain manner

deal with, handle

다루다, 취급하다, 치료하다

They treated me fairly.

accept

to answer affirmatively

admit, receive, acknowledge

받아들이다

She has accepted my proposal.

address

to give a speech to or speak to

talk to, send, mail

연설하다, 이야기하다, 부르다,
주소, 주소를 쓰다

She addressed in low tones.

arrest

to capture

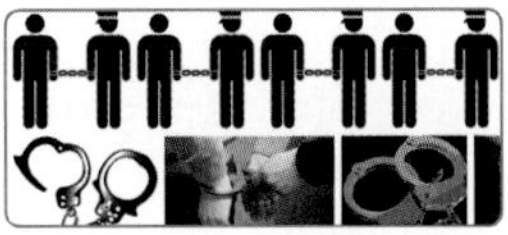

catch, seize, hold, capture

체포하다, 체포

A suspect was under arrest.

* 이미지는 구글에서 찾은 것으로, 단어와 이미지가 다를 수 있습니다. 'Test 3'에서 나만의 이미지를 그려볼 수 있습니다.

Test 1 Connecting Exercise

Score(　　/16)
Self-Evaluation

➢ 서로 맞는 것을 연결하시오.

Ⓐ 1~4 영어 단어와 우리말 뜻 연결하기

1 address	●	● 다루다, 취급하다, 치료하다
2 accept	●	● 받아들이다
3 arrest	●	● 연설하다, 이야기하다, 부르다, 주소, 주소를 쓰다
4 treat	●	● 체포하다, 체포

Ⓑ 5~8 영어 단어와 영어 설명 연결하기

5 address	●	● to deal with or regard in a certain manner
6 treat	●	● to give a speech to or speak to
7 arrest	●	● to answer affirmatively
8 accept	●	● to capture

Ⓒ 9~12 영어 단어와 동의어 연결하기

9 address	●	● deal with, handle
10 treat	●	● catch, seize, hold, capture
11 accept	●	● talk to, send, mail
12 arrest	●	● admit, receive, acknowledge

Ⓓ 13~16 우리말 뜻과 영어 단어 연결하기

13 체포하다, 체포	●	● treat
14 다루다, 취급하다, 치료하다	●	● arrest
15 받아들이다	●	● accept
16 연설하다, 이야기하다, 부르다, 주소, 주소를 쓰다	●	● address

Test 2 Writing Exercise

Score(/12)
Self-Evaluation

A 1~4 다음 단어에 맞는 뜻을 쓰시오.

1 accept ______

2 arrest ______

3 address ______

4 treat ______

B 5~8 다음 뜻에 맞는 영어 단어와 영어 동의어, 영어 설명을 쓰시오.

5 체포하다, 체포

______ ______

______

6 다루다, 취급하다, 치료하다

______ ______

______

7 받아들이다

______ ______

______

8 연설하다, 이야기하다, 부르다, 주소, 주소를 쓰다

______ ______

______

C 9~12 다음 영어 문장을 의미가 떠오를 때까지 소리 내어 읽어보시오. 1.5초 이내

9 A suspect was under arrest.

______

10 She has accepted my proposal.

______

11 She addressed in low tones.

______

12 They treated me fairly.

______

Test 3 Imaging Exercise

➢ 다음 단어에 맞는 나만의 짧은 영어 설명을 써보자. (또는 그림을 그려보자.)

treat
[triːt]

accept
[æksépt]

address
[ədrés]

arrest
[ərést]

➢ Month 01-DAY 13 영어 문장과 우리말

They treated me fairly.
그들은 나를 공정하게 대했습니다.

She has accepted my proposal.
그녀는 나의 제안을 받아들였다.

She addressed in low tones.
그녀는 낮은 음색으로 연설하였다.

A suspect was under arrest.
용의자가 체포되었다.

➢ 음원을 들으면서 소리를 무조건 따라해 보시오. (빠르기&정확도/브레인+마우스 운동)

ban

to prohibit (an action) or forbid the use of (something)

restrict, veto, forbid, boycott

금지하다, 금지

Smoking is banned in theaters.

bathe

to take a bath or to wash in a liquid

wash, cleanse, rinse, shower

씻다, 적시다, 목욕시키다

She bathed her baby everyday.

behave

to act

act, react, conduct, perform

행동하다

He behaved badly towards her.

bow

to bend the knee or body

bend, curve, yield

인사하다, 절하다

He bowed before the King.

* 이미지는 구글에서 찾은 것으로, 단어와 이미지가 다를 수 있습니다. 'Test 3'에서 나만의 이미지를 그려볼 수 있습니다.

Test 1 Connecting Exercise

Score(/16)
Self-Evaluation

➢ 서로 맞는 것을 연결하시오.

Ⓐ 1~4 영어 단어와 우리말 뜻 연결하기

1	behave	금지하다, 금지
2	ban	씻다, 적시다, 목욕시키다
3	bathe	행동하다
4	bow	인사하다, 절하다

Ⓑ 5~8 영어 단어와 영어 설명 연결하기

5	bathe	to bend the knee or body
6	ban	to prohibit (an action) or forbid the use of (something)
7	behave	to take a bath or to wash in a liquid
8	bow	to act

Ⓒ 9~12 영어 단어와 동의어 연결하기

9	bow	wash, cleanse, rinse, shower
10	bathe	restrict, veto, forbid, boycott
11	behave	act, react, conduct, perform
12	ban	bend, curve, yield

Ⓓ 13~16 우리말 뜻과 영어 단어 연결하기

13	씻다, 적시다, 목욕시키다	behave
14	행동하다	bow
15	인사하다, 절하다	ban
16	금지하다, 금지	bathe

Test 2 Writing Exercise

Score(/12)
Self-Evaluation

A 1~4 다음 단어에 맞는 뜻을 쓰시오.

1 behave ______

2 ban ______

3 bow ______

4 bathe ______

B 5~8 다음 뜻에 맞는 영어 단어와 영어 동의어, 영어 설명을 쓰시오.

5 인사하다, 절하다

______ ______

______

6 씻다, 적시다, 목욕시키다

______ ______

______

7 행동하다

______ ______

______

8 금지하다, 금지

______ ______

______

C 9~12 다음 영어 문장을 의미가 떠오를 때까지 소리 내어 읽어보시오. 1.5초 이내

9 He bowed before the King.

______

10 He behaved badly towards her.

______

11 She bathed her baby everyday.

______

12 Smoking is banned in theaters.

______

Test 3

➢ 다음 단어에 맞는 나만의 짧은 영어 설명을 써보자. (또는 그림을 그려보자.)

ban
[ban]

bathe
[beið]

behave
[bihéiv]

bow
[bau]

➢ Month 01-DAY 14 영어 문장과 우리말

Smoking is banned in theaters.
극장에서 흡연은 금지되어 있습니다.

She bathed her baby everyday.
그녀는 매일 아기를 목욕시켰습니다.

He behaved badly towards her.
그는 그녀에게 못되게 굴었다.

He bowed before the King.
그는 왕 앞에 절을 하였습니다.

Vocabulary

➢ 음원을 들으면서 소리를 무조건 따라해 보시오. (빠르기 & 정확도/브레인 + 마우스 운동)

breathe

to take air or oxygen into the lungs and expel it

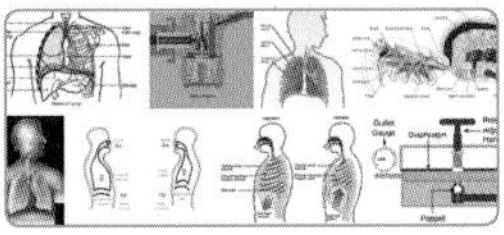

respire, inhale, exhale

숨 쉬다, 호흡하다

Always breathe through your nose.

bring, brought, brought

to carry or cause (someone or something) to come with

carry, convey, conduct

가져오다, 가지고 오다, 데리고 오다

Bring that book to me.

burn, burnt, burnt

to destroy or be destroyed by fire

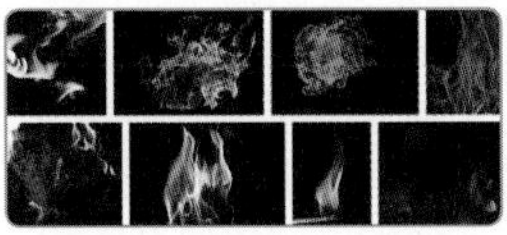

blaze, flame, damage, injure

불타다, 태우다, (불에 덴) 상처, 화상

He burnt his left hand.

burrow

to dig a hole or tunnel for habitation or refuge

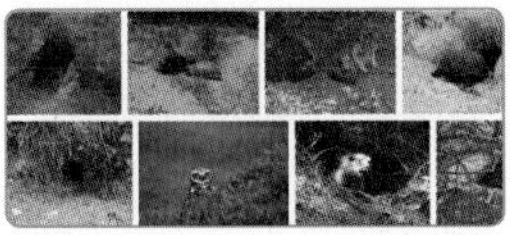

hole, shelter, tunnel

은신처나 살 집으로 굴을 파다, 토끼굴 따위

There was a rabbit's burrow.

* 이미지는 구글에서 찾은 것으로, 단어와 이미지가 다를 수 있습니다. 'Test 3'에서 나만의 이미지를 그려볼 수 있습니다.

Test 1 Connecting Exercise

Score(/16)
Self-Evaluation

≫ 서로 맞는 것을 연결하시오.

Ⓐ 1~4 영어 단어와 우리말 뜻 연결하기

1	breathe	• •	숨 쉬다, 호흡하다
2	bring, brought, brought	• •	은신처나 살 집으로 굴을 파다, 토끼굴 따위
3	burn, burnt, burnt	• •	가져오다, 가지고 오다, 데리고 오다
4	burrow	• •	불타다, 태우다, (불에 덴) 상처, 화상

Ⓑ 5~8 영어 단어와 영어 설명 연결하기

5	breathe	• •	to destroy or be destroyed by fire
6	burrow	• •	to take air or oxygen into the lungs and expel it
7	burn, burnt, burnt	• •	to carry or cause (someone or something) to come with
8	bring, brought, brought	• •	to dig a hole or tunnel for habitation or refuge

Ⓒ 9~12 영어 단어와 동의어 연결하기

9	breathe	• •	carry, convey, conduct
10	burrow	• •	respire, inhale, exhale
11	burn, burnt, burnt	• •	hole, shelter, tunnel
12	bring, brought, brought	• •	blaze, flame, damage, injure

Ⓓ 13~16 우리말 뜻과 영어 단어 연결하기

13	은신처나 살 집으로 굴을 파다, 토끼굴 따위	• •	bring, brought, brought
14	불타다, 태우다, (불에 덴) 상처, 화상	• •	burn, burnt, burnt
15	가져오다, 가지고 오다, 데리고 오다	• •	breathe
16	숨 쉬다, 호흡하다	• •	burrow

Test 2 Writing Exercise

Score(　　/12)
Self-Evaluation

Ⓐ 1~4 다음 단어에 맞는 뜻을 쓰시오.

1 burn, burnt, burnt ______________________

2 bring, brought, brought ______________________

3 burrow ______________________

4 breathe ______________________

Ⓑ 5~8 다음 뜻에 맞는 영어 단어와 영어 동의어, 영어 설명을 쓰시오.

5 가져오다, 가지고 오다, 데리고 오다

__________ ______________________

____

6 숨 쉬다, 호흡하다

__________ ______________________

____

7 은신처나 살 집으로 굴을 파다, 토끼굴 따위

__________ ______________________

____

8 불타다, 태우다, (불에 덴) 상처, 화상

__________ ______________________

____

Ⓒ 9~12 다음 영어 문장을 의미가 떠오를 때까지 소리 내어 읽어보시오. 1.5초 이내

9 He burnt his left hand.

____

10 Bring that book to me.

____

11 Always breathe through your nose.

____

12 There was a rabbit's burrow.

____

Test 3 Imaging Exercise

➢ 다음 단어에 맞는 나만의 짧은 영어 설명을 써보자. (또는 그림을 그려보자.)

breathe
[briːð]

bring, brought, brought
[briŋ, brɔːt, brɔːt]

burn, burnt, burnt
[bəːrn, bəːrnt, bəːrnt]

burrow
[bə́ːrou]

➢ Month 01-DAY 15 영어 문장과 우리말

Always breathe through your nose.
항상 코로 숨 쉬세요.

Bring that book to me.
저 책 나에게 갖다 줘.

He burnt his left hand.
그는 왼손을 데었다.

There was a rabbit's burrow.
토끼굴이 있었다.

Vocabulary

➢ 음원을 들으면서 소리를 무조건 따라해 보시오. (빠르기 & 정확도/브레인 + 마우스 운동)

calculate

to solve by a mathematical procedure

compute, reckon, figure

계산하다

Can you calculate the distance?

catch, caught, caught

to get and hold in a hand

capture, seize, arrest

붙잡다, 낚아채다

The police caught the robber.

charm

to attract or fascinate

fascinate, enchant, captivate, attract

매혹하다, 마음을 빼앗다, 매력

She charms everyone she meets.

chase

to follow rapidly in order to catch

go after, tag, pursue, follow

쫓다, 쫓아가다, 추격

The police chased the robber.

* 이미지는 구글에서 찾은 것으로, 단어와 이미지가 다를 수 있습니다. 'Test 3'에서 나만의 이미지를 그려볼 수 있습니다.

Test 1 Connecting Exercise

Score(/16)
Self-Evaluation

➢ 서로 맞는 것을 연결하시오.

Ⓐ 1~4 영어 단어와 우리말 뜻 연결하기

1	charm	•	• 쫓다, 쫓아가다, 추격
2	calculate	•	• 계산하다
3	catch, caught, caught	•	• 붙잡다, 낚아채다
4	chase	•	• 매혹하다, 마음을 빼앗다, 매력

Ⓑ 5~8 영어 단어와 영어 설명 연결하기

5	catch, caught, caught	•	• to attract or fascinate
6	chase	•	• to get and hold in a hand
7	calculate	•	• to solve by a mathematical procedure
8	charm	•	• to follow rapidly in order to catch

Ⓒ 9~12 영어 단어와 동의어 연결하기

9	charm	•	• go after, tag, pursue, follow
10	catch, caught, caught	•	• compute, reckon, figure
11	calculate	•	• capture, seize, arrest
12	chase	•	• fascinate, enchant, captivate, attract

Ⓓ 13~16 우리말 뜻과 영어 단어 연결하기

13	매혹하다, 마음을 빼앗다, 매력	•	• charm
14	계산하다	•	• catch, caught, caught
15	붙잡다, 낚아채다	•	• calculate
16	쫓다, 쫓아가다, 추격	•	• chase

Test 2 Writing Exercise

Score(/12)
Self-Evaluation

Ⓐ 1~4 다음 단어에 맞는 뜻을 쓰시오.

1 calculate ______

2 catch, caught, caught ______

3 charm ______

4 chase ______

Ⓑ 5~8 다음 뜻에 맞는 영어 단어와 영어 동의어, 영어 설명을 쓰시오.

5 계산하다

______ ______

______

6 매혹하다, 마음을 빼앗다, 매력

______ ______

______

7 쫓다, 쫓아가다, 추격

______ ______

______

8 붙잡다, 낚아채다

______ ______

______

Ⓒ 9~12 다음 영어 문장을 의미가 떠오를 때까지 소리 내어 읽어보시오. 1.5초 이내

9 She charms everyone she meets.

______

10 Can you calculate the distance?

______

11 The police caught the robber.

______

12 The police chased the robber.

______

Test 3 Imaging Exercise

➢ 다음 단어에 맞는 나만의 짧은 영어 설명을 써보자. (또는 그림을 그려보자.)

calculate
[kǽlkjulèit]

catch, caught, caught
[kætʃ, kɔːt, kɔːt]

charm
[tʃaːrm]

chase
[tʃeis]

➢ Month 01-DAY 16 영어 문장과 우리말

Can you calculate the distance?
당신은 거리를 계산할 수 있습니까?

The police caught the robber.
경찰이 강도를 붙잡았다.

She charms everyone she meets.
그녀는 그녀가 만나는 모든 사람을 매혹시킵니다.

The police chased the robber.
경찰이 강도를 쫓아가서 강도를 붙잡았습니다.

Vocabulary

➢ 음원을 들으면서 소리를 무조건 따라해 보시오. (빠르기 & 정확도/브레인 + 마우스 운동)

chuckle

to laugh quietly or to oneself

chortle, laugh, giggle, snigger

혼자서 소리작게 낄낄 웃다,
웃음 참으며 쿡쿡 웃다

He chuckled over watching TV.

churn

to agitate or stir (milk or cream)

stir up, swirl, agitate

휘젓다, 거품나게 하다

The storm churned the sea.

cling

to hold tight or adhere closely

adhere, cohere, stick to

달라붙다, 매달리다

Wet paper clings to glass.

comfort

to make a state of ease, being relaxed, and feeling no pain

ease, relax, calm down, tranquilize

편안하게 하다, 편안

The nurse comforted the patient.

* 이미지는 구글에서 찾은 것으로, 단어와 이미지가 다를 수 있습니다. 'Test 3'에서 나만의 이미지를 그려볼 수 있습니다.

Test 1 Connecting Exercise

Score(/16)
Self-Evaluation

➢ 서로 맞는 것을 연결하시오.

Ⓐ 1~4 영어 단어와 우리말 뜻 연결하기

1 comfort	•	• 달라붙다, 매달리다
2 churn	•	• 혼자서 소리작게 낄낄 웃다, 웃음 참으며 쿡쿡 웃다
3 chuckle	•	• 휘젓다, 거품나게 하다
4 cling	•	• 편안하게 하다, 편안

Ⓑ 5~8 영어 단어와 영어 설명 연결하기

5 churn	•	• to agitate or stir (milk or cream)
6 comfort	•	• to make a state of ease, being relaxed, and feeling no pain
7 cling	•	• to laugh quietly or to oneself
8 chuckle	•	• to hold tight or adhere closely

Ⓒ 9~12 영어 단어와 동의어 연결하기

9 chuckle	•	• stir up, swirl, agitate
10 comfort	•	• ease, relax, calm down, tranquilize
11 cling	•	• chortle, laugh, giggle, snigger
12 churn	•	• adhere, cohere, stick to

Ⓓ 13~16 우리말 뜻과 영어 단어 연결하기

13 혼자서 소리작게 낄낄 웃다, 웃음 참으며 쿡쿡 웃다	•	• cling
14 달라붙다, 매달리다	•	• chuckle
15 편안하게 하다, 편안	•	• churn
16 휘젓다, 거품나게 하다	•	• comfort

Test 2 Writing Exercise

Score(　　/12)
Self-Evaluation

A 1~4 다음 단어에 맞는 뜻을 쓰시오.

1 cling ______________________

2 churn ______________________

3 comfort ______________________

4 chuckle ______________________

B 5~8 다음 뜻에 맞는 영어 단어와 영어 동의어, 영어 설명을 쓰시오.

5 혼자서 소리작게 낄낄 웃다, 웃음 참으며 쿡쿡 웃다

__________ ______________________

____

6 휘젓다, 거품나게 하다

__________ ______________________

____

7 달라붙다, 매달리다

__________ ______________________

____

8 편안하게 하다, 편안

__________ ______________________

____

C 9~12 다음 영어 문장을 의미가 떠오를 때까지 소리 내어 읽어보시오. 1.5초 이내

9 The nurse comforted the patient.

____

10 He chuckled over watching TV.

____

11 The storm churned the sea.

____

12 Wet paper clings to glass.

____

Imaging Exercise
Test 3

➤ 다음 단어에 맞는 나만의 짧은 영어 설명을 써보자. (또는 그림을 그려보자.)

chuckle
[ʧʌkl]

churn
[ʧəːrn]

cling
[kliŋ]

comfort
[kʌmfərt]

➤ Month 01-DAY 17 영어 문장과 우리말

He chuckled over watching TV.
그는 TV를 보면서 웃었습니다.

The storm churned the sea.
폭풍이 바다를 뒤집어놓았다(휘저어 놓았다).

Wet paper clings to glass.
젖은 종이는 유리에 착 달라붙습니다.

The nurse comforted the patient.
간호사가 환자를 편안하게 해 주었습니다.

DAY 18 Vocabulary

➢ 음원을 들으면서 소리를 무조건 따라해 보시오. (빠르기&정확도/브레인+마우스 운동)

complain

to express feelings of pain, dissatisfaction, or resentment

find fault, grumble, grouch

불평하다, 호소하다

She complained of a headache.

conduct

to direct in action or course

manage, transmit, carry on

지휘하다, 안내하다,
운반하다, 전도하다

A police officer conducts traffic.

confuse

to make unclear

perplex, bewilder, make unclear

헷갈리게 하다, 혼동하다

I always confuse the twins.

connect

to be linked together or fasten together, link, join

join, unite, concern

연결하다, 접속하다

The Internet connects the world.

* 이미지는 구글에서 찾은 것으로, 단어와 이미지가 다를 수 있습니다. 'Test 3'에서 나만의 이미지를 그려볼 수 있습니다.

Test 1 Connecting Exercise

Score(/16)
Self-Evaluation

➢ 서로 맞는 것을 연결하시오.

Ⓐ 1~4 영어 단어와 우리말 뜻 연결하기

1 complain	연결하다, 접속하다
2 connect	불평하다, 호소하다
3 conduct	헷갈리게 하다, 혼동하다
4 confuse	지휘하다, 안내하다, 운반하다, 전도하다

Ⓑ 5~8 영어 단어와 영어 설명 연결하기

5 confuse	to direct in action or course
6 complain	to be linked together or fasten together, link, join
7 conduct	to make unclear
8 connect	to express feelings of pain, dissatisfaction, or resentment

Ⓒ 9~12 영어 단어와 동의어 연결하기

9 conduct	perplex, bewilder, make unclear
10 confuse	find fault, grumble, grouch
11 connect	manage, transmit, carry on
12 complain	join, unite, concern

Ⓓ 13~16 우리말 뜻과 영어 단어 연결하기

13 연결하다, 접속하다	complain
14 헷갈리게 하다, 혼동하다	connect
15 불평하다, 호소하다	confuse
16 지휘하다, 안내하다, 운반하다, 전도하다	conduct

Test 2 Writing Exercise

Score(　　/12)
Self-Evaluation

Ⓐ 1~4 다음 단어에 맞는 뜻을 쓰시오.

1 connect ______________________

2 conduct ______________________

3 confuse ______________________

4 complain ______________________

Ⓑ 5~8 다음 뜻에 맞는 영어 단어와 영어 동의어, 영어 설명을 쓰시오.

5 연결하다, 접속하다

__________ ______________________

____

6 지휘하다, 안내하다, 운반하다, 전도하다

__________ ______________________

____

7 불평하다, 호소하다

__________ ______________________

____

8 헷갈리게 하다, 혼동하다

__________ ______________________

____

Ⓒ 9~12 다음 영어 문장을 의미가 떠오를 때까지 소리 내어 읽어보시오. 1.5초 이내

9 She complained of a headache.

____

10 I always confuse the twins.

____

11 The Internet connects the world.

____

12 A police officer conducts traffic.

____

Test 3 Imaging Exercise

➢ 다음 단어에 맞는 나만의 짧은 영어 설명을 써보자. (또는 그림을 그려보자.)

complain
[kəmpléin]

conduct
[kándʌkt]

confuse
[kənfjúːz]

connect
[kənékt]

➢ Month 01-DAY 18 영어 문장과 우리말

She complained of a headache.
그녀는 두통을 호소했다.

A police officer conducts traffic.
경찰관이 교통을 지휘 안내하고 있습니다.

I always confuse the twins.
나는 항상 그 쌍둥이를 헷갈려 혼동한다.

The Internet connects the world.
인터넷은 세계를 연결합니다.

Vocabulary

➢ 음원을 들으면서 소리를 무조건 따라해 보시오. (빠르기&정확도/브레인+마우스 운동)

consume

to use up or spend

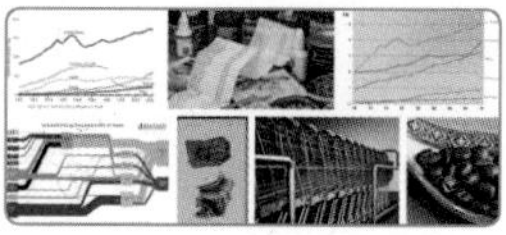

spend, expend, waste, exhaust

소비하다

My car consumes little oil.

creep, crept, crept

to move with the body close to the ground as on hands and knees, crawl

crawl

기다, 포복하다, 살금살금 걷다

Traffic creeps at that hour.

destroy

to break apart the structure of

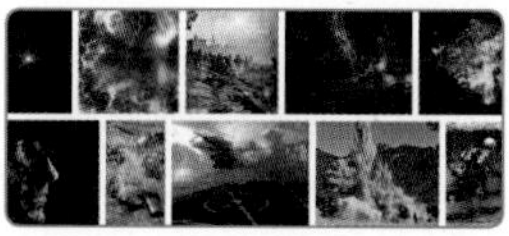

raze, demolish, ruin, wreck

파괴하다, 파멸시키다

The fire destroyed the house.

discuss

to speak with another or others about

talk about, debate, review

토론하다, 의논하다, 논의하다

They discussed the matter briefly.

* 이미지는 구글에서 찾은 것으로, 단어와 이미지가 다를 수 있습니다. 'Test 3'에서 나만의 이미지를 그려볼 수 있습니다.

Test 1 Connecting Exercise

Score(/16)
Self-Evaluation

➢ 서로 맞는 것을 연결하시오.

Ⓐ 1~4 영어 단어와 우리말 뜻 연결하기

1 creep, crept, crept	• 토론하다, 의논하다, 논의하다
2 consume	• 기다, 포복하다, 살금살금 걷다
3 destroy	• 파괴하다, 파멸시키다
4 discuss	• 소비하다

Ⓑ 5~8 영어 단어와 영어 설명 연결하기

5 consume	• to move with the body close to the ground as on hands and knees, crawl
6 destroy	• to speak with another or others about
7 discuss	• to use up or spend
8 creep, crept, crept	• to break apart the structure of

Ⓒ 9~12 영어 단어와 동의어 연결하기

9 consume	• talk about, debate, review
10 creep, crept, crept	• crawl
11 destroy	• raze, demolish, ruin, wreck
12 discuss	• spend, expend, waste, exhaust

Ⓓ 13~16 우리말 뜻과 영어 단어 연결하기

13 기다, 포복하다, 살금살금 걷다	• discuss
14 파괴하다, 파멸시키다	• destroy
15 토론하다, 의논하다, 논의하다	• creep, crept, crept
16 소비하다	• consume

Test 2 Writing Exercise

Score(/12)
Self-Evaluation

A 1~4 다음 단어에 맞는 뜻을 쓰시오.

1 consume ______
2 destroy ______
3 discuss ______
4 creep, crept, crept ______

B 5~8 다음 뜻에 맞는 영어 단어와 영어 동의어, 영어 설명을 쓰시오.

5 소비하다

______ ______

______

6 기다, 포복하다, 살금살금 걷다

______ ______

______

7 토론하다, 의논하다, 논의하다

______ ______

______

8 파괴하다, 파멸시키다

______ ______

______

C 9~12 다음 영어 문장을 의미가 떠오를 때까지 소리 내어 읽어보시오. 1.5초 이내

9 They discussed the matter briefly.

______

10 My car consumes little oil.

______

11 The fire destroyed the house.

______

12 Traffic creeps at that hour.

______

Test 3 Imaging Exercise

➢ 다음 단어에 맞는 나만의 짧은 영어 설명을 써보자. (또는 그림을 그려보자.)

consume
[kənsúːm]

creep, crept, crept
[kriːp, krept, krept]

destroy
[distrɔ́i]

discuss
[diskʌ́s]

➢ Month 01-DAY 19 영어 문장과 우리말

My car consumes little oil.
내 차는 가스가(기름이) 적게 듭니다.

Traffic creeps at that hour.
그 시간에 교통흐름은 차들이 기어갑니다.

The fire destroyed the house.
화재가 집을 파괴했습니다.

They discussed the matter briefly.
그들은 그 문제에 대해 간략하게 논의하였습니다.

DAY 20 Vocabulary

➢ 음원을 들으면서 소리를 무조건 따라해 보시오. (빠르기&정확도/브레인+마우스 운동)

dive

to plunge, especially headfirst, into water

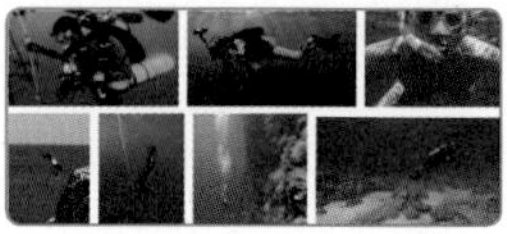

plunge, drop, jump

잠수하다, 뛰어들다,
다이빙하다, 급강하하다

He dived into a river.

drink, drank, drunk

to take a liquid into the mouth and swallow it

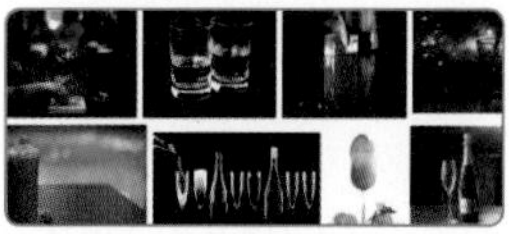

sip, imbibe, swallow liquid

(물이나 음료 등을) 마시다, 음료

You drink too much coffee.

earn

to gain or get in return for one's labor or service

get paid, make, get, receive

(일을 해서) 돈을 벌다, 돈을 받다

She earns $1500 a week.

enrage

to make violently angry or put into a rage

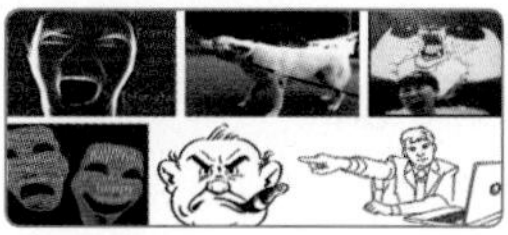

incense, infuriate, anger

화나게 하다, 격분시키다

Her arrogant attitude enraged me.

* 이미지는 구글에서 찾은 것으로, 단어와 이미지가 다를 수 있습니다. 'Test 3'에서 나만의 이미지를 그려볼 수 있습니다.

Test 1 Connecting Exercise

Score(/16)
Self-Evaluation

➢ 서로 맞는 것을 연결하시오.

A 1~4 영어 단어와 우리말 뜻 연결하기

1 drink, drank, drunk	●	● (일을 해서) 돈을 벌다, 돈을 받다
2 enrage	●	● 잠수하다, 뛰어들다, 다이빙하다, 급강하하다
3 earn	●	● (물이나 음료 등을) 마시다, 음료
4 dive	●	● 화나게 하다, 격분시키다

B 5~8 영어 단어와 영어 설명 연결하기

5 drink, drank, drunk	●	● to plunge, especially headfirst, into water
6 dive	●	● to gain or get in return for one's labor or service
7 earn	●	● to take a liquid into the mouth and swallow it
8 enrage	●	● to make violently angry or put into a rage

C 9~12 영어 단어와 동의어 연결하기

9 dive	●	● plunge, drop, jump
10 earn	●	● sip, imbibe, swallow liquid
11 enrage	●	● incense, infuriate, anger
12 drink, drank, drunk	●	● get paid, make, get, receive

D 13~16 우리말 뜻과 영어 단어 연결하기

13 잠수하다, 뛰어들다, 다이빙하다, 급강하하다	●	● earn
14 화나게 하다, 격분시키다	●	● dive
15 (물이나 음료 등을) 마시다, 음료	●	● drink, drank, drunk
16 (일을 해서) 돈을 벌다, 돈을 받다	●	● enrage

Test 2 Writing Exercise

Score(　/12)
Self-Evaluation

A 1~4 다음 단어에 맞는 뜻을 쓰시오.

1 earn ______

2 enrage ______

3 drink, drank, drunk ______

4 dive ______

B 5~8 다음 뜻에 맞는 영어 단어와 영어 동의어, 영어 설명을 쓰시오.

5 (일을 해서) 돈을 벌다, 돈을 받다

______ ______

______

6 (물이나 음료 등을) 마시다, 음료

______ ______

______

7 화나게 하다, 격분시키다

______ ______

______

8 잠수하다, 뛰어들다, 다이빙하다, 급강하하다

______ ______

______

C 9~12 다음 영어 문장을 의미가 떠오를 때까지 소리 내어 읽어보시오. 1.5초 이내

9 You drink too much coffee.

______

10 Her arrogant attitude enraged me.

______

11 He dived into a river.

______

12 She earns $1500 a week.

______

Test 3 Imaging Exercise

➤ 다음 단어에 맞는 나만의 짧은 영어 설명을 써보자. (또는 그림을 그려보자.)

dive
[daiv]

drink, drank, drunk
[driŋk, dræŋk, drʌŋk]

earn
[əːrn]

enrage
[inréidʒ]

➤ Month 01-DAY 20 영어 문장과 우리말

He dived into a river.
그는 강으로 뛰어들었습니다.

You drink too much coffee.
당신은 커피를 너무 많이 마십니다.

She earns $1500 a week.
그녀는 주급 1500달러를 받습니다.

Her arrogant attitude enraged me.
그녀의 오만한 태도가 나를 화나게 했습니다.

Month 02 Verbs

Day 01	equal, execute, expect, fasten
Day 02	fit, follow, forbid, gallop
Day 03	grip, growl, guess, handle
Day 04	hiss, hop, insist, kick
Day 05	lie, loosen, manage, mark
Day 06	mutter, object, offer, operate
Day 07	overlook, overtake, owe, pamper
Day 08	pay, peck, pour, prefer~
Day 09	punish, recall, receive, recover
Day 10	represent, shake, slide, spout
Day 11	stand, subdue, upset, accomplish
Day 12	adopt, amount, appoint, argue
Day 13	ascend, attack, attend, bear
Day 14	begin, bet, blame, bless
Day 15	browse, capture, concern, congratulate
Day 16	conquer, consist, continue, cooperate
Day 17	cover, crack, crawl, decide
Day 18	delight, differ, digest, disappear
Day 19	disappoint, doubt, doze, drain
Day 20	dream, dress, endure, engage

DAY 01 Vocabulary

➢ 음원을 들으면서 소리를 무조건 따라해 보시오. (빠르기&정확도/브레인+마우스 운동)

equal

to be equal to

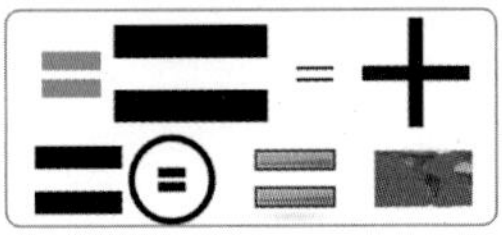

equivalent, even, identical, same

같다, 똑같다, 동일하다, 같은, 동일한

2+3=5, two plus three equals five.

execute

to put into effect or to carry out

perform, carry out

실행하다, 집행하다

I have executed a plan.

expect

to anticipate the occurrence or the coming of

anticipate, hope, await

기대하다, 기다리다, 예상하다

We expect good news today.

fasten

to attach firmly to something else, as by pinning or nailing

fix, tie, bind

단단히 매다, 고정하다

She fastened the seat belt.

* 이미지는 구글에서 찾은 것으로, 단어와 이미지가 다를 수 있습니다. 'Test 3'에서 나만의 이미지를 그려볼 수 있습니다.

Test 1 Connecting Exercise

Score(/16)
Self-Evaluation

➢ 서로 맞는 것을 연결하시오.

A 1~4 영어 단어와 우리말 뜻 연결하기

1 equal	•	• 기대하다, 기다리다, 예상하다
2 execute	•	• 실행하다, 집행하다
3 fasten	•	• 같다, 똑같다, 동일하다, 같은, 동일한
4 expect	•	• 단단히 매다, 고정하다

B 5~8 영어 단어와 영어 설명 연결하기

5 execute	•	• to attach firmly to something else, as by pinning or nailing
6 fasten	•	• to put into effect or to carry out
7 equal	•	• to anticipate the occurrence or the coming of
8 expect	•	• to be equal to

C 9~12 영어 단어와 동의어 연결하기

9 execute	•	• equivalent, even, identical, same
10 fasten	•	• perform, carry out
11 equal	•	• anticipate, hope, await
12 expect	•	• fix, tie, bind

D 13~16 우리말 뜻과 영어 단어 연결하기

13 같다, 똑같다, 동일하다, 같은, 동일한	•	• execute
14 실행하다, 집행하다	•	• equal
15 단단히 매다, 고정하다	•	• fasten
16 기대하다, 기다리다, 예상하다	•	• expect

Test 2 Writing Exercise

Score(　　/12)
Self-Evaluation

A 1~4 다음 단어에 맞는 뜻을 쓰시오.

1 execute ______________________

2 equal ______________________

3 expect ______________________

4 fasten ______________________

B 5~8 다음 뜻에 맞는 영어 단어와 영어 동의어, 영어 설명을 쓰시오.

5 실행하다, 집행하다

__________ ______________________

____

6 단단히 매다, 고정하다

__________ ______________________

____

7 같다, 똑같다, 동일하다, 같은, 동일한

__________ ______________________

____

8 기대하다, 기다리다, 예상하다

__________ ______________________

____

C 9~12 다음 영어 문장을 의미가 떠오를 때까지 소리 내어 읽어보시오. 1.5초 이내

9 I have executed a plan.

____

10 She fastened the seat belt.

____

11 2+3=5, two plus three equals five.

____

12 We expect good news today.

____

Test 3

➢ 다음 단어에 맞는 나만의 짧은 영어 설명을 써보자. (또는 그림을 그려보자.)

equal
[íːkwəl]

execute
[éksikjùːt]

expect
[ikspékt]

fasten
[fasten]

➢ Month 02-DAY 01 영어 문장과 우리말

2+3=5, two plus three equals five.
2+3은 5입니다.

I have executed a plan.
나는 계획을 실행했습니다.

We expect good news today.
우리는 오늘 좋은 소식을 기대합니다.

She fastened the seat belt.
그녀는 안전벨트(좌석벨트)를 맸습니다.

Vocabulary

➢ 음원을 들으면서 소리를 무조건 따라해 보시오. (빠르기&정확도/브레인+마우스 운동)

fit

to be the proper size and shape for

be the right size for

알맞다, 적합한, 알맞은

These shoes fit me perfectly.

follow

to come or go after

succeed, ensue, come after, go after

따르다, 따라가다, ~다음에 온다, ~뒤에 온다

The meeting follows the dinner.

forbid, forbade, forbidden

to command (someone) not to do something

ban, prohibit, proscribe

금지하다, 허락하지 않다

I forbid you to go.

gallop

to ride at full speed

run, race, rush

말이 전속력으로 달리다, 질주하다

The frightened horses galloped away.

* 이미지는 구글에서 찾은 것으로, 단어와 이미지가 다를 수 있습니다. 'Test 3'에서 나만의 이미지를 그려볼 수 있습니다.

Test 1 Connecting Exercise

Score(　　/16)
Self-Evaluation

➢ 서로 맞는 것을 연결하시오.

Ⓐ 1~4 영어 단어와 우리말 뜻 연결하기

1 follow	●	● 금지하다, 허락하지 않다
2 fit	●	● 따르다, 따라가다, ~다음에 온다, ~뒤에 온다
3 forbid, forbade, forbidden	●	● 알맞다, 적합한, 알맞은
4 gallop	●	● 말이 전속력으로 달리다, 질주하다

Ⓑ 5~8 영어 단어와 영어 설명 연결하기

5 fit	●	● to ride at full speed
6 follow	●	● to come or go after
7 gallop	●	● to command (someone) not to do something
8 forbid, forbade, forbidden	●	● to be the proper size and shape for

Ⓒ 9~12 영어 단어와 동의어 연결하기

9 fit	●	● run, race, rush
10 gallop	●	● be the right size for
11 follow	●	● succeed, ensue, come after, go after
12 forbid, forbade, forbidden	●	● ban, prohibit, proscribe

Ⓓ 13~16 우리말 뜻과 영어 단어 연결하기

13 금지하다, 허락하지 않다	●	● forbid, forbade, forbidden
14 알맞다, 적합한, 알맞은	●	● follow
15 말이 전속력으로 달리다, 질주하다	●	● gallop
16 따르다, 따라가다, ~다음에 온다, ~뒤에 온다	●	● fit

Test 2 Writing Exercise

Score(/12)
Self-Evaluation

Ⓐ 1~4 다음 단어에 맞는 뜻을 쓰시오.

1 fit ____________________

2 gallop ____________________

3 forbid, forbade, forbidden ____________________

4 follow ____________________

Ⓑ 5~8 다음 뜻에 맞는 영어 단어와 영어 동의어, 영어 설명을 쓰시오.

5 알맞다, 적합한, 알맞은

__________ ____________________

____

6 금지하다, 허락하지 않다

__________ ____________________

____

7 따르다, 따라가다, ~다음에 온다, ~뒤에 온다

__________ ____________________

____

8 말이 전속력으로 달리다, 질주하다

__________ ____________________

____

Ⓒ 9~12 다음 영어 문장을 의미가 떠오를 때까지 소리 내어 읽어보시오. 1.5초 이내

9 These shoes fit me perfectly.

____

10 The meeting follows the dinner.

____

11 I forbid you to go.

____

12 The frightened horses galloped away.

____

Test 3 Imaging Exercise

➢ 다음 단어에 맞는 나만의 짧은 영어 설명을 써보자. (또는 그림을 그려보자.)

fit
[fit]

follow
[fálou]

forbid, forbade, forbidden
[forbid, fərbǽd, fərbídn]

gallop
[gǽləp]

➢ Month 02-DAY 02 영어 문장과 우리말

These shoes fit me perfectly.
이 신발은 나에게 딱 맞습니다.

The meeting follows the dinner.
회의는 저녁식사 다음에 있습니다.

I forbid you to go.
나는 당신이 가는 것을 금지합니다.

The frightened horses galloped away.
깜짝 놀란 말들이 전속력으로 질주했습니다.

DAY 03

Vocabulary

➢ 음원을 들으면서 소리를 무조건 따라해 보시오. (빠르기 & 정확도/브레인 + 마우스 운동)

grip

to grasp or seize firmly

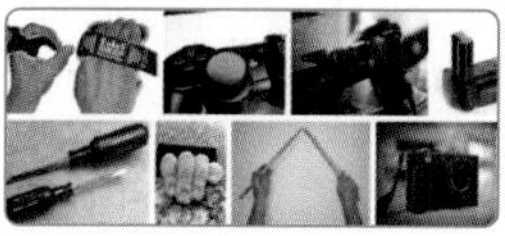

grasp, hold, catch, seize

꽉 잡다, 사로잡다, 꽉 잡음

She gripped his hand tightly.

growl

to utter a deep sound of anger or hostility, as a dog

snarl

으르렁거리다

The dog growled at us.

guess

to predict (something) without sufficient information

estimate, predict, conjecture

추측하다

I guess that is true.

handle

to operate with the hands

manipulate, operate, manage, control

처리하다, 다루다, 조종하다, 손잡이

I can handle the job.

* 이미지는 구글에서 찾은 것으로, 단어와 이미지가 다를 수 있습니다. 'Test 3'에서 나만의 이미지를 그려볼 수 있습니다.

Test 1 Connecting Exercise

Score(/16)
Self-Evaluation

➢ 서로 맞는 것을 연결하시오.

Ⓐ 1~4 영어 단어와 우리말 뜻 연결하기

1	grip	추측하다
2	handle	으르렁거리다
3	growl	꽉 잡다, 사로잡다, 꽉 잡음
4	guess	처리하다, 다루다, 조종하다, 손잡이

Ⓑ 5~8 영어 단어와 영어 설명 연결하기

5	handle	to operate with the hands
6	growl	to utter a deep sound of anger or hostility, as a dog
7	guess	to grasp or seize firmly
8	grip	to predict (something) without sufficient information

Ⓒ 9~12 영어 단어와 동의어 연결하기

9	growl	estimate, predict, conjecture
10	guess	snarl
11	handle	manipulate, operate, manage, control
12	grip	grasp, hold, catch, seize

Ⓓ 13~16 우리말 뜻과 영어 단어 연결하기

13	추측하다	grip
14	으르렁거리다	guess
15	꽉 잡다, 사로잡다, 꽉 잡음	growl
16	처리하다, 다루다, 조종하다, 손잡이	handle

Test 2 Writing Exercise

Score(/12)
Self-Evaluation

A 1~4 다음 단어에 맞는 뜻을 쓰시오.

1 grip ______

2 handle ______

3 growl ______

4 guess ______

B 5~8 다음 뜻에 맞는 영어 단어와 영어 동의어, 영어 설명을 쓰시오.

5 처리하다, 다루다, 조종하다, 손잡이

______ ______

______

6 꽉 잡다, 사로잡다, 꽉 잡음

______ ______

______

7 추측하다

______ ______

______

8 으르렁거리다

______ ______

______

C 9~12 다음 영어 문장을 의미가 떠오를 때까지 소리 내어 읽어보시오. 1.5초 이내

9 She gripped his hand tightly.

______

10 I can handle the job.

______

11 I guess that is true.

______

12 The dog growled at us.

______

Imaging Exercise

Test 3

➤ 다음 단어에 맞는 나만의 짧은 영어 설명을 써보자. (또는 그림을 그려보자.)

grip
[grip]

growl
[graul]

guess
[ges]

handle
[hǽndl]

➤ Month 02-DAY 03 영어 문장과 우리말

She gripped his hand tightly.
그녀는 그의 손을 꽉 잡았습니다.

The dog growled at us.
그 개가 우리를 보고 으르렁거렸습니다.

I guess that is true.
나는 그것이 사실일 것이라고 추측한다.

I can handle the job.
나는 그 일을 처리할 수 있습니다.

DAY 04 Vocabulary

➢ 음원을 들으면서 소리를 무조건 따라해 보시오. (빠르기 & 정확도/브레인 + 마우스 운동)

hiss

to produce or utter a hiss

siss, sizz, sibilate

쉿 하는 소리를 내다

The audience booed and hissed.

hop

to make a jump forwards or upwards

jump, bound, bounce, skip

깡충 뛰다, 깡충깡충 뛰다

I hopped down three steps.

insist

to make a determined demand for

persist, demand, require, urge

주장하다, 고집하다

I insisted on my rights.

kick

to extend the leg away from the body

strike, kicking

발로 차다

The boy kicked the dog.

* 이미지는 구글에서 찾은 것으로, 단어와 이미지가 다를 수 있습니다. 'Test 3'에서 나만의 이미지를 그려볼 수 있습니다.

Test 1 Connecting Exercise

Score(/16)
Self-Evaluation

➢ 서로 맞는 것을 연결하시오.

A 1~4 영어 단어와 우리말 뜻 연결하기

1	hiss	•	• 발로 차다
2	insist	•	• 깡충 뛰다, 깡충깡충 뛰다
3	kick	•	• 주장하다, 고집하다
4	hop	•	• 쉿 하는 소리를 내다

B 5~8 영어 단어와 영어 설명 연결하기

5	insist	•	• to produce or utter a hiss
6	hiss	•	• to make a determined demand for
7	hop	•	• to make a jump forwards or upwards
8	kick	•	• to extend the leg away from the body

C 9~12 영어 단어와 동의어 연결하기

9	hop	•	• persist, demand, require, urge
10	hiss	•	• strike, kicking
11	insist	•	• siss, sizz, sibilate
12	kick	•	• jump, bound, bounce, skip

D 13~16 우리말 뜻과 영어 단어 연결하기

13	쉿 하는 소리를 내다	•	• insist
14	깡충 뛰다, 깡충깡충 뛰다	•	• kick
15	주장하다, 고집하다	•	• hiss
16	발로 차다	•	• hop

Test 2 Writing Exercise

Score(/12)
Self-Evaluation

A 1~4 다음 단어에 맞는 뜻을 쓰시오.

1 insist ____________________

2 hiss ____________________

3 kick ____________________

4 hop ____________________

B 5~8 다음 뜻에 맞는 영어 단어와 영어 동의어, 영어 설명을 쓰시오.

5 쉿 하는 소리를 내다

__________ ____________________

____

6 깡충 뛰다, 깡충깡충 뛰다

__________ ____________________

____

7 주장하다, 고집하다

__________ ____________________

____

8 발로 차다

__________ ____________________

____

C 9~12 다음 영어 문장을 의미가 떠오를 때까지 소리 내어 읽어보시오. 1.5초 이내

9 The boy kicked the dog.

____

10 The audience booed and hissed.

____

11 I insisted on my rights.

____

12 I hopped down three steps.

____

Test 3

➢ 다음 단어에 맞는 나만의 짧은 영어 설명을 써보자. (또는 그림을 그려보자.)

hiss
[his]

hop
[hap]

insist
[insíst]

kick
[kik]

➢ Month 02-DAY 04 영어 문장과 우리말

The audience booed and hissed.
청중들이 쉬익하는 소리를 내면서 야유를 퍼부었습니다.

I hopped down three steps.
나는 세 단계 아래로 건너뛰었습니다.

I insisted on my rights.
나는 나의 권리를 주장하였습니다.

The boy kicked the dog.
아이가 개를 발로 걷어찼습니다.

➢ 음원을 들으면서 소리를 무조건 따라해 보시오. (빠르기 & 정확도/브레인 + 마우스 운동)

lie, lied, lied

to say or write as a lie

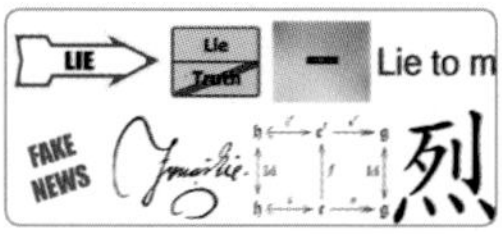

equivocate, prevaricate, fib

거짓말하다

The camera does not lie.

loosen

to make looser or less tight

loose, relax, soften

느슨하게 하다, 풀어 주다

He loosened the seat belt.

manage

to take charge of or to have charge of

direct, operate, run, handle

관리하다, 경영하다

I can manage a company.

mark

to make a visible trace

scar, scratch, imprint

표시하다, 표시

This sign marks the border.

* 이미지는 구글에서 찾은 것으로, 단어와 이미지가 다를 수 있습니다. 'Test 3'에서 나만의 이미지를 그려볼 수 있습니다.

Test 1 Connecting Exercise

Score(/16)
Self-Evaluation

➢ 서로 맞는 것을 연결하시오.

Ⓐ 1~4 영어 단어와 우리말 뜻 연결하기

1	loosen	거짓말하다
2	mark	느슨하게 하다, 풀어 주다
3	manage	관리하다, 경영하다
4	lie, lied, lied	표시하다, 표시

Ⓑ 5~8 영어 단어와 영어 설명 연결하기

5	mark	to take charge of or to have charge of
6	lie, lied, lied	to make looser or less tight
7	loosen	to make a visible trace
8	manage	to say or write as a lie

Ⓒ 9~12 영어 단어와 동의어 연결하기

9	lie, lied, lied	scar, scratch, imprint
10	loosen	equivocate, prevaricate, fib
11	manage	direct, operate, run, handle
12	mark	loose, relax, soften

Ⓓ 13~16 우리말 뜻과 영어 단어 연결하기

13	표시하다, 표시	lie, lied, lied
14	관리하다, 경영하다	loosen
15	느슨하게 하다, 풀어 주다	manage
16	거짓말하다	mark

Test 2 Writing Exercise

Score(/12)
Self-Evaluation

A 1~4 다음 단어에 맞는 뜻을 쓰시오.

1 loosen ______

2 lie, lied, lied ______

3 manage ______

4 mark ______

B 5~8 다음 뜻에 맞는 영어 단어와 영어 동의어, 영어 설명을 쓰시오.

5 거짓말하다

______ ______

______

6 관리하다, 경영하다

______ ______

______

7 표시하다, 표시

______ ______

______

8 느슨하게 하다, 풀어 주다

______ ______

______

C 9~12 다음 영어 문장을 의미가 떠오를 때까지 소리 내어 읽어보시오. 1.5초 이내

9 The camera does not lie.

______

10 He loosened the seat belt.

______

11 This sign marks the border.

______

12 I can manage a company.

______

Test 3 Imaging Exercise

➢ 다음 단어에 맞는 나만의 짧은 영어 설명을 써보자. (또는 그림을 그려보자.)

lie, lied, lied
[lai, laid, laid]

loosen
[lúːsn]

manage
[mǽnidʒ]

mark
[maːrk]

➢ Month 02-DAY 05 영어 문장과 우리말

The camera does not lie.
카메라는 거짓말을 하지 않습니다.

He loosened the seat belt.
그는 안전벨트를 느슨하게 했습니다.

I can manage a company.
나는 회사를 경영할 수 있습니다.

This sign marks the border.
이 표시는 국경을 표시합니다.

DAY 06

Vocabulary

➢ 음원을 들으면서 소리를 무조건 따라해 보시오. (빠르기&정확도/브레인+마우스 운동)

mutter

to speak or complain indistinctly in low tones

grumble, complain, murmur

중얼거리다, 구시렁거리다

He was muttering to himself.

object

to state as an objection

oppose, counter, resist

~에 반대하다

I objected to the plan.

offer

to present for acceptance

provide, give, hand

권하다, 제안하다, 제공하다, 제의

She offered me a drink.

operate

to function or cause to function

work, perform, function

작동하다, 운전하다, 수술하다

I can operate this machine.

* 이미지는 구글에서 찾은 것으로, 단어와 이미지가 다를 수 있습니다. 'Test 3'에서 나만의 이미지를 그려볼 수 있습니다.

Test 1 Connecting Exercise

Score(/16)
Self-Evaluation

➢ 서로 맞는 것을 연결하시오.

Ⓐ 1~4 영어 단어와 우리말 뜻 연결하기

1 offer	•	• 중얼거리다, 구시렁거리다
2 object	•	• 권하다, 제안하다, 제공하다, 제의
3 operate	•	• 작동하다, 운전하다, 수술하다
4 mutter	•	• ~에 반대하다

Ⓑ 5~8 영어 단어와 영어 설명 연결하기

5 mutter	•	• to function or cause to function
6 offer	•	• to speak or complain indistinctly in low tones
7 operate	•	• to present for acceptance
8 object	•	• to state as an objection

Ⓒ 9~12 영어 단어와 동의어 연결하기

9 mutter	•	• provide, give, hand
10 object	•	• oppose, counter, resist
11 offer	•	• grumble, complain, murmur
12 operate	•	• work, perform, function

Ⓓ 13~16 우리말 뜻과 영어 단어 연결하기

13 권하다, 제안하다, 제공하다, 제의	•	• offer
14 중얼거리다, 구시렁거리다	•	• mutter
15 작동하다, 운전하다, 수술하다	•	• operate
16 ~에 반대하다	•	• object

Test 2 Writing Exercise

Score(/12)
Self-Evaluation

Ⓐ 1~4 다음 단어에 맞는 뜻을 쓰시오.

1 mutter ______________________

2 offer ______________________

3 object ______________________

4 operate ______________________

Ⓑ 5~8 다음 뜻에 맞는 영어 단어와 영어 동의어, 영어 설명을 쓰시오.

5 권하다, 제안하다, 제공하다, 제의

__________ ______________________

____

6 작동하다, 운전하다, 수술하다

__________ ______________________

____

7 ~에 반대하다

__________ ______________________

____

8 중얼거리다, 구시렁거리다

__________ ______________________

____

Ⓒ 9~12 다음 영어 문장을 의미가 떠오를 때까지 소리 내어 읽어보시오. 1.5초 이내

9 I objected to the plan.

____

10 She offered me a drink.

____

11 I can operate this machine.

____

12 He was muttering to himself.

____

Test 3 Imaging Exercise

➢ 다음 단어에 맞는 나만의 짧은 영어 설명을 써보자. (또는 그림을 그려보자.)

mutter
[mʌtər]

object
[άbdʒikt]

offer
[ɔ́:fər]

operate
[άpərèit]

➢ Month 02-DAY 06 영어 문장과 우리말

He was muttering to himself.
그는 혼자서 중얼거리고 있었습니다.

I objected to the plan.
나는 그 계획에 반대했습니다.

She offered me a drink.
그녀는 나에게 음료를 권했습니다.

I can operate this machine.
나는 이 기계를 운전할 수 있습니다.

➢ **음원을 들으면서 소리를 무조건 따라해 보시오.** (빠르기&정확도/브레인+마우스 운동)

overlook

to look over from a higher place, or to fail to notice or consider

scan, survey, miss, omit

높은 데서 조망하다, 간과하다,
못 보고 지나치다

We might overlook the details.

overtake

to catch up with

outdo, exceed, get the better of

따라잡다, 따라붙다

You can't overtake that car.

owe

to be indebted to the amount of

be in debt (to)

빚이 있다, 빚지고 있다

He owes me five dollars.

pamper

to treat with excessive indulgence

indulge, coddle, spoil

응석받이로 키우다, 과보호하다,
해달라는 대로 해주다

Grandparents often pamper the children.

* 이미지는 구글에서 찾은 것으로, 단어와 이미지가 다를 수 있습니다. 'Test 3'에서 나만의 이미지를 그려볼 수 있습니다.

Test 1 Connecting Exercise

Score(　　/16)
Self-Evaluation

➢ 서로 맞는 것을 연결하시오.

Ⓐ 1~4 영어 단어와 우리말 뜻 연결하기

1 pamper	•	• 응석받이로 키우다, 과보호하다, 해달라는 대로 해주다
2 owe	•	• 빚이 있다, 빚지고 있다
3 overlook	•	• 따라잡다, 따라붙다
4 overtake	•	• 높은 데서 조망하다, 간과하다, 못 보고 지나치다

Ⓑ 5~8 영어 단어와 영어 설명 연결하기

5 owe	•	• to treat with excessive indulgence
6 pamper	•	• to catch up with
7 overtake	•	• to be indebted to the amount of
8 overlook	•	• to look over from a higher place, or to fail to notice or consider

Ⓒ 9~12 영어 단어와 동의어 연결하기

9 pamper	•	• indulge, coddle, spoil
10 overtake	•	• scan, survey, miss, omit
11 owe	•	• outdo, exceed, get the better of
12 overlook	•	• be in debt (to)

Ⓓ 13~16 우리말 뜻과 영어 단어 연결하기

13 응석받이로 키우다, 과보호하다, 해달라는 대로 해주다	•	• overlook
14 높은 데서 조망하다, 간과하다, 못 보고 지나치다	•	• pamper
15 빚이 있다, 빚지고 있다	•	• overtake
16 따라잡다, 따라붙다	•	• owe

Test 2

Writing Exercise

Score(　　/12)
Self-Evaluation

A 1~4 다음 단어에 맞는 뜻을 쓰시오.

1 overlook ______________________

2 overtake ______________________

3 pamper ______________________

4 owe ______________________

B 5~8 다음 뜻에 맞는 영어 단어와 영어 동의어, 영어 설명을 쓰시오.

5 높은 데서 조망하다, 간과하다, 못 보고 지나치다

__________ ______________________

____

6 빚이 있다, 빚지고 있다

__________ ______________________

____

7 따라잡다, 따라붙다

__________ ______________________

____

8 응석받이로 키우다, 과보호하다, 해달라는 대로 해주다

__________ ______________________

____

C 9~12 다음 영어 문장을 의미가 떠오를 때까지 소리 내어 읽어보시오. 1.5초 이내

9 He owes me five dollars.

____

10 Grandparents often pamper the children.

____

11 You can't overtake that car.

____

12 We might overlook the details.

____

Test 3

➢ 다음 단어에 맞는 나만의 짧은 영어 설명을 써보자. (또는 그림을 그려보자.)

overlook
[ou'vərlʊˌk]

overtake
[ou'vərteiˌk]

owe
[ou]

pamper
[pǽmpər]

➢ Month 02-DAY 07 영어 문장과 우리말

We might overlook the details.
우리는 세세한 것을 간과할지도 모릅니다.

You can't overtake that car.
당신은 저 차를 따라잡을 수 없습니다.

He owes me five dollars.
그는 나에게 5달러의 빚이 있습니다.

Grandparents often pamper the children.
할머니, 할아버지들은 가끔 아이들의 응석을 다 받아 줍니다.

DAY 08 Vocabulary

➢ **음원을 들으면서 소리를 무조건 따라해 보시오.** (빠르기 & 정확도/브레인 + 마우스 운동)

pay

to give money in exchange for goods or services

reward, compensate

지불하다

I paid for the tickets.

peck

to strike with the beak, or to kiss quickly and briefly

bite, hit, strike

(부리로) 쪼다, 쪼아 먹다,
가볍게 키스하다

The crow pecked his hand.

pour

to cause to stream or flow, as from a container

decant, flow, gush

쏟아붓다, 쏟아지다, 흘러나오다

Students poured into the auditorium.

prefer~

to give priority to

like better, favor

~를 더 좋아하다,
~에 우선순위를 더 두다

I prefer movie to sports.

* 이미지는 구글에서 찾은 것으로, 단어와 이미지가 다를 수 있습니다. 'Test 3'에서 나만의 이미지를 그려볼 수 있습니다.

Test 1 Connecting Exercise

Score(/16)
Self-Evaluation

➢ 서로 맞는 것을 연결하시오.

Ⓐ 1~4 영어 단어와 우리말 뜻 연결하기

1 peck	•	•	(부리로) 쪼다, 쪼아 먹다, 가볍게 키스하다
2 pour	•	•	~를 더 좋아하다, ~에 우선순위를 더 두다
3 prefer~	•	•	지불하다
4 pay	•	•	쏟아붓다, 쏟아지다, 흘러나오다

Ⓑ 5~8 영어 단어와 영어 설명 연결하기

5 pay	•	•	to strike with the beak, or to kiss quickly and briefly
6 peck	•	•	to give priority to
7 pour	•	•	to give money in exchange for goods or services
8 prefer~	•	•	to cause to stream or flow, as from a container

Ⓒ 9~12 영어 단어와 동의어 연결하기

9 prefer~	•	•	reward, compensate
10 pay	•	•	decant, flow, gush
11 pour	•	•	bite, hit, strike
12 peck	•	•	like better, favor

Ⓓ 13~16 우리말 뜻과 영어 단어 연결하기

13 지불하다	•	•	prefer~
14 ~를 더 좋아하다, ~에 우선순위를 더 두다	•	•	peck
15 쏟아붓다, 쏟아지다, 흘러나오다	•	•	pay
16 (부리로) 쪼다, 쪼아 먹다, 가볍게 키스하다	•	•	pour

Test 2 Writing Exercise

Score(/12)
Self-Evaluation

A 1~4 다음 단어에 맞는 뜻을 쓰시오.

1 pay ______

2 peck ______

3 prefer~ ______

4 pour ______

B 5~8 다음 뜻에 맞는 영어 단어와 영어 동의어, 영어 설명을 쓰시오.

5 (부리로) 쪼다, 쪼아 먹다, 가볍게 키스하다

______ ______

______

6 지불하다

______ ______

______

7 쏟아붓다, 쏟아지다, 흘러나오다

______ ______

______

8 ~를 더 좋아하다, ~에 우선순위를 더 두다

______ ______

______

C 9~12 다음 영어 문장을 의미가 떠오를 때까지 소리 내어 읽어보시오. 1.5초 이내

9 The crow pecked his hand.

______

10 I prefer movie to sports.

______

11 Students poured into the auditorium.

______

12 I paid for the tickets.

______

Test 3 Imaging Exercise

➢ 다음 단어에 맞는 나만의 짧은 영어 설명을 써보자. (또는 그림을 그려보자.)

pay
[pei]

peck
[pek]

pour
[pɔːr]

prefer~
[prifəːr]

➢ Month 02-DAY 08 영어 문장과 우리말

I paid for the tickets.
나는 티켓값을 지불했습니다.

The crow pecked his hand.
까마귀가 그의 손을 쪼았습니다.

Students poured into the auditorium.
학생들이 강당으로 쏟아져 들어왔습니다.

I prefer movie to sports.
나는 스포츠에 비해 영화를 더 좋아합니다.

Vocabulary

≫ 음원을 들으면서 소리를 무조건 따라해 보시오. (빠르기 & 정확도/브레인 + 마우스 운동)

punish

to subject to pain

castigate, penalize

벌주다, 처벌하다

He was punished for stealing.

recall

to ask or order to return, to cancel, or to remember

callback, cancel, remember

소환하다, 철회하다, 상기하다

I don't recall her name.

receive

to take or acquire

have, get, acquire

받다

I received an email yesterday.

recover

to get back or to become well again

get better, improve, get well

회복하다

He is recovering from cancer.

* 이미지는 구글에서 찾은 것으로, 단어와 이미지가 다를 수 있습니다. 'Test 3'에서 나만의 이미지를 그려볼 수 있습니다.

Test 1 Connecting Exercise

Score(/16)
Self-Evaluation

≫ 서로 맞는 것을 연결하시오.

Ⓐ 1~4 영어 단어와 우리말 뜻 연결하기

1	recover	벌주다, 처벌하다
2	recall	받다
3	receive	소환하다, 철회하다, 상기하다
4	punish	회복하다

Ⓑ 5~8 영어 단어와 영어 설명 연결하기

5	recover	to get back or to become well again
6	receive	to take or acquire
7	punish	to ask or order to return, to cancel, or to remember
8	recall	to subject to pain

Ⓒ 9~12 영어 단어와 동의어 연결하기

9	recall	callback, cancel, remember
10	punish	get better, improve, get well
11	recover	have, get, acquire
12	receive	castigate, penalize

Ⓓ 13~16 우리말 뜻과 영어 단어 연결하기

13	받다	punish
14	소환하다, 철회하다, 상기하다	recall
15	벌주다, 처벌하다	receive
16	회복하다	recover

Test 2 Writing Exercise

Score(/12)
Self-Evaluation

A 1~4 다음 단어에 맞는 뜻을 쓰시오.

1 recover ______________________

2 punish ______________________

3 receive ______________________

4 recall ______________________

B 5~8 다음 뜻에 맞는 영어 단어와 영어 동의어, 영어 설명을 쓰시오.

5 받다

______________ ______________________

____

6 벌주다, 처벌하다

______________ ______________________

____

7 회복하다

______________ ______________________

____

8 소환하다, 철회하다, 상기하다

______________ ______________________

____

C 9~12 다음 영어 문장을 의미가 떠오를 때까지 소리 내어 읽어보시오. 1.5초 이내

9 He is recovering from cancer.

____

10 I don't recall her name.

____

11 I received an email yesterday.

____

12 He was punished for stealing.

____

Test 3 Imaging Exercise

➢ 다음 단어에 맞는 나만의 짧은 영어 설명을 써보자. (또는 그림을 그려보자.)

punish
[pʌniʃ]

recall
[rikɔ́ːl]

receive
[risíːv]

recover
[rikʌvər]

➢ Month 02-DAY 09 영어 문장과 우리말

He was punished for stealing.
그는 도둑질로 처벌을 받았습니다.

I don't recall her name.
나는 그녀의 이름을 기억하지 못합니다.

I received an email yesterday.
나는 어제 이메일 한 통을 받았습니다.

He is recovering from cancer.
그는 암으로부터 회복 중에 있습니다.

Vocabulary

➢ 음원을 들으면서 소리를 무조건 따라해 보시오. (빠르기 & 정확도/브레인 + 마우스 운동)

represent

to describe or present in words, or to serve as a delegate

speak for, express, symbolize, stand for

나타내다, 표현하다, 상징하다, 대표하다

These efforts represent a change.

shake, shook, shaken

to move from side to side

tremble, shiver, quake

흔들다

The explosion shook the building.

slide, slid, slid

to cause to slide or slip

slip, skid, glide

미끄러지다

She slid into her bed.

spout

to gush forth in a rapid stream or in spurts

gush, spurt, spray, surge

내뿜다, 분출하다, 주전자의 주둥이, 입, 대롱

Water spouted from the faucet.

* 이미지는 구글에서 찾은 것으로, 단어와 이미지가 다를 수 있습니다. 'Test 3'에서 나만의 이미지를 그려볼 수 있습니다.

Test 1 Connecting Exercise

Score(/16)
Self-Evaluation

≫ 서로 맞는 것을 연결하시오.

Ⓐ 1~4 영어 단어와 우리말 뜻 연결하기

1 slide, slid, slid	•	•	미끄러지다
2 shake, shook, shaken	•	•	나타내다, 표현하다, 상징하다, 대표하다
3 represent	•	•	내뿜다, 분출하다, 주전자의 주둥이, 입, 대롱
4 spout	•	•	흔들다

Ⓑ 5~8 영어 단어와 영어 설명 연결하기

5 spout	•	•	to describe or present in words, or to serve as a delegate
6 slide, slid, slid	•	•	to gush forth in a rapid stream or in spurts
7 shake, shook, shaken	•	•	to cause to slide or slip
8 represent	•	•	to move from side to side

Ⓒ 9~12 영어 단어와 동의어 연결하기

9 slide, slid, slid	•	•	speak for, express, symbolize, stand for
10 shake, shook, shaken	•	•	gush, spurt, spray, surge
11 spout	•	•	slip, skid, glide
12 represent	•	•	tremble, shiver, quake

Ⓓ 13~16 우리말 뜻과 영어 단어 연결하기

13 내뿜다, 분출하다, 주전자의 주둥이, 입, 대롱	•	•	represent
14 흔들다	•	•	spout
15 미끄러지다	•	•	shake, shook, shaken
16 나타내다, 표현하다, 상징하다, 대표하다	•	•	slide, slid, slid

Test 2 Writing Exercise

Score(/12)
Self-Evaluation

A 1~4 다음 단어에 맞는 뜻을 쓰시오.

1 slide, slid, slid ______________________

2 represent ______________________

3 shake, shook, shaken ______________________

4 spout ______________________

B 5~8 다음 뜻에 맞는 영어 단어와 영어 동의어, 영어 설명을 쓰시오.

5 나타내다, 표현하다, 상징하다, 대표하다

______________ ______________________

____

6 미끄러지다

______________ ______________________

____

7 내뿜다, 분출하다, 주전자의 주둥이, 입, 대롱

______________ ______________________

____

8 흔들다

______________ ______________________

____

C 9~12 다음 영어 문장을 의미가 떠오를 때까지 소리 내어 읽어보시오. 1.5초 이내

9 Water spouted from the faucet.

____

10 The explosion shook the building.

____

11 These efforts represent a change.

____

12 She slid into her bed.

____

Test 3 Imaging Exercise

➢ 다음 단어에 맞는 나만의 짧은 영어 설명을 써보자. (또는 그림을 그려보자.)

represent
[rèprizént]

shake, shook, shaken
[ʃeik, ʃuk, ʃéikən]

slide, slid, slid
[slaid, slid, slid]

spout
[spaut]

➢ Month 02-DAY 10 영어 문장과 우리말

These efforts represent a change.
이러한 노력들은 어떤 변화를 의미합니다.

The explosion shook the building.
폭발로 건물이 흔들렸습니다.

She slid into her bed.
그녀는 침대로 미끄러졌습니다.

Water spouted from the faucet.
수도꼭지에서 물이 쏟아져 나왔습니다.

DAY 11 Vocabulary

➢ 음원을 들으면서 소리를 무조건 따라해 보시오. (빠르기&정확도/브레인+마우스 운동)

stand, stood, stood

to rise to an upright position on the feet

be upright, endure, withstand

일어서다, 서 있다, 참다, 견디다

I can't stand any more.

subdue

to bring under control by physical force

suppress, oppress, defeat, conquer

가라앉히다, 완화하다, 제압하다, 억제하다

He subdued the wild horse.

upset, upset, upset

to cause to overturn

overthrow, overturn, disturb

뒤집히게 하다, 기능을 방해하다, 화나게 하다, 뒤집힌, 화난

The bad news upset me.

accomplish

to bring to a goal or to finish one's mission

achieve, attain, gain

달성하다

He has accomplished his mission impossible.

* 이미지는 구글에서 찾은 것으로, 단어와 이미지가 다를 수 있습니다. 'Test 3'에서 나만의 이미지를 그려볼 수 있습니다.

Test 1 Connecting Exercise

Score(　/16)
Self-Evaluation

➢ 서로 맞는 것을 연결하시오.

Ⓐ 1~4 영어 단어와 우리말 뜻 연결하기

1	accomplish	일어서다, 서 있다, 참다, 견디다
2	upset, upset, upset	달성하다
3	stand, stood, stood	가라앉히다, 완화하다, 제압하다, 억제하다
4	subdue	뒤집히게 하다, 기능을 방해하다, 화나게 하다, 뒤집힌, 화난

Ⓑ 5~8 영어 단어와 영어 설명 연결하기

5	upset, upset, upset	to bring under control by physical force
6	subdue	to cause to overturn
7	accomplish	to rise to an upright position on the feet
8	stand, stood, stood	to bring to a goal or to finish one's mission

Ⓒ 9~12 영어 단어와 동의어 연결하기

9	accomplish	overthrow, overturn, disturb
10	upset, upset, upset	suppress, oppress, defeat, conquer
11	subdue	achieve, attain, gain
12	stand, stood, stood	be upright, endure, withstand

Ⓓ 13~16 우리말 뜻과 영어 단어 연결하기

13	일어서다, 서 있다, 참다, 견디다	stand, stood, stood
14	뒤집히게 하다, 기능을 방해하다, 화나게 하다, 뒤집힌, 화난	accomplish
15	가라앉히다, 완화하다, 제압하다, 억제하다	upset, upset, upset
16	달성하다	subdue

Test 2

Score(/12)
Self-Evaluation

Ⓐ 1~4 다음 단어에 맞는 뜻을 쓰시오.

1 stand, stood, stood ________________

2 accomplish ________________

3 subdue ________________

4 upset, upset, upset ________________

Ⓑ 5~8 다음 뜻에 맞는 영어 단어와 영어 동의어, 영어 설명을 쓰시오.

5 달성하다

________ ________________

____

6 일어서다, 서 있다, 참다, 견디다

________ ________________

____

7 가라앉히다, 완화하다, 제압하다, 억제하다

________ ________________

____

8 뒤집히게 하다, 기능을 방해하다, 화나게 하다, 뒤집힌, 화난

________ ________________

____

Ⓒ 9~12 다음 영어 문장을 의미가 떠오를 때까지 소리 내어 읽어보시오. 1.5초 이내

9 I can't stand any more.

____

10 He has accomplished his mission impossible.

____

11 The bad news upset me.

____

12 He subdued the wild horse.

____

Test 3

➢ 다음 단어에 맞는 나만의 짧은 영어 설명을 써보자. (또는 그림을 그려보자.)

stand, stood, stood
[stænd, stud, stud]

subdue
[səbdjúː]

upset, upset, upset
[ʌpset, ʌpset, ʌpset]

accomplish
[əkάmpliʃ]

➢ Month 02-DAY 11 영어 문장과 우리말

I can't stand any more.
나는 더 이상 참을 수 없습니다.

He subdued the wild horse.
그는 야생마를 굴복시켰습니다.

The bad news upset me.
안 좋은 소식이 나를 뒤집어놓았습니다.

He has accomplished his mission impossible.
그는 불가능한 임무를 완수하였다.

Vocabulary

➢ 음원을 들으면서 소리를 무조건 따라해 보시오. (빠르기&정확도/브레인+마우스 운동)

adopt

to take on the legal responsibilities as parent of

choose, select, take over

양자로 삼다, 채용하다

This company adopts a new technique.

amount

to be equal or add up

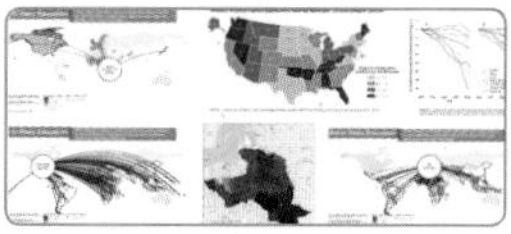

aggregate, reach, run into, total

양이 얼마가 되다, 총액, 총계

The purchases amounted to 100 dollars.

appoint

to select or designate to fill an office or a position

assign, designate, name, nominate

지명하다, 임명하다

The President appointed her the Minister.

argue

to quarrel

dispute, wrangle, quarrel, fight

논쟁하다, 말다툼하다

It is time to stop arguing.

* 이미지는 구글에서 찾은 것으로, 단어와 이미지가 다를 수 있습니다. 'Test 3'에서 나만의 이미지를 그려볼 수 있습니다.

Test 1 Connecting Exercise

Score(/16)
Self-Evaluation

➢ 서로 맞는 것을 연결하시오.

Ⓐ 1~4 영어 단어와 우리말 뜻 연결하기

1 appoint	•	• 논쟁하다, 말다툼하다
2 amount	•	• 양자로 삼다, 채용하다
3 adopt	•	• 지명하다, 임명하다
4 argue	•	• 양이 얼마가 되다, 총액, 총계

Ⓑ 5~8 영어 단어와 영어 설명 연결하기

5 amount	•	• to be equal or add up
6 appoint	•	• to quarrel
7 argue	•	• to select or designate to fill an office or a position
8 adopt	•	• to take on the legal responsibilities as parent of

Ⓒ 9~12 영어 단어와 동의어 연결하기

9 appoint	•	• choose, select, take over
10 argue	•	• aggregate, reach, run into, total
11 amount	•	• dispute, wrangle, quarrel, fight
12 adopt	•	• assign, designate, name, nominate

Ⓓ 13~16 우리말 뜻과 영어 단어 연결하기

13 양이 얼마가 되다, 총액, 총계	•	• adopt
14 양자로 삼다, 채용하다	•	• argue
15 지명하다, 임명하다	•	• amount
16 논쟁하다, 말다툼하다	•	• appoint

Test 2 Writing Exercise

Score(/12)
Self-Evaluation

Ⓐ 1~4 다음 단어에 맞는 뜻을 쓰시오.

1 amount ______
2 appoint ______
3 adopt ______
4 argue ______

Ⓑ 5~8 다음 뜻에 맞는 영어 단어와 영어 동의어, 영어 설명을 쓰시오.

5 지명하다, 임명하다

______ ______

______

6 양이 얼마가 되다, 총액, 총계

______ ______

______

7 논쟁하다, 말다툼하다

______ ______

______

8 양자로 삼다, 채용하다

______ ______

______

Ⓒ 9~12 다음 영어 문장을 의미가 떠오를 때까지 소리 내어 읽어보시오. 1.5초 이내

9 The President appointed her the Minister.

______

10 This company adopts a new technique.

______

11 The purchases amounted to 100 dollars.

______

12 It is time to stop arguing.

______

Test 3 Imaging Exercise

➤ 다음 단어에 맞는 나만의 짧은 영어 설명을 써보자. (또는 그림을 그려보자.)

adopt
[ədάpt]

amount
[əmáunt]

appoint
[əpɔ́int]

argue
[ά:rgju:]

➤ Month 02-DAY 12 영어 문장과 우리말

This company adopts a new technique.
이 회사는 새로운 기술을 채택합니다.

The purchases amounted to 100 dollars.
구매액은 100달러에 달했다.

The President appointed her the Minister.
대통령은 그녀를 장관에 임명했다.

It is time to stop arguing.
이제는 논쟁을 그칠 때입니다.

DAY 13 Vocabulary

➢ 음원을 들으면서 소리를 무조건 따라해 보시오. (빠르기&정확도/브레인+마우스 운동)

ascend

to go or move upward

mount, climb, rise

오르다, 상승하다

The airplane ascended into the clouds.

attack

to set upon in a forceful, violent, hostile, or aggressive way

assail, invade, strike (at), assault

공격하다, 공격

The enemy attacked during the night.

attend

to be present at

accompany, visit, go to

참석하다, 출석하다

Thousands of people attended the funeral.

bear, bore, born

to give birth to

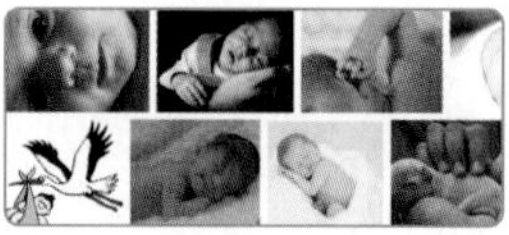

produce, yield, carry, bring

태어나다, 낳다

There are various plants bearing fruit.

* 이미지는 구글에서 찾은 것으로, 단어와 이미지가 다를 수 있습니다. 'Test 3'에서 나만의 이미지를 그려볼 수 있습니다.

Test 1 Connecting Exercise

Score(　　/16)
Self-Evaluation

➢ 서로 맞는 것을 연결하시오.

Ⓐ 1~4 영어 단어와 우리말 뜻 연결하기

1	ascend	●	● 공격하다, 공격
2	bear, bore, born	●	● 태어나다, 낳다
3	attend	●	● 오르다, 상승하다
4	attack	●	● 참석하다, 출석하다

Ⓑ 5~8 영어 단어와 영어 설명 연결하기

5	attack	●	● to set upon in a forceful, violent, hostile, or aggressive way
6	attend	●	● to give birth to
7	ascend	●	● to be present at
8	bear, bore, born	●	● to go or move upward

Ⓒ 9~12 영어 단어와 동의어 연결하기

9	attack	●	● accompany, visit, go to
10	bear, bore, born	●	● assail, invade, strike (at), assault
11	attend	●	● produce, yield, carry, bring
12	ascend	●	● mount, climb, rise

Ⓓ 13~16 우리말 뜻과 영어 단어 연결하기

13	참석하다, 출석하다	●	● bear, bore, born
14	공격하다, 공격	●	● ascend
15	태어나다, 낳다	●	● attend
16	오르다, 상승하다	●	● attack

Test 2 Writing Exercise

Score(/12)
Self-Evaluation

A 1~4 다음 단어에 맞는 뜻을 쓰시오.

1 ascend ______________________

2 attend ______________________

3 bear, bore, born ______________________

4 attack ______________________

B 5~8 다음 뜻에 맞는 영어 단어와 영어 동의어, 영어 설명을 쓰시오.

5 태어나다, 낳다

______________ ______________________

____

6 공격하다, 공격

______________ ______________________

____

7 오르다, 상승하다

______________ ______________________

____

8 참석하다, 출석하다

______________ ______________________

____

C 9~12 다음 영어 문장을 의미가 떠오를 때까지 소리 내어 읽어보시오. 1.5초 이내

9 Thousands of people attended the funeral.

____

10 There are various plants bearing fruit.

____

11 The enemy attacked during the night.

____

12 The airplane ascended into the clouds.

____

Test 3 Imaging Exercise

➢ 다음 단어에 맞는 나만의 짧은 영어 설명을 써보자. (또는 그림을 그려보자.)

ascend
[əsénd]

attack
[ətǽk]

attend
[əténd]

bear, bore, born
[bɛər, bɔːr, bɔːrn]

➢ Month 02-DAY 13 영어 문장과 우리말

The airplane ascended into the clouds.
비행기가 구름 속으로 올라갔다.

The enemy attacked during the night.
적들이 밤중에 공격했다.

Thousands of people attended the funeral.
수천 명의 사람들이 장례식에 참석했다.

There are various plants bearing fruit.
열매를 맺는 다양한 식물이 있습니다.

DAY 14 Vocabulary

➢ 음원을 들으면서 소리를 무조건 따라해 보시오. (빠르기&정확도/브레인+마우스 운동)

begin, began, begun

to start

start, commence, launch, initiate

시작하다

My name begins with a C.

bet

to stake (an amount) in a bet

stake, wager, gamble

내기로 걸다

I bet she will be there.

blame

to find fault with

accuse, criticize, denounce

비난하다, 욕하다

Don't blame children for the failure.

bless

to make holy by religious rite

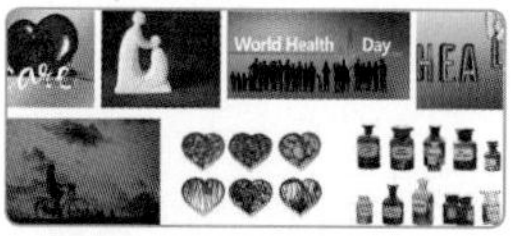

praise, thank, sanctify

보호하다, 축복하다, 은총을 베풀다

God bless you.

* 이미지는 구글에서 찾은 것으로, 단어와 이미지가 다를 수 있습니다. 'Test 3'에서 나만의 이미지를 그려볼 수 있습니다.

Test 1 Connecting Exercise

Score(　　/16)
Self-Evaluation

➢ 서로 맞는 것을 연결하시오.

Ⓐ 1~4 영어 단어와 우리말 뜻 연결하기

1	blame	•	• 보호하다, 축복하다, 은총을 베풀다
2	bet	•	• 시작하다
3	bless	•	• 비난하다, 욕하다
4	begin, began, begun	•	• 내기로 걸다

Ⓑ 5~8 영어 단어와 영어 설명 연결하기

5	blame	•	• to start
6	bless	•	• to stake (an amount) in a bet
7	bet	•	• to find fault with
8	begin, began, begun	•	• to make holy by religious rite

Ⓒ 9~12 영어 단어와 동의어 연결하기

9	blame	•	• start, commence, launch, initiate
10	bet	•	• praise, thank, sanctify
11	begin, began, begun	•	• stake, wager, gamble
12	bless	•	• accuse, criticize, denounce

Ⓓ 13~16 우리말 뜻과 영어 단어 연결하기

13	시작하다	•	• bet
14	보호하다, 축복하다, 은총을 베풀다	•	• begin, began, begun
15	내기로 걸다	•	• bless
16	비난하다, 욕하다	•	• blame

Test 2 Writing Exercise

Score(/12)
Self-Evaluation

Ⓐ 1~4 다음 단어에 맞는 뜻을 쓰시오.

1 bet ____________________

2 bless ____________________

3 blame ____________________

4 begin, began, begun ____________________

Ⓑ 5~8 다음 뜻에 맞는 영어 단어와 영어 동의어, 영어 설명을 쓰시오.

5 시작하다

____________ ____________________

____

6 내기로 걸다

____________ ____________________

____

7 보호하다, 축복하다, 은총을 베풀다

____________ ____________________

____

8 비난하다, 욕하다

____________ ____________________

____

Ⓒ 9~12 다음 영어 문장을 의미가 떠오를 때까지 소리 내어 읽어보시오. 1.5초 이내

9 I bet she will be there.

____

10 My name begins with a C.

____

11 God bless you.

____

12 Don't blame children for the failure.

____

Test 3 Imaging Exercise

➢ 다음 단어에 맞는 나만의 짧은 영어 설명을 써보자. (또는 그림을 그려보자.)

begin, began, begun
[bigín, bigǽn, bigʌn]

bet
[bet]

blame
[bleim]

bless
[bles]

➢ Month 02-DAY 14 영어 문장과 우리말

My name begins with a C.
제 이름은 C로 시작합니다.

I bet she will be there.
나는 그녀가 거기에 있을 거라는 데 내기를 건다(거기에 있을 거라고 확신한다).

Don't blame children for the failure.
어린이들에게 실패했다고 책망하지 마라.

God bless you.
당신에게 신의 은총이 있기를.

Vocabulary

➢ 음원을 들으면서 소리를 무조건 따라해 보시오. (빠르기&정확도/브레인+마우스 운동)

browse

to look through or over (something) casually

skim, scan, glance at, look through

방목하다, 띄엄띄엄 읽다, 웹을 검색하다

I browsed websites on the internet.

capture

to take by force

arrest, seize, catch

포획하다, 붙잡다

He captured the queen in chess.

concern

to have to do with

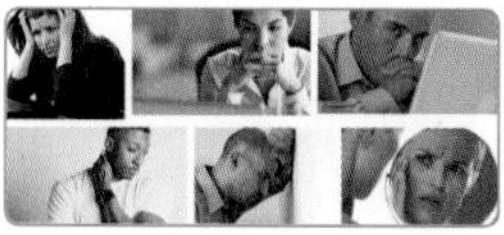

relate to, have to do with

관계하다, 관련 있다, 관여하다, 관심

This problem concerns all of us.

congratulate

to express pleasure to (a person) on a happy occasion

celebrate, commemorate, felicitate

축하하다

I congratulated her on her promotion.

* 이미지는 구글에서 찾은 것으로, 단어와 이미지가 다를 수 있습니다. 'Test 3'에서 나만의 이미지를 그려볼 수 있습니다.

Test 1 Connecting Exercise

Score(　　/16)
Self-Evaluation

➢ 서로 맞는 것을 연결하시오.

Ⓐ 1~4 영어 단어와 우리말 뜻 연결하기

1 concern ●	● 방목하다, 띄엄띄엄 읽다, 웹을 검색하다
2 congratulate ●	● 관계하다, 관련 있다, 관여하다, 관심
3 capture ●	● 축하하다
4 browse ●	● 포획하다, 붙잡다

Ⓑ 5~8 영어 단어와 영어 설명 연결하기

5 concern ●	● to express pleasure to (a person) on a happy occasion
6 browse ●	● to take by force
7 congratulate ●	● to have to do with
8 capture ●	● to look through or over (something) casually

Ⓒ 9~12 영어 단어와 동의어 연결하기

9 concern ●	● arrest, seize, catch
10 browse ●	● celebrate, commemorate, felicitate
11 congratulate ●	● skim, scan, glance at, look through
12 capture ●	● relate to, have to do with

Ⓓ 13~16 우리말 뜻과 영어 단어 연결하기

13 축하하다 ●	● capture
14 관계하다, 관련 있다, 관여하다, 관심 ●	● browse
15 포획하다, 붙잡다 ●	● congratulate
16 방목하다, 띄엄띄엄 읽다, 웹을 검색하다 ●	● concern

Test 2 Writing Exercise

Score(/12)
Self-Evaluation

Ⓐ 1~4 다음 단어에 맞는 뜻을 쓰시오.

1 browse ______________________

2 concern ______________________

3 congratulate ______________________

4 capture ______________________

Ⓑ 5~8 다음 뜻에 맞는 영어 단어와 영어 동의어, 영어 설명을 쓰시오.

5 방목하다, 띄엄띄엄 읽다, 웹을 검색하다

______________ ______________________

____

6 축하하다

______________ ______________________

____

7 포획하다, 붙잡다

______________ ______________________

____

8 관계하다, 관련 있다, 관여하다, 관심

______________ ______________________

____

Ⓒ 9~12 다음 영어 문장을 의미가 떠오를 때까지 소리 내어 읽어보시오. 1.5초 이내

9 I browsed websites on the internet.

____

10 He captured the queen in chess.

____

11 This problem concerns all of us.

____

12 I congratulated her on her promotion.

____

Test 3 Imaging Exercise

➢ 다음 단어에 맞는 나만의 짧은 영어 설명을 써보자. (또는 그림을 그려보자.)

browse
[brauz]

capture
[kǽptʃər]

concern
[kənsə́ːrn]

congratulate
[kəngrǽtʃulèit]

➢ Month 02-DAY 15 영어 문장과 우리말

I browsed websites on the internet.
나는 인터넷에서 웹사이트를 검색했다.

He captured the queen in chess.
그는 체스게임에서 여왕을 잡았다.

This problem concerns all of us.
이 문제는 우리 모두와 관련 있습니다.

I congratulated her on her promotion.
나는 그녀에게 그녀의 승진을 축하했다.

Vocabulary

➢ 음원을 들으면서 소리를 무조건 따라해 보시오. (빠르기&정확도/브레인+마우스 운동)

conquer

to gain by military force or win in war

defeat, win, subdue

정복하다

The Roman Empire conquered the world.

consist

to be composed of or to be made up

compose, comprise, constitute

이루어지다, 구성되다

Syrup consists of sugar and water.

continue

to go on or keep on

last, endure, persist, keep on

계속하다

The meeting continued for another hour.

cooperate

to work or act together

collaborate, work together

협력하다, 협조하다

He cooperated with the police investigation.

* 이미지는 구글에서 찾은 것으로, 단어와 이미지가 다를 수 있습니다. 'Test 3'에서 나만의 이미지를 그려볼 수 있습니다.

Test 1 Connecting Exercise

Score(　　/16)
Self-Evaluation

➢ 서로 맞는 것을 연결하시오.

Ⓐ 1~4 영어 단어와 우리말 뜻 연결하기

1 consist	●	● 정복하다
2 continue	●	● 협력하다, 협조하다
3 conquer	●	● 이루어지다, 구성되다
4 cooperate	●	● 계속하다

Ⓑ 5~8 영어 단어와 영어 설명 연결하기

5 conquer	●	● to go on or keep on
6 cooperate	●	● to work or act together
7 consist	●	● to gain by military force or win in war
8 continue	●	● to be composed of or to be made up

Ⓒ 9~12 영어 단어와 동의어 연결하기

9 cooperate	●	● compose, comprise, constitute
10 conquer	●	● collaborate, work together
11 consist	●	● last, endure, persist, keep on
12 continue	●	● defeat, win, subdue

Ⓓ 13~16 우리말 뜻과 영어 단어 연결하기

13 협력하다, 협조하다	●	● continue
14 정복하다	●	● cooperate
15 이루어지다, 구성되다	●	● conquer
16 계속하다	●	● consist

Test 2 Writing Exercise

Score(/12)
Self-Evaluation

Ⓐ 1~4 다음 단어에 맞는 뜻을 쓰시오.

1 cooperate ______

2 consist ______

3 conquer ______

4 continue ______

Ⓑ 5~8 다음 뜻에 맞는 영어 단어와 영어 동의어, 영어 설명을 쓰시오.

5 계속하다

______ ______

______

6 협력하다, 협조하다

______ ______

______

7 정복하다

______ ______

______

8 이루어지다, 구성되다

______ ______

______

Ⓒ 9~12 다음 영어 문장을 의미가 떠오를 때까지 소리 내어 읽어보시오. 1.5초 이내

9 He cooperated with the police investigation.

______

10 Syrup consists of sugar and water.

______

11 The Roman Empire conquered the world.

______

12 The meeting continued for another hour.

______

Test 3 Imaging Exercise

➢ 다음 단어에 맞는 나만의 짧은 영어 설명을 써보자. (또는 그림을 그려보자.)

conquer
[kάŋkər]

consist
[kənsíst]

continue
[kəntínjuː]

cooperate
[kouάpərèit]

➢ Month 02-DAY 16 영어 문장과 우리말

The Roman Empire conquered the world.
로마제국은 세계를 정복했다.

Syrup consists of sugar and water.
시럽은 설탕과 물로 이루어져 있습니다.

The meeting continued for another hour.
회의가 한 시간 더 계속되었습니다.

He cooperated with the police investigation.
그는 경찰수사에 협조하였습니다.

DAY 17 Vocabulary

≫ 음원을 들으면서 소리를 무조건 따라해 보시오. (빠르기 & 정확도/브레인 + 마우스 운동)

cover

to place or spread something over so as to protect or conceal

carpet, coat, hide, conceal

덮다, 가리다

Snow covered the fields and mountains.

crack

to break without separation of parts

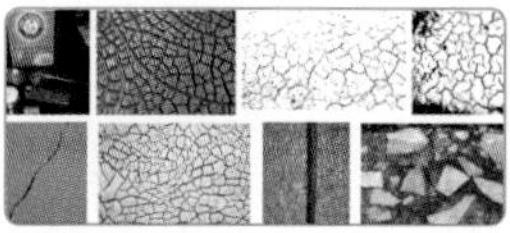

break, fissure, crevice

완전히 깨지지 않고 금이 가다, 깨지다, 균열, 크랙

The vase was cracked but unbroken.

crawl

to move slowly by dragging the body along the ground

creep

기다, 기어가다

The baby crawled across the floor.

decide

to solve or conclude

determine, solve, conclude

결정하다

We should decide what to do.

* 이미지는 구글에서 찾은 것으로, 단어와 이미지가 다를 수 있습니다. 'Test 3'에서 나만의 이미지를 그려볼 수 있습니다.

Test 1 Connecting Exercise

Score(　　/16)
Self-Evaluation

➢ 서로 맞는 것을 연결하시오.

Ⓐ 1~4 영어 단어와 우리말 뜻 연결하기

1 crack	•	• 덮다, 가리다
2 decide	•	• 결정하다
3 crawl	•	• 기다, 기어가다
4 cover	•	• 완전히 깨지지 않고 금이 가다, 깨지다, 균열, 크랙

Ⓑ 5~8 영어 단어와 영어 설명 연결하기

5 decide	•	• to place or spread something over so as to protect or conceal
6 crack	•	• to break without separation of parts
7 crawl	•	• to move slowly by dragging the body along the ground
8 cover	•	• to solve or conclude

Ⓒ 9~12 영어 단어와 동의어 연결하기

9 crack	•	• carpet, coat, hide, conceal
10 cover	•	• break, fissure, crevice
11 crawl	•	• determine, solve, conclude
12 decide	•	• creep

Ⓓ 13~16 우리말 뜻과 영어 단어 연결하기

13 완전히 깨지지 않고 금이 가다, 깨지다, 균열, 크랙	•	• crack
14 기다, 기어가다	•	• crawl
15 덮다, 가리다	•	• decide
16 결정하다	•	• cover

Test 2 Writing Exercise

Score(/12)
Self-Evaluation

Month 02

A 1~4 다음 단어에 맞는 뜻을 쓰시오.

1 cover ______________________

2 crack ______________________

3 crawl ______________________

4 decide ______________________

B 5~8 다음 뜻에 맞는 영어 단어와 영어 동의어, 영어 설명을 쓰시오.

5 완전히 깨지지 않고 금이 가다, 깨지다, 균열, 크랙

__________ ______________________

____

6 결정하다

__________ ______________________

____

7 기다, 기어가다

__________ ______________________

____

8 덮다, 가리다

__________ ______________________

____

C 9~12 다음 영어 문장을 의미가 떠오를 때까지 소리 내어 읽어보시오. 1.5초 이내

9 We should decide what to do.

____

10 Snow covered the fields and mountains.

____

11 The baby crawled across the floor.

____

12 The vase was cracked but unbroken.

____

Test 3 Imaging Exercise

➢ 다음 단어에 맞는 나만의 짧은 영어 설명을 써보자. (또는 그림을 그려보자.)

cover
[kʌvər]

crack
[kræk]

crawl
[krɔːl]

decide
[disáid]

➢ Month 02-DAY 17 영어 문장과 우리말

Snow covered the fields and mountains.
눈이 산과 들판을 뒤덮었습니다.

The vase was cracked but unbroken.
꽃병이 금이 갔지만 깨지지는 않았습니다.

The baby crawled across the floor.
아기가 바닥을 기어다녔습니다.

We should decide what to do.
우리는 할 일을 결정해야 합니다(무엇을 할 지 결정해야 합니다).

➢ 음원을 들으면서 소리를 무조건 따라해 보시오. (빠르기&정확도/브레인+마우스 운동)

delight

to take great pleasure

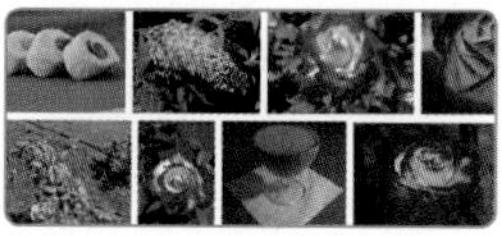

please, satisfy

기쁨을 주다, 즐겁게 하다, 기뻐하다, 기쁨

This old movie still delights people.

differ

to be dissimilar or unlike in nature, quality, amount, or form

disagree, diverge, vary

다르다, 의견을 달리하다

Ambition and dream differ from greed.

digest

to convert (food) into simpler chemical compounds

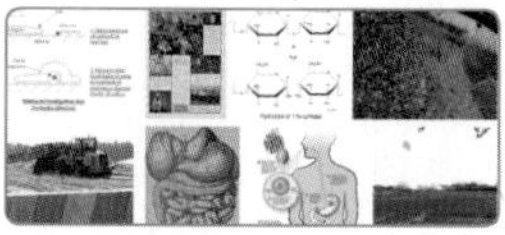

ingest, absorb, assimilate, summary

소화하다, 요약하다, 요약, 요약집

She couldn't digest food properly.

disappear

to pass out of sight

vanish, go away, fade away

사라지다, 없어지다

The moon disappeared behind the clouds.

* 이미지는 구글에서 찾은 것으로, 단어와 이미지가 다를 수 있습니다. 'Test 3'에서 나만의 이미지를 그려볼 수 있습니다.

Test 1 Connecting Exercise

Score(/16)
Self-Evaluation

➢ 서로 맞는 것을 연결하시오.

Ⓐ 1~4 영어 단어와 우리말 뜻 연결하기

1 differ	●	● 다르다, 의견을 달리하다
2 disappear	●	● 사라지다, 없어지다
3 digest	●	● 소화하다, 요약하다, 요약, 요약집
4 delight	●	● 기쁨을 주다, 즐겁게 하다, 기뻐하다, 기쁨

Ⓑ 5~8 영어 단어와 영어 설명 연결하기

5 delight	●	● to take great pleasure
6 digest	●	● to pass out of sight
7 disappear	●	● to be dissimilar or unlike in nature, quality, amount, or form
8 differ	●	● to convert (food) into simpler chemical compounds

Ⓒ 9~12 영어 단어와 동의어 연결하기

9 differ	●	● ingest, absorb, assimilate, summary
10 delight	●	● vanish, go away, fade away
11 disappear	●	● disagree, diverge, vary
12 digest	●	● please, satisfy

Ⓓ 13~16 우리말 뜻과 영어 단어 연결하기

13 다르다, 의견을 달리하다	●	● differ
14 기쁨을 주다, 즐겁게 하다, 기뻐하다, 기쁨	●	● disappear
15 소화하다, 요약하다, 요약, 요약집	●	● digest
16 사라지다, 없어지다	●	● delight

Test 2 Writing Exercise

Score(/12)
Self-Evaluation

Ⓐ 1~4 다음 단어에 맞는 뜻을 쓰시오.

1 differ ______________________

2 digest ______________________

3 delight ______________________

4 disappear ______________________

Ⓑ 5~8 다음 뜻에 맞는 영어 단어와 영어 동의어, 영어 설명을 쓰시오.

5 기쁨을 주다, 즐겁게 하다, 기뻐하다, 기쁨

____________ ______________________

____

6 소화하다, 요약하다, 요약, 요약집

____________ ______________________

____

7 다르다, 의견을 달리하다

____________ ______________________

____

8 사라지다, 없어지다

____________ ______________________

____

Ⓒ 9~12 다음 영어 문장을 의미가 떠오를 때까지 소리 내어 읽어보시오. **1.5초 이내**

9 This old movie still delights people.

____

10 The moon disappeared behind the clouds.

____

11 Ambition and dream differ from greed.

____

12 She couldn't digest food properly.

____

Test 3

➢ 다음 단어에 맞는 나만의 짧은 영어 설명을 써보자. (또는 그림을 그려보자.)

delight
[diláit]

differ
[dífər]

digest
[daidʒést]

disappear
[dìsəpíər]

➢ Month 02-DAY 18 영어 문장과 우리말

This old movie still delights people.
이 오래된 영화는 지금도 사람들을 즐겁게 합니다.

Ambition and dream differ from greed.
꿈과 야망은 탐욕과 다릅니다.

She couldn't digest food properly.
그녀는 음식물을 제대로 소화할 수 없었습니다.

The moon disappeared behind the clouds.
달은 구름 뒤로 사라졌다.

Vocabulary

➢ 음원을 들으면서 소리를 무조건 따라해 보시오. (빠르기&정확도/브레인+마우스 운동)

disappoint

to fail to meet the expectations or hopes

dismay, discontent, dissatisfy

실망시키다, 기대에 어긋나게 하다

Many sports stars disappoint their fans.

doubt

to be uncertain about

distrust, question, query

의심하다

They doubted whether that could happen.

doze

to fall into a light sleep unintentionally (doze off)

nap, drowse, slumber, snooze

깜박 졸다, 꾸벅꾸벅 졸다, 선잠 자다

He dozed off during a lecture.

drain

to draw off (a liquid) gradually

remove, draw, empty, withdraw

물을 빼다, 물이 빠지다, 배수관, 하수구

They drained water from the pool.

* 이미지는 구글에서 찾은 것으로, 단어와 이미지가 다를 수 있습니다. 'Test 3'에서 나만의 이미지를 그려볼 수 있습니다.

Test 1 Connecting Exercise

Score(/16)
Self-Evaluation

➢ 서로 맞는 것을 연결하시오.

Ⓐ 1~4 영어 단어와 우리말 뜻 연결하기

1 drain ●	● 물을 빼다, 물이 빠지다, 배수관, 하수구
2 doubt ●	● 실망시키다, 기대에 어긋나게 하다
3 doze ●	● 깜박 졸다, 꾸벅꾸벅 졸다, 선잠 자다
4 disappoint ●	● 의심하다

Ⓑ 5~8 영어 단어와 영어 설명 연결하기

5 doze ●	● to draw off (a liquid) gradually
6 doubt ●	● to fall into a light sleep unintentionally (doze off)
7 drain ●	● to fail to meet the expectations or hopes
8 disappoint ●	● to be uncertain about

Ⓒ 9~12 영어 단어와 동의어 연결하기

9 doubt ●	● dismay, discontent, dissatisfy
10 drain ●	● remove, draw, empty, withdraw
11 doze ●	● distrust, question, query
12 disappoint ●	● nap, drowse, slumber, snooze

Ⓓ 13~16 우리말 뜻과 영어 단어 연결하기

13 실망시키다, 기대에 어긋나게 하다 ●	● doze
14 물을 빼다, 물이 빠지다, 배수관, 하수구 ●	● drain
15 의심하다 ●	● doubt
16 깜박 졸다, 꾸벅꾸벅 졸다, 선잠 자다 ●	● disappoint

Test 2 Writing Exercise

Score(　　/12)
Self-Evaluation

Ⓐ 1~4 다음 단어에 맞는 뜻을 쓰시오.

1 doubt ____________________

2 doze ____________________

3 disappoint ____________________

4 drain ____________________

Ⓑ 5~8 다음 뜻에 맞는 영어 단어와 영어 동의어, 영어 설명을 쓰시오.

5 물을 빼다, 물이 빠지다, 배수관, 하수구

____________ ____________________

____

6 의심하다

____________ ____________________

____

7 실망시키다, 기대에 어긋나게 하다

____________ ____________________

____

8 깜박 졸다, 꾸벅꾸벅 졸다, 선잠 자다

____________ ____________________

____

Ⓒ 9~12 다음 영어 문장을 의미가 떠오를 때까지 소리 내어 읽어보시오. 1.5초 이내

9 Many sports stars disappoint their fans.

____

10 They doubted whether that could happen.

____

11 He dozed off during a lecture.

____

12 They drained water from the pool.

____

Test 3 Imaging Exercise

➢ 다음 단어에 맞는 나만의 짧은 영어 설명을 써보자. (또는 그림을 그려보자.)

disappoint
[dìsəpɔ́int]

doubt
[daut]

doze
[douz]

drain
[drein]

➢ Month 02-DAY 19 영어 문장과 우리말

Many sports stars disappoint their fans.
많은 스포츠 스타들이 그들의 팬들을 실망시킵니다.

They doubted whether that could happen.
그들은 그것이 일어날 수 있는지 의심했습니다.

He dozed off during a lecture.
그는 강의 도중 깜박 졸았습니다.

They drained water from the pool.
그들은 수영장에서 물을 빼냈습니다.

Vocabulary

➢ 음원을 들으면서 소리를 무조건 따라해 보시오. (빠르기&정확도/브레인+마우스 운동)

dream

to see or imagine in sleep

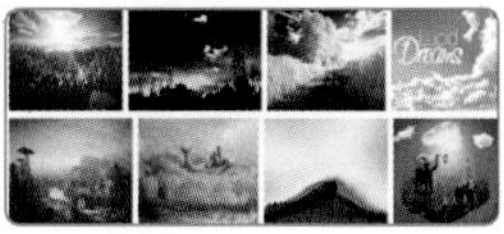

have dreams, have a dream, ambition

꿈꾸다, 바라다, 꿈, 희망

Last night I dreamed about you.

dress

to put clothes on

clothe, decorate, adorn

옷을 입다, 입히다, 장식하다, 드레스, 옷

I got dressed and went downstairs.

endure

to undergo (hardship) without yielding

bear, stand, undergo

참다, 견디다

I have endured years of hardship.

engage

to begin to employ

employ, hire, promise, engross

고용하다, (결혼을) 약속하다, (주의를) 끌다

He engaged me as his assistant.

* 이미지는 구글에서 찾은 것으로, 단어와 이미지가 다를 수 있습니다. 'Test 3'에서 나만의 이미지를 그려볼 수 있습니다.

Test 1 Connecting Exercise

Score(/16)
Self-Evaluation

➢ 서로 맞는 것을 연결하시오.

Ⓐ 1~4 영어 단어와 우리말 뜻 연결하기

1	engage	• •	고용하다, (결혼을) 약속하다, (주의를) 끌다
2	dress	• •	옷을 입다, 입히다, 장식하다, 드레스, 옷
3	endure	• •	참다, 견디다
4	dream	• •	꿈꾸다, 바라다, 꿈, 희망

Ⓑ 5~8 영어 단어와 영어 설명 연결하기

5	dream	• •	to begin to employ
6	endure	• •	to see or imagine in sleep
7	engage	• •	to put clothes on
8	dress	• •	to undergo (hardship) without yielding

Ⓒ 9~12 영어 단어와 동의어 연결하기

9	endure	• •	employ, hire, promise, engross
10	engage	• •	clothe, decorate, adorn
11	dream	• •	have dreams, have a dream, ambition
12	dress	• •	bear, stand, undergo

Ⓓ 13~16 우리말 뜻과 영어 단어 연결하기

13	꿈꾸다, 바라다, 꿈, 희망	• •	dream
14	참다, 견디다	• •	engage
15	고용하다, (결혼을) 약속하다, (주의를) 끌다	• •	endure
16	옷을 입다, 입히다, 장식하다, 드레스, 옷	• •	dress

Test 2 Writing Exercise

Score(/12)
Self-Evaluation

Ⓐ 1~4 다음 단어에 맞는 뜻을 쓰시오.

1 dress ______________________

2 engage ______________________

3 dream ______________________

4 endure ______________________

Ⓑ 5~8 다음 뜻에 맞는 영어 단어와 영어 동의어, 영어 설명을 쓰시오.

5 꿈꾸다, 바라다, 꿈, 희망

__________ ______________________

____

6 고용하다, (결혼을) 약속하다, (주의를) 끌다

__________ ______________________

____

7 참다, 견디다

__________ ______________________

____

8 옷을 입다, 입히다, 장식하다, 드레스, 옷

__________ ______________________

____

Ⓒ 9~12 다음 영어 문장을 의미가 떠오를 때까지 소리 내어 읽어보시오. 1.5초 이내

9 Last night I dreamed about you.

____

10 I have endured years of hardship.

____

11 He engaged me as his assistant.

____

12 I got dressed and went downstairs.

____

Test 3 Imaging Exercise

➢ 다음 단어에 맞는 나만의 짧은 영어 설명을 써보자. (또는 그림을 그려보자.)

dream
[driːm]

dress
[dres]

endure
[indjúər]

engage
[ingéidʒ]

➢ Month 02-DAY 20 영어 문장과 우리말

Last night I dreamed about you.
어젯밤에 당신 꿈을 꾸었습니다.

I got dressed and went downstairs.
나는 옷을 입고 아래층으로 내려갔습니다.

I have endured years of hardship.
나는 수년간의 고난을 견뎌냈습니다.

He engaged me as his assistant.
그는 나를 그의 조수로 고용했습니다.

Month 03 Verbs

Day 01 entertain, exchange, exclude, express
Day 02 feed, fill, flow, flutter
Day 03 gag, glide, glitter, grab
Day 04 greet, harm, ignore, infuriate
Day 05 instruct, intrude, kiss, lift
Day 06 locate, misunderstand, nod, notice
Day 07 observe, overflow, overwhelm, pluck
Day 08 polish, prong, release, resist
Day 09 respect, restore, rush, rustle
Day 10 seek, seize, settle, sew
Day 11 shout, shut, slip, smile
Day 12 stalk, stare, succeed, talk
Day 13 tan, tear, understand, vary
Day 14 ache, aid, aim, apologize
Day 15 appear, arrange, avoid, bark
Day 16 beat, borrow, breeze, bury
Day 17 celebrate, chirp, collect, contain
Day 18 contrast, dash, defend, depart
Day 19 distract, disturb, drag, drip
Day 20 educate, encourage, escape, excel

DAY 01 Vocabulary

➢ 음원을 들으면서 소리를 무조건 따라해 보시오. (빠르기 & 정확도/브레인 + 마우스 운동)

entertain

to provide amusement or enjoyment for (a person or audience)

amuse, please, delight

즐겁게 해주다

He entertained us with funny stories.

exchange

to give and receive (information, ideas, etc)

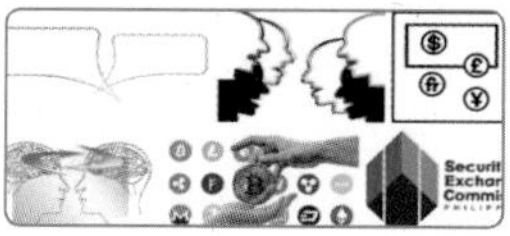

interchange, trade

교환하다, 환전하다

I have exchanged USD for EUR.

exclude

to keep out or prevent from entering

forbid, boycott, embargo, prohibit

배제하다, 제외하다

They excluded her from the meeting.

express

to put into words

state, speak, say, tell

표현하다, 급행의, 곧바로 가는, 급행(열차,버스 등)

He expressed his ideas very clearly.

* 이미지는 구글에서 찾은 것으로, 단어와 이미지가 다를 수 있습니다. 'Test 3'에서 나만의 이미지를 그려볼 수 있습니다.

Test 1 Connecting Exercise

Score(　　/16)
Self-Evaluation

➢ 서로 맞는 것을 연결하시오.

Ⓐ 1~4 영어 단어와 우리말 뜻 연결하기

1 exclude	•	• 배제하다, 제외하다
2 exchange	•	• 표현하다, 급행의, 곧바로 가는, 급행(열차,버스 등)
3 entertain	•	• 교환하다, 환전하다
4 express	•	• 즐겁게 해주다

Ⓑ 5~8 영어 단어와 영어 설명 연결하기

5 exchange	•	• to give and receive (information, ideas, etc)
6 exclude	•	• to keep out or prevent from entering
7 express	•	• to put into words
8 entertain	•	• to provide amusement or enjoyment for (a person or audience)

Ⓒ 9~12 영어 단어와 동의어 연결하기

9 exclude	•	• forbid, boycott, embargo, prohibit
10 express	•	• interchange, trade
11 exchange	•	• amuse, please, delight
12 entertain	•	• state, speak, say, tell

Ⓓ 13~16 우리말 뜻과 영어 단어 연결하기

13 즐겁게 해주다	•	• express
14 배제하다, 제외하다	•	• exclude
15 교환하다, 환전하다	•	• entertain
16 표현하다, 급행의, 곧바로 가는, 급행(열차,버스 등)	•	• exchange

Test 2 Writing Exercise

Score(/12)
Self-Evaluation

Ⓐ 1~4 다음 단어에 맞는 뜻을 쓰시오.

1 exclude ______

2 exchange ______

3 entertain ______

4 express ______

Ⓑ 5~8 다음 뜻에 맞는 영어 단어와 영어 동의어, 영어 설명을 쓰시오.

5 즐겁게 해주다

______ ______

______

6 표현하다, 급행의, 곧바로 가는, 급행(열차,버스 등)

______ ______

______

7 교환하다, 환전하다

______ ______

______

8 배제하다, 제외하다

______ ______

______

Ⓒ 9~12 다음 영어 문장을 의미가 떠오를 때까지 소리 내어 읽어보시오. 1.5초 이내

9 He entertained us with funny stories.

______

10 I have exchanged USD for EUR.

______

11 They excluded her from the meeting.

______

12 He expressed his ideas very clearly.

______

Test 3 Imaging Exercise

➤ 다음 단어에 맞는 나만의 짧은 영어 설명을 써보자. (또는 그림을 그려보자.)

entertain
[èntərtéin]

exchange
[ikstʃéindʒ]

exclude
[iksklúːd]

express
[iksprés]

➤ Month 03-DAY 01 영어 문장과 우리말

He entertained us with funny stories.
그는 재미있는 이야기로 우리를 즐겁게 했습니다.

I have exchanged USD for EUR.
나는 미국달러를 주고 유로화를 받아 환전하였습니다.

They excluded her from the meeting.
그들은 그녀를 회의에서 제외시켰습니다.

He expressed his ideas very clearly.
그는 그의 아이디어를 매우 명료하게 표현하였습니다.

DAY 02 Vocabulary

➢ 음원을 들으면서 소리를 무조건 따라해 보시오. (빠르기&정확도/브레인+마우스 운동)

feed, fed, fed

to give food to

provide, supply

기르다, 먹이다,
~을 ~에게 먹이다, 주다

I feed fish to the cat.

fill

to put something into a container or to make full

fill up, make full

채우다, 가득 메우다, 가득 차다

Thousands of people filled the streets.

flow

to move along in a stream

run, move, pass, stream

흐르다, 흘러가다

The river flows to the sea.

flutter

to wave or flap rapidly in an irregular manner

flap, flicker, ripple, fluctuate

펄럭거리다, 펄럭이다

A butterfly is fluttering its wings.

* 이미지는 구글에서 찾은 것으로, 단어와 이미지가 다를 수 있습니다. 'Test 3'에서 나만의 이미지를 그려볼 수 있습니다.

Test 1 Connecting Exercise

Score(/16)
Self-Evaluation

≫ 서로 맞는 것을 연결하시오.

Ⓐ 1~4 영어 단어와 우리말 뜻 연결하기

1	fill	• •	채우다, 가득 메우다, 가득 차다
2	flutter	• •	기르다, 먹이다, ~을 ~에게 먹이다, 주다
3	flow	• •	펄럭거리다, 펄럭이다
4	feed, fed, fed	• •	흐르다, 흘러가다

Ⓑ 5~8 영어 단어와 영어 설명 연결하기

5	fill	• •	to give food to
6	flutter	• •	to put something into a container or to make full
7	flow	• •	to wave or flap rapidly in an irregular manner
8	feed, fed, fed	• •	to move along in a stream

Ⓒ 9~12 영어 단어와 동의어 연결하기

9	feed, fed, fed	• •	provide, supply
10	fill	• •	fill up, make full
11	flutter	• •	run, move, pass, stream
12	flow	• •	flap, flicker, ripple, fluctuate

Ⓓ 13~16 우리말 뜻과 영어 단어 연결하기

13	흐르다, 흘러가다	• •	flutter
14	채우다, 가득 메우다, 가득 차다	• •	fill
15	기르다, 먹이다, ~을 ~에게 먹이다, 주다	• •	feed, fed, fed
16	펄럭거리다, 펄럭이다	• •	flow

Test 2 Writing Exercise

Score(/12)
Self-Evaluation

A 1~4 다음 단어에 맞는 뜻을 쓰시오.

1 feed, fed, fed ______

2 fill ______

3 flow ______

4 flutter ______

B 5~8 다음 뜻에 맞는 영어 단어와 영어 동의어, 영어 설명을 쓰시오.

5 흐르다, 흘러가다

______ ______

______

6 펄럭거리다, 펄럭이다

______ ______

______

7 채우다, 가득 메우다, 가득 차다

______ ______

______

8 기르다, 먹이다, ~을 ~에게 먹이다, 주다

______ ______

______

C 9~12 다음 영어 문장을 의미가 떠오를 때까지 소리 내어 읽어보시오. 1.5초 이내

9 Thousands of people filled the streets.

______

10 A butterfly is fluttering its wings.

______

11 The river flows to the sea.

______

12 I feed fish to the cat.

______

Test 3

➢ 다음 단어에 맞는 나만의 짧은 영어 설명을 써보자. (또는 그림을 그려보자.)

feed, fed, fed
[fi:d, fed, fed]

fill
[fil]

flow
[flou]

flutter
[flʌtər]

➢ Month 03-DAY 02 영어 문장과 우리말

I feed fish to the cat.
나는 고양이에게 물고기를 먹입니다.

Thousands of people filled the streets.
수천 명의 사람들이 거리를 가득 메웠습니다.

The river flows to the sea.
강물은 흘러 바다로 갑니다(강은 바다로 흘러갑니다).

A butterfly is fluttering its wings.
나비가 날개를 펄럭이고 있습니다.

DAY 03

Vocabulary

➢ 음원을 들으면서 소리를 무조건 따라해 보시오. (빠르기&정확도/브레인+마우스 운동)

gag

to prevent from speaking by using a gag, or to make jokes

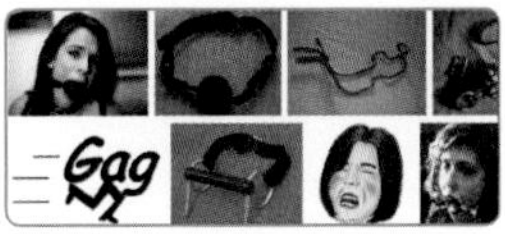

suppress, subdue, silence, joke

재갈을 물리다, 입을 틀어막다, 재갈, 웃기다

I gagged him with a towel.

glide

to move in a smooth, effortless manner

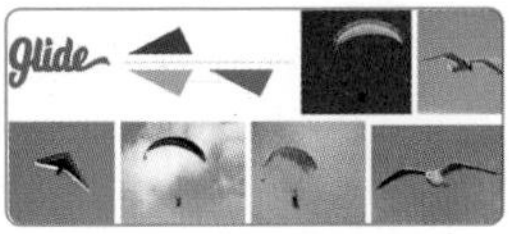

slip, sail, slide

미끄러지다, 활주하다

The dancers glided across the floor.

glitter

to reflect light in bright flashes

flash, shine, sparkle, flare

반짝이다, 빛나다

The sun glittered on the snow.

grab

to seize or grasp suddenly

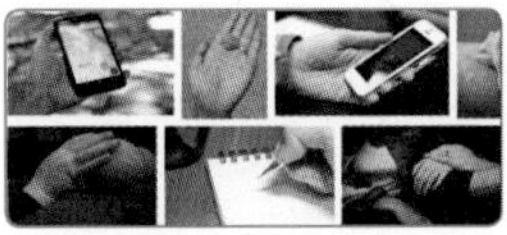

snatch, catch, capture, seize

잡아채다, 움켜쥐다

She grabbed the letter from me.

* 이미지는 구글에서 찾은 것으로, 단어와 이미지가 다를 수 있습니다. 'Test 3'에서 나만의 이미지를 그려볼 수 있습니다.

Test 1 Connecting Exercise

Score(/16)
Self-Evaluation

≫ 서로 맞는 것을 연결하시오.

A 1~4 영어 단어와 우리말 뜻 연결하기

1	grab	미끄러지다, 활주하다
2	gag	잡아채다, 움켜쥐다
3	glide	재갈을 물리다, 입을 틀어막다, 재갈, 웃기다
4	glitter	반짝이다, 빛나다

B 5~8 영어 단어와 영어 설명 연결하기

5	gag	to move in a smooth, effortless manner
6	glitter	to reflect light in bright flashes
7	glide	to seize or grasp suddenly
8	grab	to prevent from speaking by using a gag, or to make jokes

C 9~12 영어 단어와 동의어 연결하기

9	grab	snatch, catch, capture, seize
10	glitter	flash, shine, sparkle, flare
11	gag	slip, sail, slide
12	glide	suppress, subdue, silence, joke

D 13~16 우리말 뜻과 영어 단어 연결하기

13	미끄러지다, 활주하다	glide
14	재갈을 물리다, 입을 틀어막다, 재갈, 웃기다	glitter
15	반짝이다, 빛나다	gag
16	잡아채다, 움켜쥐다	grab

Test 2 Writing Exercise

Score(/12)
Self-Evaluation

A 1~4 다음 단어에 맞는 뜻을 쓰시오.

1 glide ______________________

2 grab ______________________

3 gag ______________________

4 glitter ______________________

B 5~8 다음 뜻에 맞는 영어 단어와 영어 동의어, 영어 설명을 쓰시오.

5 미끄러지다, 활주하다

______________ ______________________

____

6 반짝이다, 빛나다

______________ ______________________

____

7 재갈을 물리다, 입을 틀어막다, 재갈, 웃기다

______________ ______________________

____

8 잡아채다, 움켜쥐다

______________ ______________________

____

C 9~12 다음 영어 문장을 의미가 떠오를 때까지 소리 내어 읽어보시오. 1.5초 이내

9 The sun glittered on the snow.

____

10 She grabbed the letter from me.

____

11 I gagged him with a towel.

____

12 The dancers glided across the floor.

____

Test 3 Imaging Exercise

➢ 다음 단어에 맞는 나만의 짧은 영어 설명을 써보자. (또는 그림을 그려보자.)

gag
[gæg]

glide
[glaid]

glitter
[glítər]

grab
[græb]

➢ Month 03-DAY 03 영어 문장과 우리말

I gagged him with a towel.
나는 수건으로 그의 입을 틀어막았습니다.

The dancers glided across the floor.
댄서들은 바닥을 미끄러지듯 움직였습니다.

The sun glittered on the snow.
태양은 눈 위에서 빛났습니다.

She grabbed the letter from me.
그녀는 나한테서 편지를 낚아채 갔습니다.

➢ 음원을 들으면서 소리를 무조건 따라해 보시오. (빠르기&정확도/브레인+마우스 운동)

greet

to express greetings, or to receive with a specified reaction

salute, nod to, say hello to

인사하다, 맞이하다, (특별하게) 받아넘기다

He greeted us with a smile.

harm

to injure physically, morally, or mentally

injure, damage, hurt

해롭게 하다, 피해를 입히다, 손해, 해로움

This product may harm the environment.

ignore

to refuse to notice or to pay no attention to

disregard, neglect, disregard

무시하다

She said her husband ignored her.

infuriate

to make angry or make furious

upset, enrage, anger, make angry

격노하게 만들다, 격분시키다, 화나게 하다

I was infuriated by his words.

* 이미지는 구글에서 찾은 것으로, 단어와 이미지가 다를 수 있습니다. 'Test 3'에서 나만의 이미지를 그려볼 수 있습니다.

Test 1 Connecting Exercise

Score(　　/16)
Self-Evaluation

≫ 서로 맞는 것을 연결하시오.

Ⓐ 1~4 영어 단어와 우리말 뜻 연결하기

1 harm	•	• 해롭게 하다, 피해를 입히다, 손해, 해로움
2 ignore	•	• 무시하다
3 greet	•	• 격노하게 만들다, 격분시키다, 화나게 하다
4 infuriate	•	• 인사하다, 맞이하다, (특별하게) 받아넘기다

Ⓑ 5~8 영어 단어와 영어 설명 연결하기

5 greet	•	• to express greetings, or to receive with a specified reaction
6 ignore	•	• to make angry or make furious
7 infuriate	•	• to refuse to notice or to pay no attention to
8 harm	•	• to injure physically, morally, or mentally

Ⓒ 9~12 영어 단어와 동의어 연결하기

9 harm	•	• upset, enrage, anger, make angry
10 ignore	•	• salute, nod to, say hello to
11 infuriate	•	• injure, damage, hurt
12 greet	•	• disregard, neglect, disregard

Ⓓ 13~16 우리말 뜻과 영어 단어 연결하기

13 인사하다, 맞이하다, (특별하게) 받아넘기다	•	• harm
14 격노하게 만들다, 격분시키다, 화나게 하다	•	• greet
15 무시하다	•	• infuriate
16 해롭게 하다, 피해를 입히다, 손해, 해로움	•	• ignore

Test 2 Writing Exercise

Score(/12)
Self-Evaluation

Ⓐ 1~4 다음 단어에 맞는 뜻을 쓰시오.

1 ignore ______________________

2 infuriate ______________________

3 greet ______________________

4 harm ______________________

Ⓑ 5~8 다음 뜻에 맞는 영어 단어와 영어 동의어, 영어 설명을 쓰시오.

5 격노하게 만들다, 격분시키다, 화나게 하다

__________ ______________________

____

6 해롭게 하다, 피해를 입히다, 손해, 해로움

__________ ______________________

____

7 인사하다, 맞이하다, (특별하게) 받아넘기다

__________ ______________________

____

8 무시하다

__________ ______________________

____

Ⓒ 9~12 다음 영어 문장을 의미가 떠오를 때까지 소리 내어 읽어보시오. 1.5초 이내

9 I was infuriated by his words.

____

10 He greeted us with a smile.

____

11 She said her husband ignored her.

____

12 This product may harm the environment.

____

Test 3 Imaging Exercise

➢ 다음 단어에 맞는 나만의 짧은 영어 설명을 써보자. (또는 그림을 그려보자.)

greet
[griːt]

harm
[haːrm]

ignore
[ignɔ́ːr]

infuriate
[infjúərièit]

➢ Month 03-DAY 04 영어 문장과 우리말

He greeted us with a smile.
그는 우리를 웃으면서 맞이했습니다.

This product may harm the environment.
이 제품은 환경에 해를 끼칠 수 있습니다.

She said her husband ignored her.
그녀는 그의 남편이 그녀를 무시했다고 말했습니다.

I was infuriated by his words.
나는 그의 말에 격분하였습니다.

DAY 05 Vocabulary

➢ 음원을 들으면서 소리를 무조건 따라해 보시오. (빠르기&정확도/브레인+마우스 운동)

instruct

to teach or train, or to give orders to

educate, teach, train, order

가르치다, 지시하다, 시키다

I instructed the students in math.

intrude

to go or bring in without invitation, permission, or welcome

invade, interfere with, interrupt

침입하다, 방해하다

They intruded on our dinner party.

kiss

to touch with the lips as an expression of affection

touch with the lips

키스하다, 키스

My mother kissed me every morning.

lift

to carry from a lower to a higher position

raise, rise, elevate, hoist

들어 올리다, 올라가다, 올려짐

I couldn't lift the box.

* 이미지는 구글에서 찾은 것으로, 단어와 이미지가 다를 수 있습니다. 'Test 3'에서 나만의 이미지를 그려볼 수 있습니다.

Test 1 Connecting Exercise

Score(/16)
Self-Evaluation

➢ 서로 맞는 것을 연결하시오.

Ⓐ 1~4 영어 단어와 우리말 뜻 연결하기

1 instruct	•	• 들어 올리다, 올라가다, 올려짐
2 lift	•	• 침입하다, 방해하다
3 intrude	•	• 가르치다, 지시하다, 시키다
4 kiss	•	• 키스하다, 키스

Ⓑ 5~8 영어 단어와 영어 설명 연결하기

5 instruct	•	• to go or bring in without invitation, permission, or welcome
6 intrude	•	• to carry from a lower to a higher position
7 kiss	•	• to touch with the lips as an expression of affection
8 lift	•	• to teach or train, or to give orders to

Ⓒ 9~12 영어 단어와 동의어 연결하기

9 kiss	•	• touch with the lips
10 instruct	•	• educate, teach, train, order
11 lift	•	• raise, rise, elevate, hoist
12 intrude	•	• invade, interfere with, interrupt

Ⓓ 13~16 우리말 뜻과 영어 단어 연결하기

13 침입하다, 방해하다	•	• instruct
14 들어 올리다, 올라가다, 올려짐	•	• intrude
15 가르치다, 지시하다, 시키다	•	• kiss
16 키스하다, 키스	•	• lift

Test 2 Writing Exercise

Score(/12)
Self-Evaluation

A 1~4 다음 단어에 맞는 뜻을 쓰시오.

1 lift ______

2 instruct ______

3 kiss ______

4 intrude ______

B 5~8 다음 뜻에 맞는 영어 단어와 영어 동의어, 영어 설명을 쓰시오.

5 침입하다, 방해하다

______ ______

______

6 키스하다, 키스

______ ______

______

7 들어 올리다, 올라가다, 올려짐

______ ______

______

8 가르치다, 지시하다, 시키다

______ ______

______

C 9~12 다음 영어 문장을 의미가 떠오를 때까지 소리 내어 읽어보시오. 1.5초 이내

9 I instructed the students in math.

______

10 My mother kissed me every morning.

______

11 They intruded on our dinner party.

______

12 I couldn't lift the box.

______

Test 3

➢ 다음 단어에 맞는 나만의 짧은 영어 설명을 써보자. (또는 그림을 그려보자.)

instruct
[instrʌkt]

intrude
[intrúːd]

kiss
[kis]

lift
[lift]

➢ Month 03-DAY 05 영어 문장과 우리말

I instructed the students in math.
나는 학생들에게 수학을 가르쳤습니다.

They intruded on our dinner party.
그들은 우리 저녁 파티에 쳐들어 왔습니다.

My mother kissed me every morning.
어머니는 매일 아침 나에게 키스를 해 주었습니다.

I couldn't lift the box.
나는 그 박스를 들 수 없었습니다.

DAY 06 Vocabulary

➢ 음원을 들으면서 소리를 무조건 따라해 보시오. (빠르기&정확도/브레인+마우스 운동)

locate

to determine the position or to place at a certain location

place, situate, position, find

위치하다, 위치시키다,
(위치를) 알다, 찾아내다

I can locate the lost smartphone.

misunderstand, misunderstood, misunderstood

to understand incorrectly

misinterpret, misread

오해하다

Sorry, I misunderstood what you said.

nod

to lower and raise the head quickly

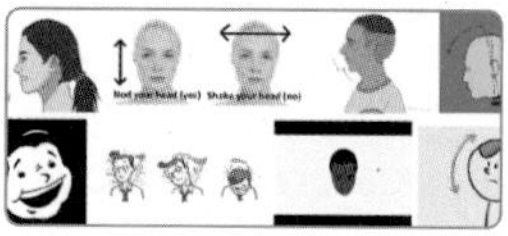

agree, assent, bow

(고개를) 끄덕이다

She said nothing but simply nodded.

notice

to become aware of

observe, see, perceive, detect

알아차리다, 통지, 통보,
고시, 알림

I noticed her leave the room.

* 이미지는 구글에서 찾은 것으로, 단어와 이미지가 다를 수 있습니다. 'Test 3'에서 나만의 이미지를 그려볼 수 있습니다.

Test 1 Connecting Exercise

Score(/16)
Self-Evaluation

➢ 서로 맞는 것을 연결하시오.

Ⓐ 1~4 영어 단어와 우리말 뜻 연결하기

1 notice	•	• 위치하다, 위치시키다, (위치를) 알다, 찾아내다
2 nod	•	• (고개를) 끄덕이다
3 locate	•	• 알아차리다, 통지, 통보, 고시, 알림
4 misunderstand, misunderstood, misunderstood	•	• 오해하다

Ⓑ 5~8 영어 단어와 영어 설명 연결하기

5 misunderstand, misunderstood, misunderstood	•	• to lower and raise the head quickly
6 notice	•	• to understand incorrectly
7 nod	•	• to determine the position or to place at a certain location
8 locate	•	• to become aware of

Ⓒ 9~12 영어 단어와 동의어 연결하기

9 nod	•	• misinterpret, misread
10 locate	•	• agree, assent, bow
11 misunderstand, misunderstood, misunderstood	•	• place, situate, position, find
12 notice	•	• observe, see, perceive, detect

Ⓓ 13~16 우리말 뜻과 영어 단어 연결하기

13 알아차리다, 통지, 통보, 고시, 알림	•	• misunderstand, misunderstood, misunderstood
14 (고개를) 끄덕이다	•	• nod
15 위치하다, 위치시키다, (위치를) 알다, 찾아내다	•	• locate
16 오해하다	•	• notice

Test 2 Writing Exercise

Score(/12)
Self-Evaluation

A 1~4 다음 단어에 맞는 뜻을 쓰시오.

1 notice ____________

2 locate ____________

3 nod ____________

4 misunderstand, misunderstood, misunderstood ____________

B 5~8 다음 뜻에 맞는 영어 단어와 영어 동의어, 영어 설명을 쓰시오.

5 위치하다, 위치시키다, (위치를) 알다, 찾아내다

____________ ____________

____

6 (고개를) 끄덕이다

____________ ____________

____

7 오해하다

____________ ____________

____

8 알아차리다, 통지, 통보, 고시, 알림

____________ ____________

____

C 9~12 다음 영어 문장을 의미가 떠오를 때까지 소리 내어 읽어보시오. 1.5초 이내

9 I noticed her leave the room.

____

10 She said nothing but simply nodded.

____

11 Sorry, I misunderstood what you said.

____

12 I can locate the lost smartphone.

____

Test 3 Imaging Exercise

➢ 다음 단어에 맞는 나만의 짧은 영어 설명을 써보자. (또는 그림을 그려보자.)

locate
[lóukeit]

misunderstand, misunderstood, misunderstood
[mi,səndərstæ'nd, mìsʌndərstúd, mìsʌndərstúd]

nod
[nad]

notice
[nóutis]

➢ Month 03-DAY 06 영어 문장과 우리말

I can locate the lost smartphone.
나는 잃어버린 스마트폰의 위치를 찾을 수 있습니다.

Sorry, I misunderstood what you said.
미안합니다, 당신이 말했던 것을 오해했습니다.

She said nothing but simply nodded.
그녀는 아무말 없이 고개만 끄덕였습니다.

I noticed her leave the room.
나는 그녀가 방에서 나가는 것을 알았습니다.

Vocabulary

➢ 음원을 들으면서 소리를 무조건 따라해 보시오. (빠르기 & 정확도/브레인 + 마우스 운동)

observe

to watch attentively

see, watch, notice

보다, 관찰하다, 준수하다, 지키다

She observed his actions with interest.

overflow

to flow or run over the top

flood, spill over

넘쳐흐르다, 넘쳐나다, 과잉, 과다

The river has overflowed its banks.

overwhelm

to surge over and submerge

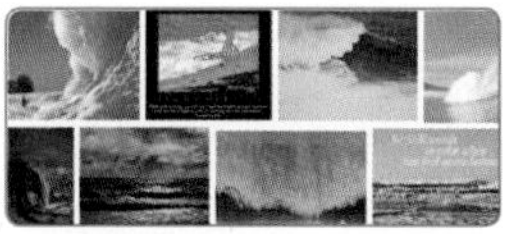

engulf, flood, flush

뒤덮다, 압도하다, 휩쓸리다

Waves are overwhelming the rocky coast.

pluck

to remove or detach by grasping and pulling abruptly

pick, draw, snatch

잡아 뜯다, 뽑다

He plucked feathers from a chicken.

* 이미지는 구글에서 찾은 것으로, 단어와 이미지가 다를 수 있습니다. 'Test 3'에서 나만의 이미지를 그려볼 수 있습니다.

Test 1 Connecting Exercise

Score(/16)
Self-Evaluation

➢ 서로 맞는 것을 연결하시오.

Ⓐ 1~4 영어 단어와 우리말 뜻 연결하기

1	overflow	•	• 잡아 뜯다, 뽑다
2	observe	•	• 뒤덮다, 압도하다, 휩쓸리다
3	pluck	•	• 보다, 관찰하다, 준수하다, 지키다
4	overwhelm	•	• 넘쳐흐르다, 넘쳐나다, 과잉, 과다

Ⓑ 5~8 영어 단어와 영어 설명 연결하기

5	overflow	•	• to remove or detach by grasping and pulling abruptly
6	pluck	•	• to flow or run over the top
7	overwhelm	•	• to surge over and submerge
8	observe	•	• to watch attentively

Ⓒ 9~12 영어 단어와 동의어 연결하기

9	overflow	•	• flood, spill over
10	overwhelm	•	• pick, draw, snatch
11	observe	•	• engulf, flood, flush
12	pluck	•	• see, watch, notice

Ⓓ 13~16 우리말 뜻과 영어 단어 연결하기

13	넘쳐흐르다, 넘쳐나다, 과잉, 과다	•	• observe
14	보다, 관찰하다, 준수하다, 지키다	•	• overflow
15	뒤덮다, 압도하다, 휩쓸리다	•	• overwhelm
16	잡아 뜯다, 뽑다	•	• pluck

Test 2 Writing Exercise

Score(/12)
Self-Evaluation

Ⓐ 1~4 다음 단어에 맞는 뜻을 쓰시오.

1 pluck ______

2 overflow ______

3 observe ______

4 overwhelm ______

Ⓑ 5~8 다음 뜻에 맞는 영어 단어와 영어 동의어, 영어 설명을 쓰시오.

5 보다, 관찰하다, 준수하다, 지키다

______ ______

______

6 넘쳐흐르다, 넘쳐나다, 과잉, 과다

______ ______

______

7 잡아 뜯다, 뽑다

______ ______

______

8 뒤덮다, 압도하다, 휩쓸리다

______ ______

______

Ⓒ 9~12 다음 영어 문장을 의미가 떠오를 때까지 소리 내어 읽어보시오. 1.5초 이내

9 She observed his actions with interest.

______

10 He plucked feathers from a chicken.

______

11 The river has overflowed its banks.

______

12 Waves are overwhelming the rocky coast.

______

Test 3 Imaging Exercise

➢ 다음 단어에 맞는 나만의 짧은 영어 설명을 써보자. (또는 그림을 그려보자.)

observe
[əbzə́:rv]

overflow
[ou'vərflou,]

overwhelm
[òuvərhwélm]

pluck
[plʌk]

➢ Month 03-DAY 07 영어 문장과 우리말

She observed his actions with interest.
그녀는 그의 행동을 흥미롭게 관찰했습니다.

The river has overflowed its banks.
강물이 둑을 넘쳐흘렀습니다.

Waves are overwhelming the rocky coast.
파도가 바위 해안선을 뒤덮고 있습니다.

He plucked feathers from a chicken.
그는 닭 털을 잡아 뽑았습니다.

DAY 08 Vocabulary

➢ **음원을 들으면서 소리를 무조건 따라해 보시오.** (빠르기&정확도/브레인+마우스 운동)

polish

to make smooth and shiny by rubbing or chemical action

shine, rub, clean, burnish

닦다, 광택을 내다, 광택이 나다

Every morning he polished his shoes.

prong

to pierce or stab with or as if with a prong

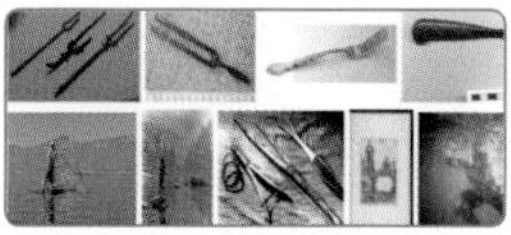

prick, a branch, a fork

찌르다, 꿰뚫다, 파헤치다, 뾰족한 끝, 뾰족한 갈래

This is a three - pronged fork.

release

to set free from confinement or bondage

set free, issue, publish

놓아주다, 공개하다, 출시하다

They released a new movie yesterday.

resist

to take action in opposition to

fight, refuse, battle against

저항하다, 억제하다

The soldiers resisted the enemy attack.

* 이미지는 구글에서 찾은 것으로, 단어와 이미지가 다를 수 있습니다. 'Test 3'에서 나만의 이미지를 그려볼 수 있습니다.

Test 1 Connecting Exercise

Score(　/16)
Self-Evaluation

➢ 서로 맞는 것을 연결하시오.

Ⓐ 1~4 영어 단어와 우리말 뜻 연결하기

1 prong	•	• 저항하다, 억제하다
2 polish	•	• 닦다, 광택을 내다, 광택이 나다
3 release	•	• 놓아주다, 공개하다, 출시하다
4 resist	•	• 찌르다, 꿰뚫다, 파헤치다, 뾰족한 끝, 뾰족한 갈래

Ⓑ 5~8 영어 단어와 영어 설명 연결하기

5 resist	•	• to set free from confinement or bondage
6 polish	•	• to make smooth and shiny by rubbing or chemical action
7 prong	•	• to pierce or stab with or as if with a prong
8 release	•	• to take action in opposition to

Ⓒ 9~12 영어 단어와 동의어 연결하기

9 polish	•	• prick, a branch, a fork
10 prong	•	• shine, rub, clean, burnish
11 resist	•	• fight, refuse, battle against
12 release	•	• set free, issue, publish

Ⓓ 13~16 우리말 뜻과 영어 단어 연결하기

13 찌르다, 꿰뚫다, 파헤치다, 뾰족한 끝, 뾰족한 갈래	•	• polish
14 닦다, 광택을 내다, 광택이 나다	•	• prong
15 놓아주다, 공개하다, 출시하다	•	• resist
16 저항하다, 억제하다	•	• release

Test 2 Writing Exercise

Score(/12)
Self-Evaluation

Ⓐ 1~4 다음 단어에 맞는 뜻을 쓰시오.

1 resist ______________________

2 prong ______________________

3 polish ______________________

4 release ______________________

Ⓑ 5~8 다음 뜻에 맞는 영어 단어와 영어 동의어, 영어 설명을 쓰시오.

5 놓아주다, 공개하다, 출시하다

______________ ______________________

____

6 닦다, 광택을 내다, 광택이 나다

______________ ______________________

____

7 찌르다, 꿰뚫다, 파헤치다, 뾰족한 끝, 뾰족한 갈래

______________ ______________________

____

8 저항하다, 억제하다

______________ ______________________

____

Ⓒ 9~12 다음 영어 문장을 의미가 떠오를 때까지 소리 내어 읽어보시오. 1.5초 이내

9 The soldiers resisted the enemy attack.

____

10 Every morning he polished his shoes.

____

11 They released a new movie yesterday.

____

12 This is a three - pronged fork.

____

Test 3 Imaging Exercise

➢ 다음 단어에 맞는 나만의 짧은 영어 설명을 써보자. (또는 그림을 그려보자.)

polish
[póuliʃ]

prong
[prɔːŋ]

release
[rilíːs]

resist
[rizíst]

➢ Month 03-DAY 08 영어 문장과 우리말

Every morning he polished his shoes.
매일 아침 그는 그의 구두를 닦았습니다.

This is a three - pronged fork.
이것은 세 갈래의 포크입니다.

They released a new movie yesterday.
그들은 어제 새 영화를 개봉했습니다.

The soldiers resisted the enemy attack.
군인들은 적의 공격에 저항했습니다.

DAY 09 Vocabulary

➢ 음원을 들으면서 소리를 무조건 따라해 보시오. (빠르기 & 정확도/브레인 + 마우스 운동)

respect

to have an attitude of esteem towards

regard, honour, admire, esteem

존경하다, 존중하다

I want you to respect me.

restore

to return (something) to an original or former condition

rebuild, reconstruct

회복하다, 복구하다

We will restore her to health.

rush

to move, act, or progress with speed, swiftly, or rapidly

run, flow, hurry, hasten

달려가다, 서두르다, 재촉하다, 혼잡

Someone inside the building rushed out.

rustle

to move with soft fluttering or crackling sounds

crackle, whisper, swish

바스락바스락 소리 내다

The leaves rustled in the wind.

* 이미지는 구글에서 찾은 것으로, 단어와 이미지가 다를 수 있습니다. 'Test 3'에서 나만의 이미지를 그려볼 수 있습니다.

Test 1 Connecting Exercise

Score(/16)
Self-Evaluation

➢ 서로 맞는 것을 연결하시오.

Ⓐ 1~4 영어 단어와 우리말 뜻 연결하기

1	respect	회복하다, 복구하다
2	rustle	존경하다, 존중하다
3	rush	달려가다, 서두르다, 재촉하다, 혼잡
4	restore	바스락바스락 소리 내다

Ⓑ 5~8 영어 단어와 영어 설명 연결하기

5	rustle	to return (something) to an original or former condition
6	restore	to move with soft fluttering or crackling sounds
7	respect	to move, act, or progress with speed, swiftly, or rapidly
8	rush	to have an attitude of esteem towards

Ⓒ 9~12 영어 단어와 동의어 연결하기

9	rush	rebuild, reconstruct
10	rustle	regard, honour, admire, esteem
11	restore	crackle, whisper, swish
12	respect	run, flow, hurry, hasten

Ⓓ 13~16 우리말 뜻과 영어 단어 연결하기

13	존경하다, 존중하다	rush
14	회복하다, 복구하다	respect
15	바스락바스락 소리 내다	rustle
16	달려가다, 서두르다, 재촉하다, 혼잡	restore

Test 2 Writing Exercise

Score(/12)
Self-Evaluation

A 1~4 다음 단어에 맞는 뜻을 쓰시오.

1 restore ______

2 rush ______

3 rustle ______

4 respect ______

B 5~8 다음 뜻에 맞는 영어 단어와 영어 동의어, 영어 설명을 쓰시오.

5 회복하다, 복구하다

______ ______

______

6 달려가다, 서두르다, 재촉하다, 혼잡

______ ______

______

7 바스락바스락 소리 내다

______ ______

______

8 존경하다, 존중하다

______ ______

______

C 9~12 다음 영어 문장을 의미가 떠오를 때까지 소리 내어 읽어보시오. 1.5초 이내

9 The leaves rustled in the wind.

______

10 I want you to respect me.

______

11 Someone inside the building rushed out.

______

12 We will restore her to health.

______

Test 3 Imaging Exercise

➢ 다음 단어에 맞는 나만의 짧은 영어 설명을 써보자. (또는 그림을 그려보자.)

respect
[rispékt]

restore
[ristɔ́ːr]

rush
[rʌʃ]

rustle
[rʌsl]

➢ Month 03-DAY 09 영어 문장과 우리말

I want you to respect me.
나는 당신이 나를 존중해 주기를 원합니다.

We will restore her to health.
우리는 그녀를 건강한 상태로 회복시킬 것입니다.

Someone inside the building rushed out.
빌딩 안의 누군가가 달려나왔습니다.

The leaves rustled in the wind.
나뭇잎이 바람에 우수수 소리를 냅니다.

DAY 10 Vocabulary

➢ 음원을 들으면서 소리를 무조건 따라해 보시오. (빠르기 & 정확도 / 브레인 + 마우스 운동)

seek

to try to locate or discover

look for, search for

찾다, 추구하다

All animals seek their prey everyday.

seize

to grasp suddenly and forcibly

grab, grip, grasp

잡다, 붙잡다

He seized her by the arm.

settle

to put in order; arrange in a desired state or condition

decide, establish, determine

결정하다, 자리 잡다

I settled myself in the armchair.

sew

to make, repair, or fasten by stitching, as with a needle and thread

stitch, patch, seam

꿰매다

She sewed her own wedding dress.

* 이미지는 구글에서 찾은 것으로, 단어와 이미지가 다를 수 있습니다. 'Test 3'에서 나만의 이미지를 그려볼 수 있습니다.

Test 1 Connecting Exercise

Score(/16)
Self-Evaluation

➢ 서로 맞는 것을 연결하시오.

Ⓐ 1~4 영어 단어와 우리말 뜻 연결하기

1 seize	●	●	결정하다, 자리 잡다
2 settle	●	●	꿰매다
3 sew	●	●	찾다, 추구하다
4 seek	●	●	잡다, 붙잡다

Ⓑ 5~8 영어 단어와 영어 설명 연결하기

5 seize	●	●	to make, repair, or fasten by stitching, as with a needle and thread
6 settle	●	●	to put in order; arrange in a desired state or condition
7 seek	●	●	to grasp suddenly and forcibly
8 sew	●	●	to try to locate or discover

Ⓒ 9~12 영어 단어와 동의어 연결하기

9 sew	●	●	stitch, patch, seam
10 settle	●	●	decide, establish, determine
11 seek	●	●	look for, search for
12 seize	●	●	grab, grip, grasp

Ⓓ 13~16 우리말 뜻과 영어 단어 연결하기

13 잡다, 붙잡다	●	●	sew
14 찾다, 추구하다	●	●	seize
15 결정하다, 자리 잡다	●	●	seek
16 꿰매다	●	●	settle

Test 2 Writing Exercise

Score(/12)
Self-Evaluation

A 1~4 다음 단어에 맞는 뜻을 쓰시오.

1 sew ______________________

2 seize ______________________

3 settle ______________________

4 seek ______________________

B 5~8 다음 뜻에 맞는 영어 단어와 영어 동의어, 영어 설명을 쓰시오.

5 결정하다, 자리 잡다

______________ ______________________

____

6 잡다, 붙잡다

______________ ______________________

____

7 꿰매다

______________ ______________________

____

8 찾다, 추구하다

______________ ______________________

____

C 9~12 다음 영어 문장을 의미가 떠오를 때까지 소리 내어 읽어보시오. 1.5초 이내

9 I settled myself in the armchair.

____

10 He seized her by the arm.

____

11 She sewed her own wedding dress.

____

12 All animals seek their prey everyday.

____

Test 3 Imaging Exercise

➢ 다음 단어에 맞는 나만의 짧은 영어 설명을 써보자. (또는 그림을 그려보자.)

seek
[siːk]

seize
[siːz]

settle
[sétl]

sew
[sou]

➢ Month 03-DAY 10 영어 문장과 우리말

All animals seek their prey everyday.
모든 동물들은 매일 그들의 먹이를 찾습니다.

He seized her by the arm.
그는 그녀의 팔을 붙잡았습니다.

I settled myself in the armchair.
나는 안락의자에 자리 잡았습니다.

She sewed her own wedding dress.
그녀는 그녀 자신의 웨딩드레스를 바느질했습니다.

DAY 11
Vocabulary

➢ 음원을 들으면서 소리를 무조건 따라해 보시오. (빠르기 & 정확도/브레인 + 마우스 운동)

shout

to utter (something) in a loud cry

yell, scream, roar

소리치다, 외치다

We began to shout for help.

shut

to move into a closed position

close, secure, fasten, seal

~을 닫다, 잠그다

Shut your eyes and don't look.

slip

to move smoothly, easily, and quietly

slide, glide

미끄러지다, 미끄러지듯 놓치다, (실수로) 미끄러져 넘어지다

The cup slipped from her hand.

smile

to have or form a smile

grin

웃다, 미소를 짓다, 웃음

He smiled whenever I saw him.

* 이미지는 구글에서 찾은 것으로, 단어와 이미지가 다를 수 있습니다. 'Test 3'에서 나만의 이미지를 그려볼 수 있습니다.

Test 1 Connecting Exercise

Score(/16)
Self-Evaluation

➢ 서로 맞는 것을 연결하시오.

Ⓐ 1~4 영어 단어와 우리말 뜻 연결하기

1 smile	•	• 소리치다, 외치다
2 shut	•	• ~을 닫다, 잠그다
3 slip	•	• 웃다, 미소를 짓다, 웃음
4 shout	•	• 미끄러지다, 미끄러지듯 놓치다, (실수로) 미끄러져 넘어지다

Ⓑ 5~8 영어 단어와 영어 설명 연결하기

5 smile	•	• to move into a closed position
6 shout	•	• to have or form a smile
7 shut	•	• to utter (something) in a loud cry
8 slip	•	• to move smoothly, easily, and quietly

Ⓒ 9~12 영어 단어와 동의어 연결하기

9 slip	•	• close, secure, fasten, seal
10 smile	•	• yell, scream, roar
11 shout	•	• grin
12 shut	•	• slide, glide

Ⓓ 13~16 우리말 뜻과 영어 단어 연결하기

13 ~을 닫다, 잠그다	•	• smile
14 웃다, 미소를 짓다, 웃음	•	• slip
15 소리치다, 외치다	•	• shut
16 미끄러지다, 미끄러지듯 놓치다, (실수로) 미끄러져 넘어지다	•	• shout

Test 2 Writing Exercise

Score(/12)
Self-Evaluation

Ⓐ 1~4 다음 단어에 맞는 뜻을 쓰시오.

1 slip ______________________

2 shout ______________________

3 shut ______________________

4 smile ______________________

Ⓑ 5~8 다음 뜻에 맞는 영어 단어와 영어 동의어, 영어 설명을 쓰시오.

5 미끄러지다, 미끄러지듯 놓치다, (실수로) 미끄러져 넘어지다

______________ ______________________

____

6 웃다, 미소를 짓다, 웃음

______________ ______________________

____

7 소리치다, 외치다

______________ ______________________

____

8 ~을 닫다, 잠그다

______________ ______________________

____

Ⓒ 9~12 다음 영어 문장을 의미가 떠오를 때까지 소리 내어 읽어보시오. 1.5초 이내

9 He smiled whenever I saw him.

____

10 The cup slipped from her hand.

____

11 Shut your eyes and don't look.

____

12 We began to shout for help.

____

Test 3

➢ 다음 단어에 맞는 나만의 짧은 영어 설명을 써보자. (또는 그림을 그려보자.)

shout
[ʃaut]

shut
[ʃʌt]

slip
[slip]

smile
[smail]

➢ Month 03-DAY 11 영어 문장과 우리말

We began to shout for help.
우리는 도와달라고 소리치기 시작했습니다.

Shut your eyes and don't look.
(당신의) 눈을 감고 보지 마세요.

The cup slipped from her hand.
컵이 그녀의 손에서 미끄러졌습니다.

He smiled whenever I saw him.
그는 내가 그를 볼 때마다 항상 미소지었습니다.

DAY 12 Vocabulary

➢ **음원을 들으면서 소리를 무조건 따라해 보시오.** (빠르기&정확도/브레인+마우스 운동)

stalk

to pursue or track (prey) stealthily

pursue, follow, track, stem

가만히 뒤를 밟다, 집요하게 추근대다, 대, 줄기

The hunter was stalking the deer.

stare

to look at directly and fixedly

gaze, look

빤히 쳐다보다

She stared me in the eyes.

succeed

to accomplish an aim

triumph, win, follow, come after

목표를 달성하다, 성공하다, ~가 ~ 다음에 오다, 이어지다

I succeeded in getting the job.

talk

to exchange thoughts or opinions in spoken or sign language

speak, chat, converse, communicate

말하다, 이야기하다

Let's talk instead of fighting.

* 이미지는 구글에서 찾은 것으로, 단어와 이미지가 다를 수 있습니다. 'Test 3'에서 나만의 이미지를 그려볼 수 있습니다.

Test 1 Connecting Exercise

Score(　/16)
Self-Evaluation

➢ 서로 맞는 것을 연결하시오.

Ⓐ 1~4 영어 단어와 우리말 뜻 연결하기

1 stare	●	● 말하다, 이야기하다
2 succeed	●	● 목표를 달성하다, 성공하다, ~가 ~ 다음에 오다, 이어지다
3 talk	●	● 빤히 쳐다보다
4 stalk	●	● 가만히 뒤를 밟다, 집요하게 추근대다, 대, 줄기

Ⓑ 5~8 영어 단어와 영어 설명 연결하기

5 stare	●	● to exchange thoughts or opinions in spoken or sign language
6 talk	●	● to pursue or track (prey) stealthily
7 succeed	●	● to look at directly and fixedly
8 stalk	●	● to accomplish an aim

Ⓒ 9~12 영어 단어와 동의어 연결하기

9 stalk	●	● speak, chat, converse, communicate
10 talk	●	● triumph, win, follow, come after
11 succeed	●	● gaze, look
12 stare	●	● pursue, follow, track, stem

Ⓓ 13~16 우리말 뜻과 영어 단어 연결하기

13 가만히 뒤를 밟다, 집요하게 추근대다, 대, 줄기	●	● talk
14 목표를 달성하다, 성공하다, ~가 ~ 다음에 오다, 이어지다	●	● succeed
15 말하다, 이야기하다	●	● stare
16 빤히 쳐다보다	●	● stalk

Test 2 Writing Exercise

Score(/12)
Self-Evaluation

Ⓐ 1~4 다음 단어에 맞는 뜻을 쓰시오.

1 stare ______________________

2 succeed ______________________

3 talk ______________________

4 stalk ______________________

Ⓑ 5~8 다음 뜻에 맞는 영어 단어와 영어 동의어, 영어 설명을 쓰시오.

5 말하다, 이야기하다

______________ ______________________

____

6 빤히 쳐다보다

______________ ______________________

____

7 가만히 뒤를 밟다, 집요하게 추근대다, 대, 줄기

______________ ______________________

____

8 목표를 달성하다, 성공하다, ~가 ~ 다음에 오다, 이어지다

______________ ______________________

____

Ⓒ 9~12 다음 영어 문장을 의미가 떠오를 때까지 소리 내어 읽어보시오. 1.5초 이내

9 She stared me in the eyes.

____

10 I succeeded in getting the job.

____

11 Let's talk instead of fighting.

____

12 The hunter was stalking the deer.

____

Test 3 Imaging Exercise

➢ 다음 단어에 맞는 나만의 짧은 영어 설명을 써보자. (또는 그림을 그려보자.)

stalk
[stɔːk]

stare
[stɛər]

succeed
[səksíːd]

talk
[tɔːk]

➢ Month 03-DAY 12 영어 문장과 우리말

The hunter was stalking the deer.
사냥꾼이 사슴을 쫓고 있었습니다.

She stared me in the eyes.
그녀는 나의 눈을 똑바로 쳐다보았습니다.

I succeeded in getting the job.
나는 취업하는 데 성공했습니다.

Let's talk instead of fighting.
싸우지 말고 말로 합시다.

Vocabulary

➢ 음원을 들으면서 소리를 무조건 따라해 보시오. (빠르기 & 정확도/브레인 + 마우스 운동)

tan

to become darker from exposure to the sun

sunburn, suntan

햇볕에 태우다

She was tanned by the sun.

tear

to pull apart or into pieces by force

rend, rip, split, cleave

찢다, 조각내다, 분해하다, 찢어지다, 조각나다

This fabric does not tear easily.

understand, understood, understood

to know thoroughly or to become aware of

comprehend, apprehend, know

이해하다, 알아듣다

I understand what they're saying.

vary

to show or cause changes in

change, shift, differ, be different

달라지다, 변하다, 다르다

The temperature varied throughout the day.

* 이미지는 구글에서 찾은 것으로, 단어와 이미지가 다를 수 있습니다. 'Test 3'에서 나만의 이미지를 그려볼 수 있습니다.

Test 1 Connecting Exercise

Score(/16)
Self-Evaluation

≫ 서로 맞는 것을 연결하시오.

A 1~4 영어 단어와 우리말 뜻 연결하기

1	tear	달라지다, 변하다, 다르다
2	vary	햇볕에 태우다
3	tan	찢다, 조각내다, 분해하다, 찢어지다, 조각나다
4	understand, understood, understood	이해하다, 알아듣다

B 5~8 영어 단어와 영어 설명 연결하기

5	tan	to show or cause changes in
6	understand, understood, understood	to become darker from exposure to the sun
7	tear	to pull apart or into pieces by force
8	vary	to know thoroughly or to become aware of

C 9~12 영어 단어와 동의어 연결하기

9	tear	change, shift, differ, be different
10	tan	comprehend, apprehend, know
11	understand, understood, understood	rend, rip, split, cleave
12	vary	sunburn, suntan

D 13~16 우리말 뜻과 영어 단어 연결하기

13	찢다, 조각내다, 분해하다, 찢어지다, 조각나다	tan
14	햇볕에 태우다	vary
15	달라지다, 변하다, 다르다	understand, understood, understood
16	이해하다, 알아듣다	tear

Test 2 Writing Exercise

Score(/12)
Self-Evaluation

A 1~4 다음 단어에 맞는 뜻을 쓰시오.

1 tan ______

2 understand, understood, understood ______

3 tear ______

4 vary ______

B 5~8 다음 뜻에 맞는 영어 단어와 영어 동의어, 영어 설명을 쓰시오.

5 햇볕에 태우다

______ ______

______

6 이해하다, 알아듣다

______ ______

______

7 찢다, 조각내다, 분해하다, 찢어지다, 조각나다

______ ______

______

8 달라지다, 변하다, 다르다

______ ______

______

C 9~12 다음 영어 문장을 의미가 떠오를 때까지 소리 내어 읽어보시오. 1.5초 이내

9 This fabric does not tear easily.

______

10 I understand what they're saying.

______

11 She was tanned by the sun.

______

12 The temperature varied throughout the day.

______

Test 3 Imaging Exercise

➢ 다음 단어에 맞는 나만의 짧은 영어 설명을 써보자. (또는 그림을 그려보자.)

tan
[tæn]

tear
[tiər]

understand, understood, understood
[ʌndərstǽnd, ʌndərstúd, ʌndərstúd]

vary
[vέəri]

➢ Month 03-DAY 13 영어 문장과 우리말

She was tanned by the sun.
그녀는 햇볕에 검게 탔다.

This fabric does not tear easily.
이 천은 쉽게 찢어지지 않습니다.

I understand what they're saying.
나는 그들이 무엇을 말하고 있는지를 알고 있습니다.

The temperature varied throughout the day.
기온이 하루 내내 변하였습니다.

DAY 14 Vocabulary

➢ 음원을 들으면서 소리를 무조건 따라해 보시오. (빠르기&정확도/브레인+마우스 운동)

ache

to suffer a pain

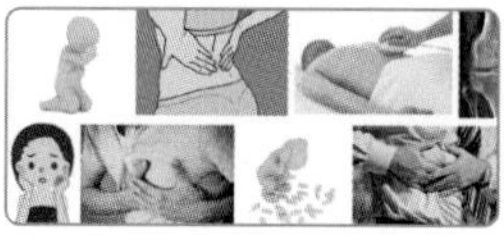

hurt, burn, pain

아프다, 아픔

My heart ached for the starving people.

aid

to provide assistance or support, give a hand

help, support, serve, assist

돕다, 원조하다, 도움, 원조

He aided the players in their victory.

aim

to direct (something like a gun or camera) toward a point

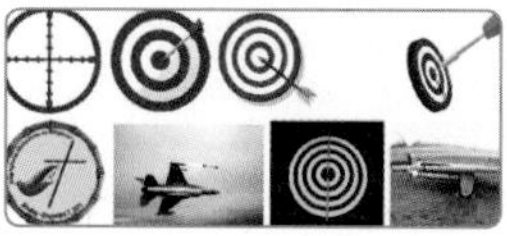

point, propose, intend

겨누다, 목표, 목적

The sniper aimed at the target carefully.

apologize

to make excuse for

excuse, say sorry, express regret

사죄하다, 사과하다

I apologized to her for my rudeness.

* 이미지는 구글에서 찾은 것으로, 단어와 이미지가 다를 수 있습니다. 'Test 3'에서 나만의 이미지를 그려볼 수 있습니다.

Test 1 Connecting Exercise

Score(/16)
Self-Evaluation

➢ 서로 맞는 것을 연결하시오.

A 1~4 영어 단어와 우리말 뜻 연결하기

1	aim	겨누다, 목표, 목적
2	ache	돕다, 원조하다, 도움, 원조
3	apologize	사죄하다, 사과하다
4	aid	아프다, 아픔

B 5~8 영어 단어와 영어 설명 연결하기

5	apologize	to direct (something like a gun or camera) toward a point
6	aid	to suffer a pain
7	ache	to provide assistance or support, give a hand
8	aim	to make excuse for

C 9~12 영어 단어와 동의어 연결하기

9	apologize	point, propose, intend
10	ache	hurt, burn, pain
11	aim	excuse, say sorry, express regret
12	aid	help, support, serve, assist

D 13~16 우리말 뜻과 영어 단어 연결하기

13	아프다, 아픔	ache
14	돕다, 원조하다, 도움, 원조	aid
15	사죄하다, 사과하다	apologize
16	겨누다, 목표, 목적	aim

Test 2 Writing Exercise

Score(　　/12)
Self-Evaluation

A 1~4 다음 단어에 맞는 뜻을 쓰시오.

1 ache ____________

2 aim ____________

3 aid ____________

4 apologize ____________

B 5~8 다음 뜻에 맞는 영어 단어와 영어 동의어, 영어 설명을 쓰시오.

5 돕다, 원조하다, 도움, 원조

____________ ____________

____

6 겨누다, 목표, 목적

____________ ____________

____

7 사죄하다, 사과하다

____________ ____________

____

8 아프다, 아픔

____________ ____________

____

C 9~12 다음 영어 문장을 의미가 떠오를 때까지 소리 내어 읽어보시오. 2초 이내

9 The sniper aimed at the target carefully.

____

10 My heart ached for the starving people.

____

11 He aided the players in their victory.

____

12 I apologized to her for my rudeness.

____

Test 3 Imaging Exercise

➢ 다음 단어에 맞는 나만의 짧은 영어 설명을 써보자. (또는 그림을 그려보자.)

ache
[eik]

aid
[eid]

aim
[eim]

apologize
[əpɑ́lədʒàiz]

➢ Month 03-DAY 14 영어 문장과 우리말

My heart ached for the starving people.
굶주리는 사람들로 내 마음이 아프다.

He aided the players in their victory.
그는 선수들의 승리를 도왔다.

The sniper aimed at the target carefully.
저격수는 목표를 조심스럽게 겨누었다.

I apologized to her for my rudeness.
나는 그녀에게 나의 무례함에 대하여 사과하였다.

Vocabulary

➢ 음원을 들으면서 소리를 무조건 따라해 보시오. (빠르기&정확도/브레인+마우스 운동)

appear

to become visible or to come into sight

emerge, issue, look, show

나타나다

A man suddenly appeared in the doorway.

arrange

to put into a specific order

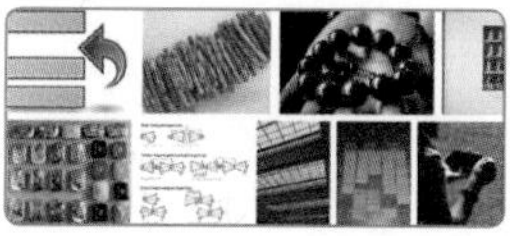

array, deploy, organize, prepare for

정리하다, 준비하다

She arranged shoes in a neat row.

avoid

to keep away from or to prevent from happening

prevent, hinder, refrain from

피하다

The train stopped to avoid a collision.

bark

to utter in a loud, harsh voice of a dog

yap, yell, yelp

개가 짖다, 개 짖는 소리

A dog barked at the stranger loudly.

* 이미지는 구글에서 찾은 것으로, 단어와 이미지가 다를 수 있습니다. 'Test 3'에서 나만의 이미지를 그려볼 수 있습니다.

Test 1 Connecting Exercise

Score(/16)
Self-Evaluation

➢ 서로 맞는 것을 연결하시오.

Ⓐ 1~4 영어 단어와 우리말 뜻 연결하기

1 appear	•	• 개가 짖다, 개 짖는 소리
2 bark	•	• 나타나다
3 arrange	•	• 정리하다, 준비하다
4 avoid	•	• 피하다

Ⓑ 5~8 영어 단어와 영어 설명 연결하기

5 bark	•	• to utter in a loud, harsh voice of a dog
6 avoid	•	• to put into a specific order
7 appear	•	• to keep away from or to prevent from happening
8 arrange	•	• to become visible or to come into sight

Ⓒ 9~12 영어 단어와 동의어 연결하기

9 appear	•	• yap, yell, yelp
10 arrange	•	• array, deploy, organize, prepare for
11 bark	•	• prevent, hinder, refrain from
12 avoid	•	• emerge, issue, look, show

Ⓓ 13~16 우리말 뜻과 영어 단어 연결하기

13 나타나다	•	• appear
14 피하다	•	• arrange
15 정리하다, 준비하다	•	• bark
16 개가 짖다, 개 짖는 소리	•	• avoid

Test 2 Writing Exercise

Score(　/12)
Self-Evaluation

Month 03

A 1~4 다음 단어에 맞는 뜻을 쓰시오.

1 arrange ____________________

2 appear ____________________

3 avoid ____________________

4 bark ____________________

B 5~8 다음 뜻에 맞는 영어 단어와 영어 동의어, 영어 설명을 쓰시오.

5 정리하다, 준비하다

__________ ____________________

____

6 나타나다

__________ ____________________

____

7 피하다

__________ ____________________

____

8 개가 짖다, 개 짖는 소리

__________ ____________________

____

C 9~12 다음 영어 문장을 의미가 떠오를 때까지 소리 내어 읽어보시오. 2초 이내

9 She arranged shoes in a neat row.

____

10 The train stopped to avoid a collision.

____

11 A dog barked at the stranger loudly.

____

12 A man suddenly appeared in the doorway.

____

Test 3 Imaging Exercise

➢ 다음 단어에 맞는 나만의 짧은 영어 설명을 써보자. (또는 그림을 그려보자.)

appear
[əpíər]

arrange
[əréindʒ]

avoid
[əvɔ́id]

bark
[baːrk]

➢ Month 03-DAY 15 영어 문장과 우리말

A man suddenly appeared in the doorway.
한 남자가 문간에 갑자기 나타났다.

She arranged shoes in a neat row.
그녀는 신발을 가지런히 정렬하였다.

The train stopped to avoid a collision.
열차가 충돌을 피하기 위하여 멈추었습니다.

A dog barked at the stranger loudly.
개가 낯선 이에게 큰 소리로 짖었다.

DAY 16 Vocabulary

➢ 음원을 들으면서 소리를 무조건 따라해 보시오. (빠르기 & 정확도/브레인 + 마우스 운동)

beat

to strike or hit repeatedly

batter, hit, strike, knock

때리다, 이기다

The rain was beating against the window.

borrow

to take or obtain with the promise to return

lend, take on loan

(움직일 수 있는 물건에 한정하여) 빌리다

I borrowed this book from the library.

breeze

to move quickly, casually, smoothly, or easily

blow

부드럽게 움직이다, 산들바람 불다, 미풍

The south wind breezed over the fields.

bury

to put in the ground and cover with earth

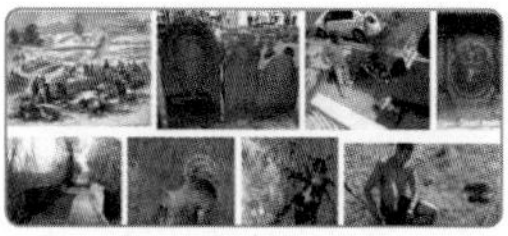

entomb, inearth, hide, cover

파묻다, 묻히다, 가리다, 덮다

She buried her face in the pillows.

* 이미지는 구글에서 찾은 것으로, 단어와 이미지가 다를 수 있습니다. 'Test 3'에서 나만의 이미지를 그려볼 수 있습니다.

Test 1 Connecting Exercise

Score(/16)
Self-Evaluation

➢ 서로 맞는 것을 연결하시오.

Ⓐ 1~4 영어 단어와 우리말 뜻 연결하기

1 breeze	•	• (움직일 수 있는 물건에 한정하여) 빌리다
2 borrow	•	• 부드럽게 움직이다, 산들바람 불다, 미풍
3 bury	•	• 때리다, 이기다
4 beat	•	• 파묻다, 묻히다, 가리다, 덮다

Ⓑ 5~8 영어 단어와 영어 설명 연결하기

5 bury	•	• to take or obtain with the promise to return
6 breeze	•	• to strike or hit repeatedly
7 borrow	•	• to put in the ground and cover with earth
8 beat	•	• to move quickly, casually, smoothly, or easily

Ⓒ 9~12 영어 단어와 동의어 연결하기

9 borrow	•	• lend, take on loan
10 breeze	•	• entomb, inearth, hide, cover
11 beat	•	• blow
12 bury	•	• batter, hit, strike, knock

Ⓓ 13~16 우리말 뜻과 영어 단어 연결하기

13 때리다, 이기다	•	• bury
14 부드럽게 움직이다, 산들바람 불다, 미풍	•	• borrow
15 (움직일 수 있는 물건에 한정하여) 빌리다	•	• beat
16 파묻다, 묻히다, 가리다, 덮다	•	• breeze

Test 2 Writing Exercise

Score(/12)
Self-Evaluation

Ⓐ 1~4 다음 단어에 맞는 뜻을 쓰시오.

1 breeze ______

2 borrow ______

3 bury ______

4 beat ______

Ⓑ 5~8 다음 뜻에 맞는 영어 단어와 영어 동의어, 영어 설명을 쓰시오.

5 (움직일 수 있는 물건에 한정하여) 빌리다

______ ______

______

6 파묻다, 묻히다, 가리다, 덮다

______ ______

______

7 때리다, 이기다

______ ______

______

8 부드럽게 움직이다, 산들바람 불다, 미풍

______ ______

______

Ⓒ 9~12 다음 영어 문장을 의미가 떠오를 때까지 소리 내어 읽어보시오. 2초 이내

9 I borrowed this book from the library.

______

10 The south wind breezed over the fields.

______

11 She buried her face in the pillows.

______

12 The rain was beating against the window.

______

Test 3 Imaging Exercise

➢ 다음 단어에 맞는 나만의 짧은 영어 설명을 써보자. (또는 그림을 그려보자.)

beat
[biːt]

borrow
[bάrou]

breeze
[briːz]

bury
[béri]

➢ Month 03-DAY 16 영어 문장과 우리말

The rain was beating against the window.
비가 창문을 때리고 있었습니다.

I borrowed this book from the library.
나는 도서관에서 이 책을 빌렸다.

The south wind breezed over the fields.
남풍이 온 들판에 산들산들 불어왔다.

She buried her face in the pillows.
그녀는 베개에 얼굴을 묻었다.

DAY 17 Vocabulary

➢ 음원을 들으면서 소리를 무조건 따라해 보시오. (빠르기&정확도/브레인+마우스 운동)

celebrate

to observe (a birthday, anniversary, etc)

commemorate, rejoice

축하하다, 기념하다, 맞이하다

He celebrates his ninetieth birthday next month.

chirp

the short, sharp sound made by small birds or insects

peep, cheep, tweet, twitter

짹짹 울다

The birds were chirping in the bushes.

collect

to bring together in a group

gather, accumulate, assemble

수집하다, 모으다

They are collecting information from the Internet.

contain

to have, keep, include within limits

include, hold, have, involve

포함하다, 함유하다

This box contains a pair of shoes.

* 이미지는 구글에서 찾은 것으로, 단어와 이미지가 다를 수 있습니다. 'Test 3'에서 나만의 이미지를 그려볼 수 있습니다.

Test 1 Connecting Exercise

Score(　　/16)
Self-Evaluation

➢ 서로 맞는 것을 연결하시오.

Ⓐ 1~4 영어 단어와 우리말 뜻 연결하기

1 celebrate	•	• 수집하다, 모으다
2 collect	•	• 짹짹 울다
3 chirp	•	• 포함하다, 함유하다
4 contain	•	• 축하하다, 기념하다, 맞이하다

Ⓑ 5~8 영어 단어와 영어 설명 연결하기

5 collect	•	• to have, keep, include within limits
6 chirp	•	• to bring together in a group
7 celebrate	•	• the short, sharp sound made by small birds or insects
8 contain	•	• to observe (a birthday, anniversary, etc)

Ⓒ 9~12 영어 단어와 동의어 연결하기

9 celebrate	•	• include, hold, have, involve
10 contain	•	• gather, accumulate, assemble
11 chirp	•	• commemorate, rejoice
12 collect	•	• peep, cheep, tweet, twitter

Ⓓ 13~16 우리말 뜻과 영어 단어 연결하기

13 수집하다, 모으다	•	• celebrate
14 짹짹 울다	•	• chirp
15 축하하다, 기념하다, 맞이하다	•	• contain
16 포함하다, 함유하다	•	• collect

Test 2 Writing Exercise

Score(/12)
Self-Evaluation

Ⓐ 1~4 다음 단어에 맞는 뜻을 쓰시오.

1 chirp ____________________

2 celebrate ____________________

3 collect ____________________

4 contain ____________________

Ⓑ 5~8 다음 뜻에 맞는 영어 단어와 영어 동의어, 영어 설명을 쓰시오.

5 수집하다, 모으다

__________ ____________________

____

6 축하하다, 기념하다, 맞이하다

__________ ____________________

____

7 포함하다, 함유하다

__________ ____________________

____

8 짹짹 울다

__________ ____________________

____

Ⓒ 9~12 다음 영어 문장을 의미가 떠오를 때까지 소리 내어 읽어보시오. 2초 이내

9 This box contains a pair of shoes.

____

10 The birds were chirping in the bushes.

____

11 They are collecting information from the Internet.

____

12 He celebrates his ninetieth birthday next month.

____

Test 3

➢ 다음 단어에 맞는 나만의 짧은 영어 설명을 써보자. (또는 그림을 그려보자.)

celebrate
[séləbrèit]

chirp
[ʧəːrp]

collect
[kάlekt]

contain
[kəntéin]

➢ Month 03-DAY 17 영어 문장과 우리말

He celebrates his ninetieth birthday next month.
그는 다음달 90회 생일을 맞이합니다.

The birds were chirping in the bushes.
수풀 속에서 새들이 짹짹 울고 있었습니다.

They are collecting information from the Internet.
그들은 인터넷에서 정보를 수집하고 있습니다.

This box contains a pair of shoes.
이 상자(박스)에는 구두 한켤레가 담겨 있습니다.

DAY 18 Vocabulary

➢ 음원을 들으면서 소리를 무조건 따라해 보시오. (빠르기&정확도/브레인+마우스 운동)

contrast

to compare in order to show unlikeness or differences

compare, collate, set against

대조하다, 비교하다, 비교, 대조

Before buying I contrasted A with B.

dash

to move with haste, to run quickly and suddenly

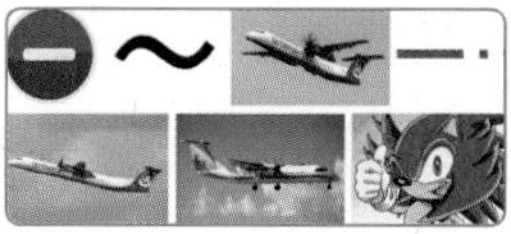

rush, crash

갑자기 빠르게 달리다, 돌진하다

You must dash to catch your train.

defend

to make or keep safe from danger, attack, or harm

protect, guard, shield

방어하다, 지키다, 보호하다

A vaccine defends the body from infection.

depart

to go away

leave, deviate, diverge

출발하다, 떠나다, 벗어나다, 죽다

They departed for the islands at dawn.

* 이미지는 구글에서 찾은 것으로, 단어와 이미지가 다를 수 있습니다. 'Test 3'에서 나만의 이미지를 그려볼 수 있습니다.

Test 1 Connecting Exercise

Score(/16)
Self-Evaluation

➢ 서로 맞는 것을 연결하시오.

Ⓐ 1~4 영어 단어와 우리말 뜻 연결하기

1 depart	•	• 방어하다, 지키다, 보호하다
2 contrast	•	• 대조하다, 비교하다, 비교, 대조
3 defend	•	• 출발하다, 떠나다, 벗어나다, 죽다
4 dash	•	• 갑자기 빠르게 달리다, 돌진하다

Ⓑ 5~8 영어 단어와 영어 설명 연결하기

5 contrast	•	• to compare in order to show unlikeness or differences
6 depart	•	• to move with haste, to run quickly and suddenly
7 dash	•	• to make or keep safe from danger, attack, or harm
8 defend	•	• to go away

Ⓒ 9~12 영어 단어와 동의어 연결하기

9 depart	•	• compare, collate, set against
10 contrast	•	• rush, crash
11 defend	•	• protect, guard, shield
12 dash	•	• leave, deviate, diverge

Ⓓ 13~16 우리말 뜻과 영어 단어 연결하기

13 출발하다, 떠나다, 벗어나다, 죽다	•	• depart
14 대조하다, 비교하다, 비교, 대조	•	• contrast
15 갑자기 빠르게 달리다, 돌진하다	•	• dash
16 방어하다, 지키다, 보호하다	•	• defend

Test 2 Writing Exercise

Score(　　/12)
Self-Evaluation

A 1~4 다음 단어에 맞는 뜻을 쓰시오.

1 contrast ______________________

2 defend ______________________

3 dash ______________________

4 depart ______________________

B 5~8 다음 뜻에 맞는 영어 단어와 영어 동의어, 영어 설명을 쓰시오.

5 출발하다, 떠나다, 벗어나다, 죽다

______________ ______________________

____

6 대조하다, 비교하다, 비교, 대조

______________ ______________________

____

7 방어하다, 지키다, 보호하다

______________ ______________________

____

8 갑자기 빠르게 달리다, 돌진하다

______________ ______________________

____

C 9~12 다음 영어 문장을 의미가 떠오를 때까지 소리 내어 읽어보시오. 2초 이내

9 A vaccine defends the body from infection.

____

10 You must dash to catch your train.

____

11 Before buying I contrasted A with B.

____

12 They departed for the islands at dawn.

____

➢ 다음 단어에 맞는 나만의 짧은 영어 설명을 써보자. (또는 그림을 그려보자.)

contrast
[kəntrǽst]

dash
[dæʃ]

defend
[difénd]

depart
[dipɑ́:rt]

➢ Month 03-DAY 18 영어 문장과 우리말

Before buying I contrasted A with B.
구입하기 전에 나는 A와 B를 대조(비교)해 보았습니다.

You must dash to catch your train.
당신은 열차를 타기 위해 서둘러 달려야 합니다.

A vaccine defends the body from infection.
백신은 감염으로부터 몸을 보호합니다.

They departed for the islands at dawn.
그들은 새벽에 섬으로 떠났습니다.

➢ 음원을 들으면서 소리를 무조건 따라해 보시오. (빠르기&정확도/브레인+마우스 운동)

distract

to divide or confuse the attention of (a person)

divert, sidetrack, draw away

흐트러뜨리다, 산만하게 하다, 벗어나게 하다

Smartphones sometimes distract us from our concentration.

disturb

to interfere with

interrupt, hinder, bother, disrupt

방해하다, 교란시키다, 귀찮게 하다

Actually I didn't want to disturb you.

drag

to pull or be pulled with force, esp along the ground or other surface

pull, draw, haul, trail

끌다, 질질 끌다, 끌리다

He dragged his chair towards the table.

drip

to fall in drops

dribble, drop, trickle

물방울이 똑똑 떨어지다

Water is dripping from that leaky faucet.

* 이미지는 구글에서 찾은 것으로, 단어와 이미지가 다를 수 있습니다. 'Test 3'에서 나만의 이미지를 그려볼 수 있습니다.

Test 1 Connecting Exercise

Score(　　/16)
Self-Evaluation

➢ 서로 맞는 것을 연결하시오.

Ⓐ 1~4 영어 단어와 우리말 뜻 연결하기

1 distract	•	• 물방울이 똑똑 떨어지다
2 drag	•	• 흐트러뜨리다, 산만하게 하다, 벗어나게 하다
3 drip	•	• 방해하다, 교란시키다, 귀찮게 하다
4 disturb	•	• 끌다, 질질 끌다, 끌리다

Ⓑ 5~8 영어 단어와 영어 설명 연결하기

5 distract	•	• to interfere with
6 drip	•	• to fall in drops
7 disturb	•	• to pull or be pulled with force, esp along the ground or other surface
8 drag	•	• to divide or confuse the attention of (a person)

Ⓒ 9~12 영어 단어와 동의어 연결하기

9 drip	•	• divert, sidetrack, draw away
10 distract	•	• pull, draw, haul, trail
11 drag	•	• interrupt, hinder, bother, disrupt
12 disturb	•	• dribble, drop, trickle

Ⓓ 13~16 우리말 뜻과 영어 단어 연결하기

13 물방울이 똑똑 떨어지다	•	• drag
14 끌다, 질질 끌다, 끌리다	•	• disturb
15 흐트러뜨리다, 산만하게 하다, 벗어나게 하다	•	• distract
16 방해하다, 교란시키다, 귀찮게 하다	•	• drip

Test 2 Writing Exercise

Score(/12)
Self-Evaluation

A 1~4 다음 단어에 맞는 뜻을 쓰시오.

1 drip ______________________

2 disturb ______________________

3 drag ______________________

4 distract ______________________

B 5~8 다음 뜻에 맞는 영어 단어와 영어 동의어, 영어 설명을 쓰시오.

5 끌다, 질질 끌다, 끌리다

______________ ______________________

____

6 물방울이 똑똑 떨어지다

______________ ______________________

____

7 흐트러뜨리다, 산만하게 하다, 벗어나게 하다

______________ ______________________

____

8 방해하다, 교란시키다, 귀찮게 하다

______________ ______________________

____

C 9~12 다음 영어 문장을 의미가 떠오를 때까지 소리 내어 읽어보시오. 2초 이내

9 He dragged his chair towards the table.

____

10 Water is dripping from that leaky faucet.

____

11 Actually I didn't want to disturb you.

____

12 Smartphones sometimes distract us from our concentration.

____

Test 3 Imaging Exercise

➢ 다음 단어에 맞는 나만의 짧은 영어 설명을 써보자. (또는 그림을 그려보자.)

distract
[distrǽkt]

disturb
[distə́ːrb]

drag
[dræg]

drip
[drip]

➢ Month 03-DAY 19 영어 문장과 우리말

Smartphones sometimes distract us from our concentration.
스마트폰은 때때로 우리의 집중력을 흐트려뜨립니다.

Actually I didn't want to disturb you.
사실 나는 당신을 방해하고 싶지 않았습니다.

He dragged his chair towards the table.
그는 의자를 테이블 쪽으로 끌고 갔습니다.

Water is dripping from that leaky faucet.
새는 수도꼭지에서 물방울이 똑똑 떨어집니다.

DAY 20 Vocabulary

➢ 음원을 들으면서 소리를 무조건 따라해 보시오. (빠르기 & 정확도/브레인 + 마우스 운동)

educate

to develop the powers of (a person) by schooling

teach, train, coach, instruct

교육하다

He was educated at a private school.

encourage

to inspire with hope, courage, or confidence

cheer, embolden, hearten, inspire

격려하다, 용기를 북돋다

You must encourage him to try again.

escape

to get free

flee, elude, evade

탈출하다, 도망가다, 도망, 탈출

A prisoner has escaped from a jail.

excel

to do or be better than

surpass, exceed, outstrip, stand out

우수하다, 뛰어나다

He excelled in mathematics and at sports.

* 이미지는 구글에서 찾은 것으로, 단어와 이미지가 다를 수 있습니다. 'Test 3'에서 나만의 이미지를 그려볼 수 있습니다.

Test 1 Connecting Exercise

Score(/16)
Self-Evaluation

➢ 서로 맞는 것을 연결하시오.

Ⓐ 1~4 영어 단어와 우리말 뜻 연결하기

1 escape	•	• 우수하다, 뛰어나다
2 excel	•	• 격려하다, 용기를 북돋다
3 educate	•	• 탈출하다, 도망가다, 도망, 탈출
4 encourage	•	• 교육하다

Ⓑ 5~8 영어 단어와 영어 설명 연결하기

5 excel	•	• to inspire with hope, courage, or confidence
6 educate	•	• to get free
7 escape	•	• to do or be better than
8 encourage	•	• to develop the powers of (a person) by schooling

Ⓒ 9~12 영어 단어와 동의어 연결하기

9 encourage	•	• cheer, embolden, hearten, inspire
10 educate	•	• teach, train, coach, instruct
11 excel	•	• flee, elude, evade
12 escape	•	• surpass, exceed, outstrip, stand out

Ⓓ 13~16 우리말 뜻과 영어 단어 연결하기

13 교육하다	•	• excel
14 우수하다, 뛰어나다	•	• educate
15 격려하다, 용기를 북돋다	•	• escape
16 탈출하다, 도망가다, 도망, 탈출	•	• encourage

Test 2 Writing Exercise

Score(/12)
Self-Evaluation

A 1~4 다음 단어에 맞는 뜻을 쓰시오.

1 escape ______

2 encourage ______

3 educate ______

4 excel ______

B 5~8 다음 뜻에 맞는 영어 단어와 영어 동의어, 영어 설명을 쓰시오.

5 격려하다, 용기를 북돋다

______ ______

______

6 탈출하다, 도망가다, 도망, 탈출

______ ______

______

7 교육하다

______ ______

______

8 우수하다, 뛰어나다

______ ______

______

C 9~12 다음 영어 문장을 의미가 떠오를 때까지 소리 내어 읽어보시오. 2초 이내

9 You must encourage him to try again.

______

10 A prisoner has escaped from a jail.

______

11 He excelled in mathematics and at sports.

______

12 He was educated at a private school.

______

Test 3

➢ 다음 단어에 맞는 나만의 짧은 영어 설명을 써보자. (또는 그림을 그려보자.)

educate
[édʒukèit]

encourage
[inkə́ːridʒ]

escape
[iskéip]

excel
[iksél]

➢ Month 03-DAY 20 영어 문장과 우리말

He was educated at a private school.
그는 사립학교에서 교육받았습니다.

You must encourage him to try again.
당신은 그가 다시 시도할 수 있도록 용기를 북돋아 주어야 합니다.

A prisoner has escaped from a jail.
죄수가 감옥에서 탈출하였습니다.

He excelled in mathematics and at sports.
그는 수학과 스포츠에서 뛰어났습니다.

Month 04 Verbs

Day 01 excuse, exhibit, exist, explain
Day 02 flick, free, glow, grow
Day 03 hike, hold, horrify, hurry
Day 04 impress, injure, introduce, invade
Day 05 jog, join, kidnap, kneel
Day 06 knock, lay, lead, light
Day 07 marry, memorize, misuse, note
Day 08 occur, organize, overjoy, praise
Day 09 pretend, prick, protest, rejoice
Day 10 remain, remark, repeat, replace
Day 11 reply, return, sacrifice, select
Day 12 serve, shoot, shriek, sightsee
Day 13 sink, skid, sow, spend
Day 14 steal, stick, stir, stretch
Day 15 thaw, throw, try, unlock
Day 16 unmask, utter, abstain, admire
Day 17 announce, broadcast, burden, challenge
Day 18 charge, check, choose, command
Day 19 communicate, construct, count, create
Day 20 deal, decorate, deliver, dial

Vocabulary

➢ 음원을 들으면서 소리를 무조건 따라해 보시오. (빠르기&정확도/브레인+마우스 운동)

excuse

to make allowance for

forgive, pardon, allow

용서하다, 허용하다, 용서, 허용

I'll excuse your carelessness this time.

exhibit

to put something on public display

show, display, reveal

전시하다, 보이다, 공개하다

She exhibited her paintings at a gallery.

exist

to have actual being

be, subsist

존재하다

Scientists believe that the alien does exist.

explain

to make plain or comprehensible

describe, explicate

설명하다

We explained our plan to the committee.

* 이미지는 구글에서 찾은 것으로, 단어와 이미지가 다를 수 있습니다. 'Test 3'에서 나만의 이미지를 그려볼 수 있습니다.

Test 1 Connecting Exercise

Score(/16)
Self-Evaluation

≫ 서로 맞는 것을 연결하시오.

Ⓐ 1~4 영어 단어와 우리말 뜻 연결하기

1 exist ●	● 존재하다
2 exhibit ●	● 설명하다
3 explain ●	● 전시하다, 보이다, 공개하다
4 excuse ●	● 용서하다, 허용하다, 용서, 허용

Ⓑ 5~8 영어 단어와 영어 설명 연결하기

5 explain ●	● to make allowance for
6 excuse ●	● to have actual being
7 exhibit ●	● to put something on public display
8 exist ●	● to make plain or comprehensible

Ⓒ 9~12 영어 단어와 동의어 연결하기

9 exist ●	● describe, explicate
10 explain ●	● forgive, pardon, allow
11 excuse ●	● be, subsist
12 exhibit ●	● show, display, reveal

Ⓓ 13~16 우리말 뜻과 영어 단어 연결하기

13 용서하다, 허용하다, 용서, 허용 ●	● exhibit
14 존재하다 ●	● excuse
15 전시하다, 보이다, 공개하다 ●	● explain
16 설명하다 ●	● exist

Test 2 Writing Exercise

Score(/12)
Self-Evaluation

Month 04

A 1~4 다음 단어에 맞는 뜻을 쓰시오.

1 exist ______

2 exhibit ______

3 excuse ______

4 explain ______

B 5~8 다음 뜻에 맞는 영어 단어와 영어 동의어, 영어 설명을 쓰시오.

5 용서하다, 허용하다, 용서, 허용

______ ______

______

6 설명하다

______ ______

______

7 전시하다, 보이다, 공개하다

______ ______

______

8 존재하다

______ ______

______

C 9~12 다음 영어 문장을 의미가 떠오를 때까지 소리 내어 읽어보시오. 2초 이내

9 I'll excuse your carelessness this time.

______

10 Scientists believe that the alien does exist.

______

11 We explained our plan to the committee.

______

12 She exhibited her paintings at a gallery.

______

Test 3 Imaging Exercise

➢ 다음 단어에 맞는 나만의 짧은 영어 설명을 써보자. (또는 그림을 그려보자.)

excuse
[ikskjú:z]

exhibit
[igzíbit]

exist
[igzíst]

explain
[ikspléin]

➢ Month 04-DAY 01 영어 문장과 우리말

I'll excuse your carelessness this time.
이번에는 당신의 부주의를 용서하겠습니다.

She exhibited her paintings at a gallery.
그녀는 갤러리에서 그녀의 그림들을 전시하였습니다.

Scientists believe that the alien does exist.
과학자들은 외계인이 존재한다고 믿습니다.

We explained our plan to the committee.
우리는 우리의 계획을 위원회에 설명하였습니다.

DAY 02

Vocabulary

➢ 음원을 들으면서 소리를 무조건 따라해 보시오. (빠르기 & 정확도/브레인 + 마우스 운동)

flick

to touch or hit with a light quick blow or fillip

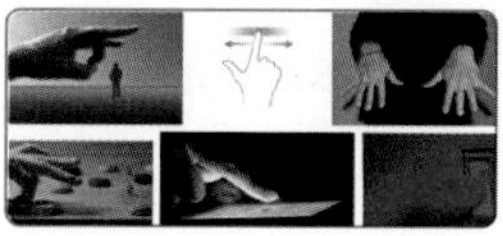

fillip, flip, hit, touch

(손가락으로) 가볍게 치다, 톡톡 치다, 빠르게 움직이다

The snake's tongue flicked in and out.

free

to make free, as from confinement or oppression

loose, unloose, release, liberate

자유롭게 하다, 자유의, 무료의, ~가 없는, 비어있는

I was at last freed from fear.

glow

to shine brightly and steadily

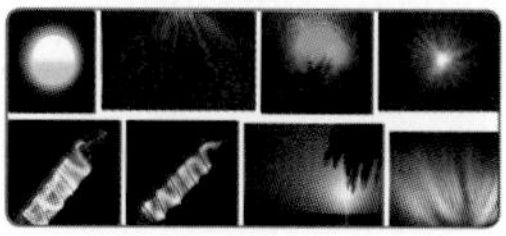

glitter, shine, flash, brighten

빨갛게 빛을 내다, 빛나다

The firewood was glowing in the fire.

grow, grew, grown

to expand or increase

get bigger, get taller

자라다, 크다, 성장하다

The business grew under a new owner.

* 이미지는 구글에서 찾은 것으로, 단어와 이미지가 다를 수 있습니다. 'Test 3'에서 나만의 이미지를 그려볼 수 있습니다.

Test 1 Connecting Exercise

Score(/16)
Self-Evaluation

➢ 서로 맞는 것을 연결하시오.

Ⓐ 1~4 영어 단어와 우리말 뜻 연결하기

1 glow ●	● (손가락으로) 가볍게 치다, 톡톡 치다, 빠르게 움직이다
2 free ●	● 빨갛게 빛을 내다, 빛나다
3 flick ●	● 자라다, 크다, 성장하다
4 grow, grew, grown ●	● 자유롭게 하다, 자유의, 무료의, ~가 없는, 비어있는

Ⓑ 5~8 영어 단어와 영어 설명 연결하기

5 free ●	● to make free, as from confinement or oppression
6 grow, grew, grown ●	● to touch or hit with a light quick blow or fillip
7 glow ●	● to shine brightly and steadily
8 flick ●	● to expand or increase

Ⓒ 9~12 영어 단어와 동의어 연결하기

9 flick ●	● loose, unloose, release, liberate
10 free ●	● get bigger, get taller
11 glow ●	● glitter, shine, flash, brighten
12 grow, grew, grown ●	● fillip, flip, hit, touch

Ⓓ 13~16 우리말 뜻과 영어 단어 연결하기

13 자라다, 크다, 성장하다 ●	● free
14 자유롭게 하다, 자유의, 무료의, ~가 없는, 비어있는 ●	● grow, grew, grown
15 빨갛게 빛을 내다, 빛나다 ●	● glow
16 (손가락으로) 가볍게 치다, 톡톡 치다, 빠르게 움직이다 ●	● flick

Test 2 Writing Exercise

Score(/12)
Self-Evaluation

A 1~4 다음 단어에 맞는 뜻을 쓰시오.

1 glow ______

2 free ______

3 flick ______

4 grow, grew, grown ______

B 5~8 다음 뜻에 맞는 영어 단어와 영어 동의어, 영어 설명을 쓰시오.

5 자라다, 크다, 성장하다

______ ______

______

6 (손가락으로) 가볍게 치다, 톡톡 치다, 빠르게 움직이다

______ ______

______

7 빨갛게 빛을 내다, 빛나다

______ ______

______

8 자유롭게 하다, 자유의, 무료의, ~가 없는, 비어있는

______ ______

______

C 9~12 다음 영어 문장을 의미가 떠오를 때까지 소리 내어 읽어보시오. 2초 이내

9 The snake's tongue flicked in and out.

______

10 The firewood was glowing in the fire.

______

11 I was at last freed from fear.

______

12 The business grew under a new owner.

______

Test 3

➢ 다음 단어에 맞는 나만의 짧은 영어 설명을 써보자. (또는 그림을 그려보자.)

flick
[flik]

free
[friː]

glow
[glou]

grow, grew, grown
[grou, gruː, groun]

➢ Month 04-DAY 02 영어 문장과 우리말

The snake's tongue flicked in and out.
뱀의 혀가 날름거렸습니다.

I was at last freed from fear.
나는 마침내 두려움에서 자유로워졌습니다(벗어났습니다).

The firewood was glowing in the fire.
장작이 빨갛게 불타고 있었습니다.

The business grew under a new owner.
새로운 주인으로 사업은 성장했습니다.

DAY 03 Vocabulary

➢ 음원을 들으면서 소리를 무조건 따라해 보시오. (빠르기 & 정확도/브레인 + 마우스 운동)

hike

to travel over on foot

walk, trek

도보여행을 하다, 하이킹, 도보여행

I have hiked all over South Korea.

hold, held, held

to keep in one's grasp

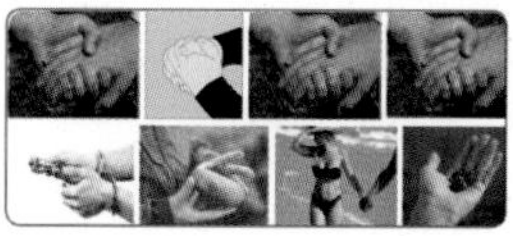

keep, grasp, maintain, possess

붙잡다, 꽉 쥐다, 지탱하다,
유지하다, 가지다

Hold this bowl for a moment, please.

horrify

to cause to feel horror

terrify, frighten

소름 끼치게 하다, 무섭게 하다,
공포심을 느끼게 하다

I was horrified when I saw these.

hurry

to move or act with speed or haste

speed, hasten, make haste

서두르다, 서두름

'Hurry up' means
'do something more quickly'.

* 이미지는 구글에서 찾은 것으로, 단어와 이미지가 다를 수 있습니다. 'Test 3'에서 나만의 이미지를 그려볼 수 있습니다.

Test 1 Connecting Exercise

Score(/16)
Self-Evaluation

➢ 서로 맞는 것을 연결하시오.

Ⓐ 1~4 영어 단어와 우리말 뜻 연결하기

1 hike	•	• 서두르다, 서두름
2 horrify	•	• 소름 끼치게 하다, 무섭게 하다, 공포심을 느끼게 하다
3 hurry	•	• 붙잡다, 꽉 쥐다, 지탱하다, 유지하다, 가지다
4 hold, held, held	•	• 도보여행을 하다, 하이킹, 도보여행

Ⓑ 5~8 영어 단어와 영어 설명 연결하기

5 hike	•	• to travel over on foot
6 hold, held, held	•	• to keep in one's grasp
7 horrify	•	• to move or act with speed or haste
8 hurry	•	• to cause to feel horror

Ⓒ 9~12 영어 단어와 동의어 연결하기

9 horrify	•	• terrify, frighten
10 hike	•	• walk, trek
11 hold, held, held	•	• keep, grasp, maintain, possess
12 hurry	•	• speed, hasten, make haste

Ⓓ 13~16 우리말 뜻과 영어 단어 연결하기

13 소름 끼치게 하다, 무섭게 하다, 공포심을 느끼게 하다	•	• hike
14 도보여행을 하다, 하이킹, 도보여행	•	• horrify
15 붙잡다, 꽉 쥐다, 지탱하다, 유지하다, 가지다	•	• hold, held, held
16 서두르다, 서두름	•	• hurry

Test 2 Writing Exercise

Score(/12)
Self-Evaluation

Ⓐ 1~4 다음 단어에 맞는 뜻을 쓰시오.

1 hurry ______

2 hike ______

3 hold, held, held ______

4 horrify ______

Ⓑ 5~8 다음 뜻에 맞는 영어 단어와 영어 동의어, 영어 설명을 쓰시오.

5 도보여행을 하다, 하이킹, 도보여행

______ ______

______

6 붙잡다, 꽉 쥐다, 지탱하다, 유지하다, 가지다

______ ______

______

7 서두르다, 서두름

______ ______

______

8 소름 끼치게 하다, 무섭게 하다, 공포심을 느끼게 하다

______ ______

______

Ⓒ 9~12 다음 영어 문장을 의미가 떠오를 때까지 소리 내어 읽어보시오. 2초 이내

9 I have hiked all over South Korea.

______

10 Hold this bowl for a moment, please.

______

11 'Hurry up' means 'do something more quickly'.

______

12 I was horrified when I saw these.

______

Test 3 Imaging Exercise

➢ 다음 단어에 맞는 나만의 짧은 영어 설명을 써보자. (또는 그림을 그려보자.)

hike
[haik]

hold, held, held
[hould, held, held]

horrify
[hɔ́:rəfài]

hurry
[hə́:ri]

➢ Month 04-DAY 03 영어 문장과 우리말

I have hiked all over South Korea.
나는 도보여행으로 대한민국 전지역을 다녔습니다.

Hold this bowl for a moment, please.
이 그릇을 잠깐만 잡고 있어 주세요.

I was horrified when I saw these.
나는 이것들을 보았을 때 공포심을 느꼈습니다.

'Hurry up' means 'do something more quickly'.
'Hurry up'은 '더 빨리 하라'는 뜻입니다.

Vocabulary

➢ 음원을 들으면서 소리를 무조건 따라해 보시오. (빠르기 & 정확도/브레인 + 마우스 운동)

impress

to make an impression on

affect, influence, inspire

인상을 주다, 감동 주다

What impressed me most was their kindness.

injure

to cause physical or mental harm

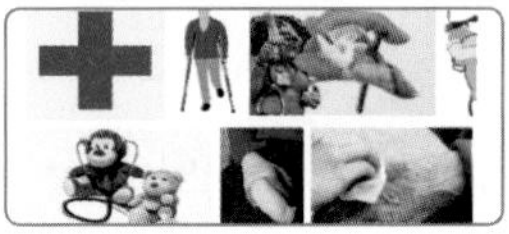

hurt, wound, harm, damage

다치게 하다, 해치다

Too much stress can injure your health.

introduce

to present (someone) by name (to another person)

acquaint, present, announce

소개하다

Let me introduce you to my mother.

invade

to enter by force in order to conquer or pillage

attack, occupy, conquer, intrude

침입하다, 침략하다

I don't want to invade your privacy.

* 이미지는 구글에서 찾은 것으로, 단어와 이미지가 다를 수 있습니다. 'Test 3'에서 나만의 이미지를 그려볼 수 있습니다.

Test 1 Connecting Exercise

Score(/16)
Self-Evaluation

➢ 서로 맞는 것을 연결하시오.

A 1~4 영어 단어와 우리말 뜻 연결하기

1 injure	•	• 인상을 주다, 감동 주다
2 impress	•	• 소개하다
3 introduce	•	• 다치게 하다, 해치다
4 invade	•	• 침입하다, 침략하다

B 5~8 영어 단어와 영어 설명 연결하기

5 introduce	•	• to enter by force in order to conquer or pillage
6 injure	•	• to present (someone) by name (to another person)
7 impress	•	• to cause physical or mental harm
8 invade	•	• to make an impression on

C 9~12 영어 단어와 동의어 연결하기

9 injure	•	• affect, influence, inspire
10 introduce	•	• attack, occupy, conquer, intrude
11 impress	•	• hurt, wound, harm, damage
12 invade	•	• acquaint, present, announce

D 13~16 우리말 뜻과 영어 단어 연결하기

13 침입하다, 침략하다	•	• introduce
14 다치게 하다, 해치다	•	• injure
15 인상을 주다, 감동 주다	•	• invade
16 소개하다	•	• impress

Test 2 Writing Exercise

Score(　　/12)
Self-Evaluation

A 1~4 다음 단어에 맞는 뜻을 쓰시오.

1 introduce ______

2 injure ______

3 impress ______

4 invade ______

B 5~8 다음 뜻에 맞는 영어 단어와 영어 동의어, 영어 설명을 쓰시오.

5 침입하다, 침략하다

______ ______

______

6 다치게 하다, 해치다

______ ______

______

7 인상을 주다, 감동 주다

______ ______

______

8 소개하다

______ ______

______

C 9~12 다음 영어 문장을 의미가 떠오를 때까지 소리 내어 읽어보시오. 2초 이내

9 I don't want to invade your privacy.

______

10 Let me introduce you to my mother.

______

11 Too much stress can injure your health.

______

12 What impressed me most was their kindness.

______

Test 3 Imaging Exercise

➢ 다음 단어에 맞는 나만의 짧은 영어 설명을 써보자. (또는 그림을 그려보자.)

impress
[imprés]

injure
[índʒər]

introduce
[ìntrədjúːs]

invade
[invéid]

➢ Month 04-DAY 04 영어 문장과 우리말

What impressed me most was their kindness.
나에게 가장 인상깊었던 것은 그들의 친절함이었다.

Too much stress can injure your health.
과도한 스트레스가 당신의 건강을 해칠 수 있습니다.

Let me introduce you to my mother.
당신을 우리 어머니에게 소개시켜드리겠습니다.

I don't want to invade your privacy.
당신의 사생활을 침범하고 싶지 않습니다.

DAY 05 Vocabulary

➢ 음원을 들으면서 소리를 무조건 따라해 보시오. (빠르기 & 정확도/브레인 + 마우스 운동)

jog

to run or move slowly

run, race

천천히 달리다

We're jogging along in the morning.

join

to put or bring together

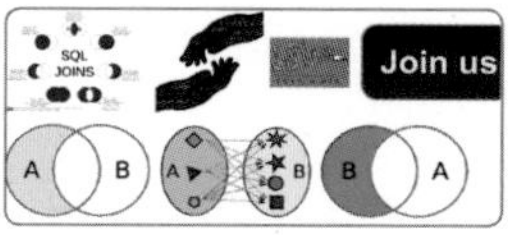

combine, unite, enrol in, enlist in

합류하다, 참가하다, 가입하다

He joined the Army five years ago.

kidnap

to abduct or confine (a person) forcibly

abduct

납치하다, 유괴하다

His son was kidnapped by some kidnappers.

kneel, knelt, knelt

to go down or rest on one or both knees

kneeling

무릎 꿇다, 무릎 꿇음

She knelt on the floor and prayed.

* 이미지는 구글에서 찾은 것으로, 단어와 이미지가 다를 수 있습니다. 'Test 3'에서 나만의 이미지를 그려볼 수 있습니다.

Test 1 Connecting Exercise

Score(/16)
Self-Evaluation

≫ 서로 맞는 것을 연결하시오.

Ⓐ 1~4 영어 단어와 우리말 뜻 연결하기

1	join	•	• 무릎 꿇다, 무릎 꿇음
2	jog	•	• 천천히 달리다
3	kidnap	•	• 납치하다, 유괴하다
4	kneel, knelt, knelt	•	• 합류하다, 참가하다, 가입하다

Ⓑ 5~8 영어 단어와 영어 설명 연결하기

5	join	•	• to go down or rest on one or both knees
6	kneel, knelt, knelt	•	• to put or bring together
7	jog	•	• to run or move slowly
8	kidnap	•	• to abduct or confine (a person) forcibly

Ⓒ 9~12 영어 단어와 동의어 연결하기

9	kidnap	•	• combine, unite, enrol in, enlist in
10	jog	•	• abduct
11	kneel, knelt, knelt	•	• kneeling
12	join	•	• run, race

Ⓓ 13~16 우리말 뜻과 영어 단어 연결하기

13	무릎 꿇다, 무릎 꿇음	•	• jog
14	납치하다, 유괴하다	•	• kneel, knelt, knelt
15	천천히 달리다	•	• kidnap
16	합류하다, 참가하다, 가입하다	•	• join

Test 2 Writing Exercise

Score(/12)
Self-Evaluation

A 1~4 다음 단어에 맞는 뜻을 쓰시오.

1 jog ______

2 join ______

3 kneel, knelt, knelt ______

4 kidnap ______

B 5~8 다음 뜻에 맞는 영어 단어와 영어 동의어, 영어 설명을 쓰시오.

5 무릎 꿇다, 무릎 꿇음

______ ______

______

6 납치하다, 유괴하다

______ ______

______

7 천천히 달리다

______ ______

______

8 합류하다, 참가하다, 가입하다

______ ______

______

C 9~12 다음 영어 문장을 의미가 떠오를 때까지 소리 내어 읽어보시오. 2초 이내

9 He joined the Army five years ago.

______

10 She knelt on the floor and prayed.

______

11 We're jogging along in the morning.

______

12 His son was kidnapped by some kidnappers.

______

Test 3 Imaging Exercise

➢ 다음 단어에 맞는 나만의 짧은 영어 설명을 써보자. (또는 그림을 그려보자.)

jog
[dʒag]

join
[dʒɔin]

kidnap
[kídnæp]

kneel, knelt, knelt
[niːl, nelt, nelt]

➢ Month 04-DAY 05 영어 문장과 우리말

We're jogging along in the morning.
우리는 아침에 조깅하고 있습니다.

He joined the Army five years ago.
그는 5년 전에 군에 입대하였습니다.

His son was kidnapped by some kidnappers.
그의 아들은 납치범들에게 유괴되었습니다.

She knelt on the floor and prayed.
그녀는 바닥에 무릎을 꿇고 기도했습니다.

Vocabulary

➢ 음원을 들으면서 소리를 무조건 따라해 보시오. (빠르기 & 정확도 / 브레인 + 마우스 운동)

knock

to strike with a hard blow

strike, hit, beat, punch

두드리다, 노크하다, 때리다,
부딪히다, 두드림

I knocked my head on a door.

lay, laid, laid

to put down,
or to produce eggs

place, put down, set down

놓다, 두다,
(알을) 낳다

He laid his coat on the bed.

lead

to guide or direct in a course

guide, escort, precede

이끌다, 안내하다, 인도하다,
선두, 맨 앞

Follow me and I'll lead you.

light, lit, lighted

to cause to give out light

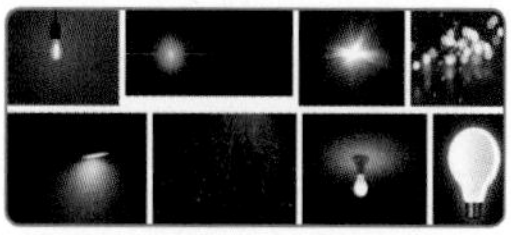

ignite, kindle, illuminate

불을 붙이다, 불을 켜다, 빛, 불,
가볍게 하다, 가벼운

The bright moon lit the road brightly.

* 이미지는 구글에서 찾은 것으로, 단어와 이미지가 다를 수 있습니다. 'Test 3'에서 나만의 이미지를 그려볼 수 있습니다.

Test 1 Connecting Exercise

Score(/16)
Self-Evaluation

➢ 서로 맞는 것을 연결하시오.

Ⓐ 1~4 영어 단어와 우리말 뜻 연결하기

1 lay, laid, laid	•	• 놓다, 두다, (알을) 낳다
2 knock	•	• 불을 붙이다, 불을 켜다, 빛, 불, 가볍게 하다, 가벼운
3 light, lit, lighted	•	• 이끌다, 안내하다, 인도하다, 선두, 맨 앞
4 lead	•	• 두드리다, 노크하다, 때리다, 부딪히다, 두드림

Ⓑ 5~8 영어 단어와 영어 설명 연결하기

5 lay, laid, laid	•	• to put down, or to produce eggs
6 knock	•	• to guide or direct in a course
7 lead	•	• to strike with a hard blow
8 light, lit, lighted	•	• to cause to give out light

Ⓒ 9~12 영어 단어와 동의어 연결하기

9 lay, laid, laid	•	• guide, escort, precede
10 knock	•	• place, put down, set down
11 light, lit, lighted	•	• strike, hit, beat, punch
12 lead	•	• ignite, kindle, illuminate

Ⓓ 13~16 우리말 뜻과 영어 단어 연결하기

13 두드리다, 노크하다, 때리다, 부딪히다, 두드림	•	• light, lit, lighted
14 불을 붙이다, 불을 켜다, 빛, 불, 가볍게 하다, 가벼운	•	• lay, laid, laid
15 놓다, 두다, (알을) 낳다	•	• knock
16 이끌다, 안내하다, 인도하다, 선두, 맨 앞	•	• lead

Test 2 Writing Exercise

Score(/12)
Self-Evaluation

Ⓐ 1~4 다음 단어에 맞는 뜻을 쓰시오.

1 light, lit, lighted ____________

2 knock ____________

3 lead ____________

4 lay, laid, laid ____________

Ⓑ 5~8 다음 뜻에 맞는 영어 단어와 영어 동의어, 영어 설명을 쓰시오.

5 불을 붙이다, 불을 켜다, 빛, 불, 가볍게 하다, 가벼운

____________ ____________

____

6 놓다, 두다, (알을) 낳다

____________ ____________

____

7 두드리다, 노크하다, 때리다, 부딪히다, 두드림

____________ ____________

____

8 이끌다, 안내하다, 인도하다, 선두, 맨 앞

____________ ____________

____

Ⓒ 9~12 다음 영어 문장을 의미가 떠오를 때까지 소리 내어 읽어보시오. 2초 이내

9 He laid his coat on the bed.

____

10 I knocked my head on a door.

____

11 The bright moon lit the road brightly.

____

12 Follow me and I'll lead you.

____

Test 3

➢ 다음 단어에 맞는 나만의 짧은 영어 설명을 써보자. (또는 그림을 그려보자.)

knock
[nak]

lay, laid, laid
[lei, leid, leid]

lead
[li:d]

light, lit, lighted
[lait, lit, laitid]

➢ Month 04-DAY 06 영어 문장과 우리말

I knocked my head on a door.
나는 문에 머리를 부딪쳤습니다.

He laid his coat on the bed.
그는 그의 코트를 침대 위에 내려놓았다.

Follow me and I'll lead you.
나를 따라오십시오. 제가 안내하겠습니다.

The bright moon lit the road brightly.
밝은 달이 도로를 밝게 비추었습니다.

Vocabulary

➢ **음원을 들으면서 소리를 무조건 따라해 보시오.** (빠르기&정확도/브레인+마우스 운동)

marry

to join in marriage

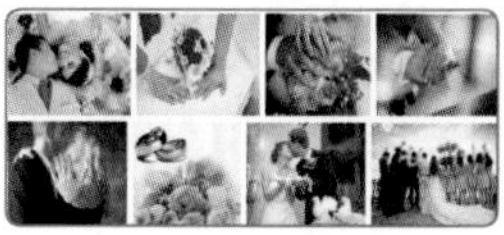

wed, get married

결혼하다

They married a month after they met.

memorize

to learn by heart or commit to memory

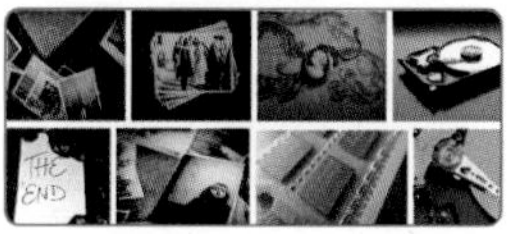

remember, learn

암기하다, 기억하다

She memorized all the details what happened.

misuse

to use incorrectly

misapply, abuse

잘못 쓰이다, 악용하다, 오용하다, 오용, 남용

The words are misused in this context.

note

to make a brief summary or to record in writing

record, message, memo

기록하다, 메모, 짧은 기록

I made a note of his address.

* 이미지는 구글에서 찾은 것으로, 단어와 이미지가 다를 수 있습니다. 'Test 3'에서 나만의 이미지를 그려볼 수 있습니다.

Test 1 Connecting Exercise

Score(　　/16)
Self-Evaluation

➢ 서로 맞는 것을 연결하시오.

Ⓐ 1~4 영어 단어와 우리말 뜻 연결하기

1 note	●	● 잘못 쓰이다, 악용하다, 오용하다, 오용, 남용
2 misuse	●	● 결혼하다
3 marry	●	● 암기하다, 기억하다
4 memorize	●	● 기록하다, 메모, 짧은 기록

Ⓑ 5~8 영어 단어와 영어 설명 연결하기

5 note	●	● to use incorrectly
6 memorize	●	● to learn by heart or commit to memory
7 misuse	●	● to make a brief summary or to record in writing
8 marry	●	● to join in marriage

Ⓒ 9~12 영어 단어와 동의어 연결하기

9 note	●	● wed, get married
10 misuse	●	● record, message, memo
11 marry	●	● misapply, abuse
12 memorize	●	● remember, learn

Ⓓ 13~16 우리말 뜻과 영어 단어 연결하기

13 잘못 쓰이다, 악용하다, 오용하다, 오용, 남용	●	● misuse
14 결혼하다	●	● memorize
15 암기하다, 기억하다	●	● marry
16 기록하다, 메모, 짧은 기록	●	● note

Test 2 Writing Exercise

Score(　　/12)
Self-Evaluation

Ⓐ 1~4 다음 단어에 맞는 뜻을 쓰시오.

1 misuse ____________________

2 marry ____________________

3 memorize ____________________

4 note ____________________

Ⓑ 5~8 다음 뜻에 맞는 영어 단어와 영어 동의어, 영어 설명을 쓰시오.

5 결혼하다

__________ __________________

____

6 기록하다, 메모, 짧은 기록

__________ __________________

____

7 잘못 쓰이다, 악용하다, 오용하다, 오용, 남용

__________ __________________

____

8 암기하다, 기억하다

__________ __________________

____

Ⓒ 9~12 다음 영어 문장을 의미가 떠오를 때까지 소리 내어 읽어보시오. 2초 이내

9 I made a note of his address.

____

10 She memorized all the details what happened.

____

11 The words are misused in this context.

____

12 They married a month after they met.

____

Test 3 Imaging Exercise

➤ 다음 단어에 맞는 나만의 짧은 영어 설명을 써보자. (또는 그림을 그려보자.)

marry
[mǽri]

memorize
[méməràiz]

misuse
[mìsjúːs]

note
[nout]

➤ Month 04-DAY 07 영어 문장과 우리말

They married a month after they met.
그들은 만난 지 한 달 만에 결혼했습니다.

She memorized all the details what happened.
그녀는 일어났던 모든 세세한 것들을 기억했습니다.

The words are misused in this context.
이 문맥에서 단어들이 잘못 쓰였습니다.

I made a note of his address.
나는 그의 주소를 노트했습니다.

➢ **음원을 들으면서 소리를 무조건 따라해 보시오.** (빠르기&정확도/브레인+마우스 운동)

occur

to take place

happen, arise, appear

일어나다, 생기다

The accident occurred at 8:40 a.m.

organize

to form (something) into a structured whole

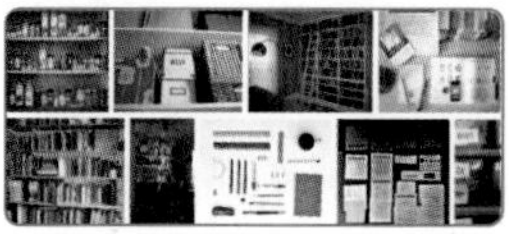

make, form, arrange, array

조직하다, 체계화하다

I always organized my thoughts before speaking.

overjoy

to fill with joy

cheer, delight, enchant

매우 기쁘게 하다, 즐겁게 하다

The economic growth overjoyed the Korean industry.

praise

to express commendation or admiration of

compliment, commend, applaud

칭찬하다, 칭찬

I have nothing but praise for her.

* 이미지는 구글에서 찾은 것으로, 단어와 이미지가 다를 수 있습니다. 'Test 3'에서 나만의 이미지를 그려볼 수 있습니다.

Test 1 Connecting Exercise

Score(/16)
Self-Evaluation

➢ 서로 맞는 것을 연결하시오.

A 1~4 영어 단어와 우리말 뜻 연결하기

1	praise	매우 기쁘게 하다, 즐겁게 하다
2	organize	조직하다, 체계화하다
3	overjoy	일어나다, 생기다
4	occur	칭찬하다, 칭찬

B 5~8 영어 단어와 영어 설명 연결하기

5	occur	to form (something) into a structured whole
6	organize	to fill with joy
7	overjoy	to express commendation or admiration of
8	praise	to take place

C 9~12 영어 단어와 동의어 연결하기

9	praise	make, form, arrange, array
10	overjoy	compliment, commend, applaud
11	occur	cheer, delight, enchant
12	organize	happen, arise, appear

D 13~16 우리말 뜻과 영어 단어 연결하기

13	일어나다, 생기다	overjoy
14	조직하다, 체계화하다	praise
15	매우 기쁘게 하다, 즐겁게 하다	occur
16	칭찬하다, 칭찬	organize

Test 2 Writing Exercise

Score(/12)
Self-Evaluation

A 1~4 다음 단어에 맞는 뜻을 쓰시오.

1 praise ______________________

2 organize ______________________

3 occur ______________________

4 overjoy ______________________

B 5~8 다음 뜻에 맞는 영어 단어와 영어 동의어, 영어 설명을 쓰시오.

5 조직하다, 체계화하다

______________ ______________________

____

6 일어나다, 생기다

______________ ______________________

____

7 칭찬하다, 칭찬

______________ ______________________

____

8 매우 기쁘게 하다, 즐겁게 하다

______________ ______________________

____

C 9~12 다음 영어 문장을 의미가 떠오를 때까지 소리 내어 읽어보시오. 2초 이내

9 I always organized my thoughts before speaking.

____

10 The accident occurred at 8:40 a.m.

____

11 I have nothing but praise for her.

____

12 The economic growth overjoyed the Korean industry.

____

Test 3 Imaging Exercise

➢ 다음 단어에 맞는 나만의 짧은 영어 설명을 써보자. (또는 그림을 그려보자.)

occur
[əkə́:r]

organize
[ɔ́:rgənàiz]

overjoy
[ou,vərʤɔi]

praise
[preiz]

➢ Month 04-DAY 08 영어 문장과 우리말

The accident occurred at 8:40 a.m.
사고는 아침 여덟시 사십분에 일어났습니다.

I always organized my thoughts before speaking.
나는 항상 말하기 전에 생각을 정리했습니다.

The economic growth overjoyed the Korean industry.
경제성장이 한국 산업을 기분 좋게 하였습니다.

I have nothing but praise for her.
나는 그녀에게 칭찬만 해 줍니다.

➢ 음원을 들으면서 소리를 무조건 따라해 보시오. (빠르기 & 정확도/브레인 + 마우스 운동)

pretend

to give a false appearance of

feign, fake

뭐뭐인 체하다

We are pretending that nothing is wrong.

prick

to pierce with a sharp point

puncture, pierce, stab

쑤시다, 찌르다, 찔리다

I pricked my finger with a needle.

protest

to express a strong objection

object, oppose, say no to

저항하다, 항의하다, 주장하다

They are protesting against the new law.

rejoice

to feel joyful or to be delighted

celebrate, delight, be happy

크게 기뻐하다, 환호하다

We rejoiced at the news of victory.

* 이미지는 구글에서 찾은 것으로, 단어와 이미지가 다를 수 있습니다. 'Test 3'에서 나만의 이미지를 그려볼 수 있습니다.

Test 1 Connecting Exercise

Score(　　/16)
Self-Evaluation

≫ 서로 맞는 것을 연결하시오.

Ⓐ 1~4 영어 단어와 우리말 뜻 연결하기

1	rejoice	•	• 뭐뭐인 체하다
2	prick	•	• 저항하다, 항의하다, 주장하다
3	protest	•	• 크게 기뻐하다, 환호하다
4	pretend	•	• 쑤시다, 찌르다, 찔리다

Ⓑ 5~8 영어 단어와 영어 설명 연결하기

5	pretend	•	• to feel joyful or to be delighted
6	prick	•	• to pierce with a sharp point
7	protest	•	• to express a strong objection
8	rejoice	•	• to give a false appearance of

Ⓒ 9~12 영어 단어와 동의어 연결하기

9	prick	•	• object, oppose, say no to
10	rejoice	•	• feign, fake
11	protest	•	• puncture, pierce, stab
12	pretend	•	• celebrate, delight, be happy

Ⓓ 13~16 우리말 뜻과 영어 단어 연결하기

13	저항하다, 항의하다, 주장하다	•	• protest
14	뭐뭐인 체하다	•	• prick
15	쑤시다, 찌르다, 찔리다	•	• rejoice
16	크게 기뻐하다, 환호하다	•	• pretend

Test 2 Writing Exercise

Score(　　/12)
Self-Evaluation

Ⓐ 1~4 다음 단어에 맞는 뜻을 쓰시오.

1 rejoice ______

2 protest ______

3 pretend ______

4 prick ______

Ⓑ 5~8 다음 뜻에 맞는 영어 단어와 영어 동의어, 영어 설명을 쓰시오.

5 뭐뭐인 체하다

______ ______

______

6 크게 기뻐하다, 환호하다

______ ______

______

7 쑤시다, 찌르다, 찔리다

______ ______

______

8 저항하다, 항의하다, 주장하다

______ ______

______

Ⓒ 9~12 다음 영어 문장을 의미가 떠오를 때까지 소리 내어 읽어보시오. 2초 이내

9 They are protesting against the new law.

______

10 We rejoiced at the news of victory.

______

11 We are pretending that nothing is wrong.

______

12 I pricked my finger with a needle.

______

Test 3

➢ 다음 단어에 맞는 나만의 짧은 영어 설명을 써보자. (또는 그림을 그려보자.)

pretend
[priténd]

prick
[prik]

protest
[próutest]

rejoice
[ridʒɔ́is]

➢ Month 04-DAY 09 영어 문장과 우리말

We are pretending that nothing is wrong.
우리는 잘못된 것이 없는 것처럼 가장하고 있습니다.

I pricked my finger with a needle.
나는 바늘로 손가락을 찔렀다.

They are protesting against the new law.
그들은 새로 만든 법에 항의하고 있습니다.

We rejoiced at the news of victory.
우리는 승리의 소식에 기뻐했습니다.

Vocabulary

➢ 음원을 들으면서 소리를 무조건 따라해 보시오. (빠르기 & 정확도/브레인 + 마우스 운동)

remain

to continue in the same state or condition

continue, stay, stay behind

남아있다, 그대로 있다

He remained at home with his family.

remark

to express briefly

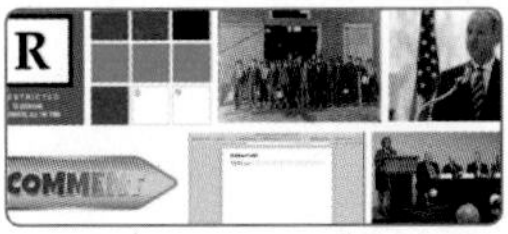

comment, say, state, note

간략히 나타내다, 말하다,
주의를 주어 표현하다, 표시하다

I remarked that I would go there.

repeat

to say again, or to do something again

iterate, reiterate, redo

반복하다, 되풀이 하다

I don't want to repeat my words.

replace

to put back into a former position or place

substitute, exchange, switch

대신하다, 교체하다

Automobiles are being replaced by electric cars.

* 이미지는 구글에서 찾은 것으로, 단어와 이미지가 다를 수 있습니다. 'Test 3'에서 나만의 이미지를 그려볼 수 있습니다.

Test 1 Connecting Exercise

Score(　　/16)
Self-Evaluation

➢ 서로 맞는 것을 연결하시오.

Ⓐ 1~4 영어 단어와 우리말 뜻 연결하기

1	repeat	•	• 남아있다, 그대로 있다
2	remark	•	• 간략히 나타내다, 말하다, 주의를 주어 표현하다, 표시하다
3	remain	•	• 반복하다, 되풀이 하다
4	replace	•	• 대신하다, 교체하다

Ⓑ 5~8 영어 단어와 영어 설명 연결하기

5	repeat	•	• to put back into a former position or place
6	remark	•	• to continue in the same state or condition
7	replace	•	• to say again, or to do something again
8	remain	•	• to express briefly

Ⓒ 9~12 영어 단어와 동의어 연결하기

9	remain	•	• iterate, reiterate, redo
10	repeat	•	• comment, say, state, note
11	remark	•	• substitute, exchange, switch
12	replace	•	• continue, stay, stay behind

Ⓓ 13~16 우리말 뜻과 영어 단어 연결하기

13	간략히 나타내다, 말하다, 주의를 주어 표현하다, 표시하다	•	• remark
14	반복하다, 되풀이 하다	•	• replace
15	남아있다, 그대로 있다	•	• repeat
16	대신하다, 교체하다	•	• remain

Test 2 Writing Exercise

Score(/12)
Self-Evaluation

A 1~4 다음 단어에 맞는 뜻을 쓰시오.

1 remain ______

2 remark ______

3 replace ______

4 repeat ______

B 5~8 다음 뜻에 맞는 영어 단어와 영어 동의어, 영어 설명을 쓰시오.

5 남아있다, 그대로 있다

______ ______

______

6 대신하다, 교체하다

______ ______

______

7 간략히 나타내다, 말하다, 주의를 주어 표현하다, 표시하다

______ ______

______

8 반복하다, 되풀이 하다

______ ______

______

C 9~12 다음 영어 문장을 의미가 떠오를 때까지 소리 내어 읽어보시오. 2초 이내

9 I remarked that I would go there.

______

10 Automobiles are being replaced by electric cars.

______

11 I don't want to repeat my words.

______

12 He remained at home with his family.

______

Test 3 Imaging Exercise

➢ 다음 단어에 맞는 나만의 짧은 영어 설명을 써보자. (또는 그림을 그려보자.)

remain
[riméin]

remark
[rimɑ́ːrk]

repeat
[ripíːt]

replace
[ripléis]

➢ Month 04-DAY 10 영어 문장과 우리말

He remained at home with his family.
그는 가족들과 집에 남았습니다.

I remarked that I would go there.
내가 거기에 갈거라고 말했습니다.

I don't want to repeat my words.
나는 내 말을 반복하고 싶지 않습니다.

Automobiles are being replaced by electric cars.
자동차는 전기자동차로 대체되고 있습니다.

DAY 11 Vocabulary

➢ 음원을 들으면서 소리를 무조건 따라해 보시오. (빠르기 & 정확도/브레인 + 마우스 운동)

reply

to make answer (to)

answer, respond, response

대답하다, 대답

She replied that she didn't want it.

return

to go or come back, as to an earlier condition or place

come back, go back, turn back

돌아가다, 돌아오다, 돌려주다

I returned to my office after lunch.

sacrifice

to give up (one thing) for (another thing)

abandon, surrender, give up

희생하다(하나를 위해 다른 것을 버리고 포기하다)

He sacrificed a sheep in the temple.

select

to make a choice or selection

choose, take, pick out

고르다, 선택하다

They selected only smart pupils for selection.

* 이미지는 구글에서 찾은 것으로, 단어와 이미지가 다를 수 있습니다. 'Test 3'에서 나만의 이미지를 그려볼 수 있습니다.

Test 1 Connecting Exercise

Score(/16)
Self-Evaluation

➢ 서로 맞는 것을 연결하시오.

Ⓐ 1~4 영어 단어와 우리말 뜻 연결하기

1 sacrifice	●	● 돌아가다, 돌아오다, 돌려주다
2 return	●	● 희생하다(하나를 위해 다른 것을 버리고 포기하다)
3 reply	●	● 고르다, 선택하다
4 select	●	● 대답하다, 대답

Ⓑ 5~8 영어 단어와 영어 설명 연결하기

5 select	●	● to go or come back, as to an earlier condition or place
6 reply	●	● to give up (one thing) for (another thing)
7 sacrifice	●	● to make a choice or selection
8 return	●	● to make answer (to)

Ⓒ 9~12 영어 단어와 동의어 연결하기

9 sacrifice	●	● choose, take, pick out
10 reply	●	● answer, respond, response
11 select	●	● abandon, surrender, give up
12 return	●	● come back, go back, turn back

Ⓓ 13~16 우리말 뜻과 영어 단어 연결하기

13 고르다, 선택하다	●	● select
14 희생하다(하나를 위해 다른 것을 버리고 포기하다)	●	● sacrifice
15 돌아가다, 돌아오다, 돌려주다	●	● return
16 대답하다, 대답	●	● reply

Test 2 Writing Exercise

Score(/12)
Self-Evaluation

Month 04

A 1~4 다음 단어에 맞는 뜻을 쓰시오.

1 return ____________________

2 sacrifice ____________________

3 select ____________________

4 reply ____________________

B 5~8 다음 뜻에 맞는 영어 단어와 영어 동의어, 영어 설명을 쓰시오.

5 대답하다, 대답

____________ ____________________

____

6 돌아가다, 돌아오다, 돌려주다

____________ ____________________

____

7 희생하다(하나를 위해 다른 것을 버리고 포기하다)

____________ ____________________

____

8 고르다, 선택하다

____________ ____________________

____

C 9~12 다음 영어 문장을 의미가 떠오를 때까지 소리 내어 읽어보시오. 2초 이내

9 I returned to my office after lunch.

____

10 They selected only smart pupils for selection.

____

11 He sacrificed a sheep in the temple.

____

12 She replied that she didn't want it.

____

Test 3 Imaging Exercise

➢ 다음 단어에 맞는 나만의 짧은 영어 설명을 써보자. (또는 그림을 그려보자.)

reply
[ripláі]

return
[ritə́ːrn]

sacrifice
[sǽkrəfàis]

select
[silékt]

➢ Month 04-DAY 11 영어 문장과 우리말

She replied that she didn't want it.
그녀는 그것을 원하지 않는다고 대답했습니다.

I returned to my office after lunch.
나는 점심 식사 후 내 사무실로 돌아왔습니다.

He sacrificed a sheep in the temple.
그는 신전에 양을 제물로 바쳤습니다.

They selected only smart pupils for selection.
그들은 선발에서 똑똑한 학생들만 선택했습니다.

Vocabulary

≫ 음원을 들으면서 소리를 무조건 따라해 보시오. (빠르기 & 정확도/브레인 + 마우스 운동)

serve

to work for (someone) as a servant, or to distribute food

work for, help, aid, assist

봉사하다, 제공하다, 날라다 주다

I served the soup to the guests.

shoot, shot, shot

to discharge or fire

discharge, fire, gush, spurt

쏘다, 발사하다

He shot an arrow into the air.

shriek

to utter a loud, sharp, shrill cry

screak, scream, screech

비명을 지르다,
날카로운 소리로 말하다, 비명

She shrieked whenever she saw a spider.

sightsee

to visit famous or interesting sights

travel, visit

관광하다

We only had three days to sightsee.

* 이미지는 구글에서 찾은 것으로, 단어와 이미지가 다를 수 있습니다. 'Test 3'에서 나만의 이미지를 그려볼 수 있습니다.

Test 1 Connecting Exercise

Score(　　/16)
Self-Evaluation

➢ 서로 맞는 것을 연결하시오.

Ⓐ 1~4 영어 단어와 우리말 뜻 연결하기

1	shriek	• • 쏘다, 발사하다
2	serve	• • 관광하다
3	sightsee	• • 봉사하다, 제공하다, 날라다 주다
4	shoot, shot, shot	• • 비명을 지르다, 날카로운 소리로 말하다, 비명

Ⓑ 5~8 영어 단어와 영어 설명 연결하기

5	sightsee	• • to visit famous or interesting sights
6	shoot, shot, shot	• • to utter a loud, sharp, shrill cry
7	shriek	• • to work for (someone) as a servant, or to distribute food
8	serve	• • to discharge or fire

Ⓒ 9~12 영어 단어와 동의어 연결하기

9	shoot, shot, shot	• • travel, visit
10	sightsee	• • screak, scream, screech
11	shriek	• • discharge, fire, gush, spurt
12	serve	• • work for, help, aid, assist

Ⓓ 13~16 우리말 뜻과 영어 단어 연결하기

13	쏘다, 발사하다	• • shriek
14	관광하다	• • shoot, shot, shot
15	봉사하다, 제공하다, 날라다 주다	• • sightsee
16	비명을 지르다, 날카로운 소리로 말하다, 비명	• • serve

Test 2 Writing Exercise

Score(/12)
Self-Evaluation

Ⓐ 1~4 다음 단어에 맞는 뜻을 쓰시오.

1 sightsee ______________________

2 serve ______________________

3 shoot, shot, shot ______________________

4 shriek ______________________

Ⓑ 5~8 다음 뜻에 맞는 영어 단어와 영어 동의어, 영어 설명을 쓰시오.

5 비명을 지르다, 날카로운 소리로 말하다, 비명

______________ ______________________

____

6 쏘다, 발사하다

______________ ______________________

____

7 관광하다

______________ ______________________

____

8 봉사하다, 제공하다, 날라다 주다

______________ ______________________

____

Ⓒ 9~12 다음 영어 문장을 의미가 떠오를 때까지 소리 내어 읽어보시오. 2초 이내

9 He shot an arrow into the air.

____

10 She shrieked whenever she saw a spider.

____

11 I served the soup to the guests.

____

12 We only had three days to sightsee.

____

Test 3

➢ 다음 단어에 맞는 나만의 짧은 영어 설명을 써보자. (또는 그림을 그려보자.)

serve
[sə:rv]

shoot, shot, shot
[ʃu:t, ʃat, ʃat]

shriek
[ʃri:k]

sightsee
[sáitsì:]

➢ Month 04-DAY 12 영어 문장과 우리말

I served the soup to the guests.
나는 손님들에게 수프를 날라다 주었습니다.

He shot an arrow into the air.
그는 공중으로 화살을 쏘았습니다.

She shrieked whenever she saw a spider.
그녀는 거미를 볼 때마다 비명을 질렀습니다.

We only had three days to sightsee.
우리는 3일간만 관광할 시간이 있었습니다.

➢ 음원을 들으면서 소리를 무조건 따라해 보시오. (빠르기&정확도/브레인+마우스 운동)

sink, sank, sunk

to go below the surface of water or another liquid

go down, go under, submerge

가라앉다

The boat was beginning to sink fast.

skid

to slide sideways, especially roughly or heavily

slide, slip, slide sideways

(거칠고 험하게) 옆으로 미끄러지다

I skidded my skates to a stop.

sow

to scatter seed over land

seed, scatter, plant

씨 뿌리다, 파종하다

Don't sow a doubt in your mind.

spend, spent, spent

to use up or to pay out (money)

consume, expend, use up

(돈, 시간을) 쓰다, 소비하다

We are spending the evening watching TV.

* 이미지는 구글에서 찾은 것으로, 단어와 이미지가 다를 수 있습니다. 'Test 3'에서 나만의 이미지를 그려볼 수 있습니다.

Test 1 Connecting Exercise

Score(/16)
Self-Evaluation

➢ 서로 맞는 것을 연결하시오.

Ⓐ 1~4 영어 단어와 우리말 뜻 연결하기

1	sink, sank, sunk	(돈, 시간을) 쓰다, 소비하다
2	skid	(거칠고 험하게) 옆으로 미끄러지다
3	spend, spent, spent	가라앉다
4	sow	씨 뿌리다, 파종하다

Ⓑ 5~8 영어 단어와 영어 설명 연결하기

5	skid	to go below the surface of water or another liquid
6	sow	to slide sideways, especially roughly or heavily
7	sink, sank, sunk	to use up or to pay out (money)
8	spend, spent, spent	to scatter seed over land

Ⓒ 9~12 영어 단어와 동의어 연결하기

9	sow	slide, slip, slide sideways
10	skid	go down, go under, submerge
11	sink, sank, sunk	consume, expend, use up
12	spend, spent, spent	seed, scatter, plant

Ⓓ 13~16 우리말 뜻과 영어 단어 연결하기

13	가라앉다	sow
14	씨 뿌리다, 파종하다	skid
15	(거칠고 험하게) 옆으로 미끄러지다	sink, sank, sunk
16	(돈, 시간을) 쓰다, 소비하다	spend, spent, spent

Test 2 Writing Exercise

Score(/12)
Self-Evaluation

A 1~4 다음 단어에 맞는 뜻을 쓰시오.

1 skid ____________________

2 sink, sank, sunk ____________________

3 sow ____________________

4 spend, spent, spent ____________________

B 5~8 다음 뜻에 맞는 영어 단어와 영어 동의어, 영어 설명을 쓰시오.

5 가라앉다

__________ ____________________

____

6 (거칠고 험하게) 옆으로 미끄러지다

__________ ____________________

____

7 씨 뿌리다, 파종하다

__________ ____________________

____

8 (돈, 시간을) 쓰다, 소비하다

__________ ____________________

____

C 9~12 다음 영어 문장을 의미가 떠오를 때까지 소리 내어 읽어보시오. 2초 이내

9 I skidded my skates to a stop.

____

10 Don't sow a doubt in your mind.

____

11 The boat was beginning to sink fast.

____

12 We are spending the evening watching TV.

____

Test 3

➢ 다음 단어에 맞는 나만의 짧은 영어 설명을 써보자. (또는 그림을 그려보자.)

sink, sank, sunk
[siŋk, sæŋk, sʌŋk]

skid
[skid]

sow
[sou]

spend, spent, spent
[spend, spent, spent]

➢ Month 04-DAY 13 영어 문장과 우리말

The boat was beginning to sink fast.
배가 빠르게 가라앉기 시작했습니다.

I skidded my skates to a stop.
나는 스케이트를 미끄러지듯 멈추게 했습니다.

Don't sow a doubt in your mind.
마음속에 의심의 종자를 심지 마세요.

We are spending the evening watching TV.
우리는 TV를 보면서 저녁시간을 보내고 있습니다.

Vocabulary

➢ 음원을 들으면서 소리를 무조건 따라해 보시오. (빠르기&정확도/브레인+마우스 운동)

steal, stole, stolen

to take (the property of another) without right or permission

thieve, rob, snitch, snatch

훔치다, 빼앗다, 털다

Someone stole my wallet on the subway.

stick, stuck, stuck

to pierce, puncture, or penetrate with a pointed instrument

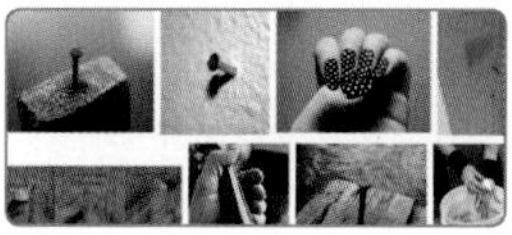

pierce, puncture, adhere, cohere

찌르다, 꽂다, 박다, 붙이다, 막대기

He stuck a needle in my back.

stir

to pass an implement through (a liquid)

mix, blend, whisk, agitate

(도구를 사용해) 휘젓다

She stirred the soup before tasting it.

stretch

to lengthen, widen, or distend

extend, expand, spread

뻗다, 펴다, 늘리다

She arched her back and stretched herself.

* 이미지는 구글에서 찾은 것으로, 단어와 이미지가 다를 수 있습니다. 'Test 3'에서 나만의 이미지를 그려볼 수 있습니다.

Test 1 Connecting Exercise

Score(/16)
Self-Evaluation

➢ 서로 맞는 것을 연결하시오.

Ⓐ 1~4 영어 단어와 우리말 뜻 연결하기

1	steal, stole, stolen	훔치다, 빼앗다, 털다
2	stick, stuck, stuck	(도구를 사용해) 휘젓다
3	stretch	찌르다, 꽂다, 박다, 붙이다, 막대기
4	stir	뻗다, 펴다, 늘리다

Ⓑ 5~8 영어 단어와 영어 설명 연결하기

5	stretch	to take (the property of another) without right or permission
6	stir	to pass an implement through (a liquid)
7	steal, stole, stolen	to pierce, puncture, or penetrate with a pointed instrument
8	stick, stuck, stuck	to lengthen, widen, or distend

Ⓒ 9~12 영어 단어와 동의어 연결하기

9	stretch	thieve, rob, snitch, snatch
10	stir	mix, blend, whisk, agitate
11	stick, stuck, stuck	pierce, puncture, adhere, cohere
12	steal, stole, stolen	extend, expand, spread

Ⓓ 13~16 우리말 뜻과 영어 단어 연결하기

13	찌르다, 꽂다, 박다, 붙이다, 막대기	stir
14	뻗다, 펴다, 늘리다	stretch
15	(도구를 사용해) 휘젓다	steal, stole, stolen
16	훔치다, 빼앗다, 털다	stick, stuck, stuck

Test 2 Writing Exercise

Score(/12)
Self-Evaluation

A 1~4 다음 단어에 맞는 뜻을 쓰시오.

1 stir ______

2 stick, stuck, stuck ______

3 stretch ______

4 steal, stole, stolen ______

B 5~8 다음 뜻에 맞는 영어 단어와 영어 동의어, 영어 설명을 쓰시오.

5 뻗다, 펴다, 늘리다

______ ______

______

6 훔치다, 빼앗다, 털다

______ ______

______

7 찌르다, 꽂다, 박다, 붙이다, 막대기

______ ______

______

8 (도구를 사용해) 휘젓다

______ ______

______

C 9~12 다음 영어 문장을 의미가 떠오를 때까지 소리 내어 읽어보시오. 2초 이내

9 She stirred the soup before tasting it.

______

10 He stuck a needle in my back.

______

11 She arched her back and stretched herself.

______

12 Someone stole my wallet on the subway.

______

Test 3 Imaging Exercise

➢ 다음 단어에 맞는 나만의 짧은 영어 설명을 써보자. (또는 그림을 그려보자.)

steal, stole, stolen
[stiːl, stoul, stóulən]

stick, stuck, stuck
[stik, stʌk, stʌk]

stir
[stəːr]

stretch
[stretʃ]

➢ Month 04-DAY 14 영어 문장과 우리말

Someone stole my wallet on the subway.
지하철에서 누가 내 지갑을 훔쳐갔다.

He stuck a needle in my back.
그는 내 등에 바늘을 꽂았습니다.

She stirred the soup before tasting it.
그녀는 맛보기 전에 수프를 휘저었습니다.

She arched her back and stretched herself.
그녀는 등을 활모양으로 젖히고 몸을 폈습니다.

DAY 15 Vocabulary

➢ 음원을 들으면서 소리를 무조건 따라해 보시오. (빠르기&정확도/브레인+마우스 운동)

thaw

to change from a frozen solid to a liquid by gradual warming

melt, dissolve, defrost, liquefy

(따뜻해져서) 녹다, 녹이다, 해동하다

Frozen food must be thawed before cooking.

throw, threw, thrown

to project or cast (something) through the air

cast, dart, hurl, fling, toss

(공중에) 던지다, 내던지다

She threw her clothes onto the bed.

try

to make an effort to do or accomplish (something)

attempt, endeavour, aim

해보다, 시도하다, 노력하다

Try learning VOCAPOD 20 minutes a day.

unlock

to undo the lock of

unfasten, open, disclose, release

자물쇠를 열다, 풀다

He unlocked the door of the car.

* 이미지는 구글에서 찾은 것으로, 단어와 이미지가 다를 수 있습니다. 'Test 3'에서 나만의 이미지를 그려볼 수 있습니다.

Test 1 Connecting Exercise

Score(/16)
Self-Evaluation

➢ 서로 맞는 것을 연결하시오.

Ⓐ 1~4 영어 단어와 우리말 뜻 연결하기

1 try	•	• (공중에) 던지다, 내던지다
2 thaw	•	• 해보다, 시도하다, 노력하다
3 throw, threw, thrown	•	• 자물쇠를 열다, 풀다
4 unlock	•	• (따뜻해져서) 녹다, 녹이다, 해동하다

Ⓑ 5~8 영어 단어와 영어 설명 연결하기

5 unlock	•	• to make an effort to do or accomplish (something)
6 try	•	• to undo the lock of
7 thaw	•	• to project or cast (something) through the air
8 throw, threw, thrown	•	• to change from a frozen solid to a liquid by gradual warming

Ⓒ 9~12 영어 단어와 동의어 연결하기

9 unlock	•	• melt, dissolve, defrost, liquefy
10 try	•	• attempt, endeavour, aim
11 thaw	•	• cast, dart, hurl, fling, toss
12 throw, threw, thrown	•	• unfasten, open, disclose, release

Ⓓ 13~16 우리말 뜻과 영어 단어 연결하기

13 (따뜻해져서) 녹다, 녹이다, 해동하다	•	• unlock
14 자물쇠를 열다, 풀다	•	• try
15 (공중에) 던지다, 내던지다	•	• thaw
16 해보다, 시도하다, 노력하다	•	• throw, threw, thrown

Test 2 Writing Exercise

Score(/12)
Self-Evaluation

A 1~4 다음 단어에 맞는 뜻을 쓰시오.

1 try

2 thaw

3 unlock

4 throw, threw, thrown

B 5~8 다음 뜻에 맞는 영어 단어와 영어 동의어, 영어 설명을 쓰시오.

5 (따뜻해져서) 녹다, 녹이다, 해동하다

6 (공중에) 던지다, 내던지다

7 해보다, 시도하다, 노력하다

8 자물쇠를 열다, 풀다

C 9~12 다음 영어 문장을 의미가 떠오를 때까지 소리 내어 읽어보시오. 2초 이내

9 Try learning VOCAPOD 20 minutes a day.

10 He unlocked the door of the car.

11 Frozen food must be thawed before cooking.

12 She threw her clothes onto the bed.

Test 3

➢ 다음 단어에 맞는 나만의 짧은 영어 설명을 써보자. (또는 그림을 그려보자.)

thaw
[θɔː]

throw, threw, thrown
[θrou, θruː, θroun]

try
[trai]

unlock
[ənla'k]

➢ Month 04-DAY 15 영어 문장과 우리말

Frozen food must be thawed before cooking.
냉동 식품은 요리하기 전에 해동시켜야 합니다.

She threw her clothes onto the bed.
그녀는 그녀의 옷을 침대 위에 던졌습니다.

Try learning VOCAPOD 20 minutes a day.
VOCAPOD을 하루 20분씩 배우도록 하세요.

He unlocked the door of the car.
그는 자동차 문을 열었습니다.

DAY 16 Vocabulary

➢ 음원을 들으면서 소리를 무조건 따라해 보시오. (빠르기&정확도/브레인+마우스 운동)

unmask

to remove a mask from or to disclose the true character of

expose, uncover, disclose

가면을 벗다, (실제 모습을) 드러내다, 노출하다

The journal article unmasked the corrupt politician.

utter

to produce or make speech sounds

speak, pronounce, complete, total, absolute

입 밖으로 소리를 내다, 소리를 내뱉다, 완전한, 절대적인

I was unable to utter a word.

abstain

to keep oneself from doing

refrain, avoid, forbear

삼가다, 조심하다

You have to abstain from alcohol and smoking.

admire

to regard with pleasure and respect

praise, appreciate, respect

감탄하다, 칭찬하다

I admired her ability as a singer songwriter.

* 이미지는 구글에서 찾은 것으로, 단어와 이미지가 다를 수 있습니다. 'Test 3'에서 나만의 이미지를 그려볼 수 있습니다.

Test 1 Connecting Exercise

Score(　/16)
Self-Evaluation

≫ 서로 맞는 것을 연결하시오.

Ⓐ 1~4 영어 단어와 우리말 뜻 연결하기

1 utter	•	• 가면을 벗다, (실제 모습을) 드러내다, 노출하다
2 admire	•	• 입 밖으로 소리를 내다, 소리를 내뱉다, 완전한, 절대적인
3 abstain	•	• 감탄하다, 칭찬하다
4 unmask	•	• 삼가다, 조심하다

Ⓑ 5~8 영어 단어와 영어 설명 연결하기

5 unmask	•	• to produce or make speech sounds
6 utter	•	• to remove a mask from or to disclose the true character of
7 admire	•	• to keep oneself from doing
8 abstain	•	• to regard with pleasure and respect

Ⓒ 9~12 영어 단어와 동의어 연결하기

9 utter	•	• expose, uncover, disclose
10 unmask	•	• refrain, avoid, forbear
11 abstain	•	• speak, pronounce, complete, total, absolute
12 admire	•	• praise, appreciate, respect

Ⓓ 13~16 우리말 뜻과 영어 단어 연결하기

13 감탄하다, 칭찬하다	•	• unmask
14 입 밖으로 소리를 내다, 소리를 내뱉다, 완전한, 절대적인	•	• admire
15 가면을 벗다, (실제 모습을) 드러내다, 노출하다	•	• utter
16 삼가다, 조심하다	•	• abstain

Test 2 Writing Exercise

Score(/12)
Self-Evaluation

A 1~4 다음 단어에 맞는 뜻을 쓰시오.

1 abstain ________________

2 unmask ________________

3 utter ________________

4 admire ________________

B 5~8 다음 뜻에 맞는 영어 단어와 영어 동의어, 영어 설명을 쓰시오.

5 감탄하다, 칭찬하다

________ ________________

____

6 입 밖으로 소리를 내다, 소리를 내뱉다, 완전한, 절대적인

________ ________________

____

7 가면을 벗다, (실제 모습을) 드러내다, 노출하다

________ ________________

____

8 삼가다, 조심하다

________ ________________

____

C 9~12 다음 영어 문장을 의미가 떠오를 때까지 소리 내어 읽어보시오. 2초 이내

9 I was unable to utter a word.

____

10 You have to abstain from alcohol and smoking.

____

11 The journal article unmasked the corrupt politician.

____

12 I admired her ability as a singer songwriter.

____

Test 3

➤ 다음 단어에 맞는 나만의 짧은 영어 설명을 써보자. (또는 그림을 그려보자.)

unmask
[ənmæ'sk]

utter
[ʌtər]

abstain
[æbstéin]

admire
[ædmáiər]

➤ Month 04-DAY 16 영어 문장과 우리말

The journal article unmasked the corrupt politician.
신문 기사는 부패한 정치인의 가면을 벗겨냈습니다.

I was unable to utter a word.
나는 한마디도 할 수 없었습니다.

You have to abstain from alcohol and smoking.
당신은 알코올과 흡연을 삼가야 합니다.

I admired her ability as a singer songwriter.
나는 그녀의 싱어송라이터로서의 능력에 감탄하였다.

DAY 17 Vocabulary

➢ 음원을 들으면서 소리를 무조건 따라해 보시오. (빠르기&정확도/브레인+마우스 운동)

announce

to make known publicly

publish, declare, advertise, broadcast

알리다, 발표하다

She anounced the news at 9 pm yesterday.

broadcast

to transmit (announcements) on radio or television

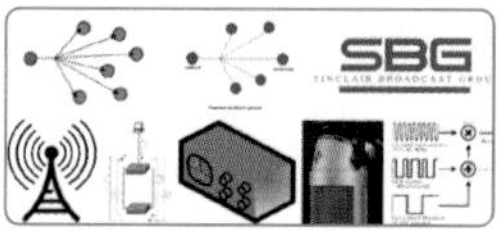

transmit, show, announce

방송하다, 방송

This is a radio station that broadcasts news.

burden

to load heavily

weigh down, load

짐 지우다, 짐, 부담

Burden means 'a heavy load that you carry'.

challenge

to call to engage in a contest, fight, or competition

try, brave

도전하다, 도전

She challenged me to a game of chess.

* 이미지는 구글에서 찾은 것으로, 단어와 이미지가 다를 수 있습니다. 'Test 3'에서 나만의 이미지를 그려볼 수 있습니다.

Test 1 Connecting Exercise

Score(/16)
Self-Evaluation

➢ 서로 맞는 것을 연결하시오.

Ⓐ 1~4 영어 단어와 우리말 뜻 연결하기

1	broadcast	•	• 방송하다, 방송
2	burden	•	• 도전하다, 도전
3	announce	•	• 알리다, 발표하다
4	challenge	•	• 짐 지우다, 짐, 부담

Ⓑ 5~8 영어 단어와 영어 설명 연결하기

5	announce	•	• to make known publicly
6	challenge	•	• to call to engage in a contest, fight, or competition
7	burden	•	• to load heavily
8	broadcast	•	• to transmit (announcements) on radio or television

Ⓒ 9~12 영어 단어와 동의어 연결하기

9	announce	•	• weigh down, load
10	challenge	•	• transmit, show, announce
11	burden	•	• try, brave
12	broadcast	•	• publish, declare, advertise, broadcast

Ⓓ 13~16 우리말 뜻과 영어 단어 연결하기

13	방송하다, 방송	•	• announce
14	알리다, 발표하다	•	• broadcast
15	도전하다, 도전	•	• challenge
16	짐 지우다, 짐, 부담	•	• burden

Test 2 Writing Exercise

Score(/12)
Self-Evaluation

Month 04

Ⓐ 1~4 다음 단어에 맞는 뜻을 쓰시오.

1 challenge ______________________

2 announce ______________________

3 broadcast ______________________

4 burden ______________________

Ⓑ 5~8 다음 뜻에 맞는 영어 단어와 영어 동의어, 영어 설명을 쓰시오.

5 알리다, 발표하다

______________ ______________________

____

6 짐 지우다, 짐, 부담

______________ ______________________

____

7 도전하다, 도전

______________ ______________________

____

8 방송하다, 방송

______________ ______________________

____

Ⓒ 9~12 다음 영어 문장을 의미가 떠오를 때까지 소리 내어 읽어보시오. 2초 이내

9 She anounced the news at 9 pm yesterday.

____

10 This is a radio station that broadcasts news.

____

11 Burden means 'a heavy load that you carry'.

____

12 She challenged me to a game of chess.

____

Test 3 Imaging Exercise

➤ 다음 단어에 맞는 나만의 짧은 영어 설명을 써보자. (또는 그림을 그려보자.)

announce
[ənáuns]

broadcast
[brɔ́ːdkæst]

burden
[bə́ːrdn]

challenge
[ʧǽlindʒ]

➤ Month 04-DAY 17 영어 문장과 우리말

She anounced the news at 9 pm yesterday.
그녀는 어제 오후 9시 뉴스를 발표했다.

This is a radio station that broadcasts news.
여기는 뉴스를 방송하는 라디오 방송국입니다.

Burden means 'a heavy load that you carry'.
Burden은 '당신이 운반하는 무거운 짐'을 의미합니다.

She challenged me to a game of chess.
그녀는 나에게 체스게임으로 도전했습니다.

Vocabulary

≫ 음원을 들으면서 소리를 무조건 따라해 보시오. (빠르기&정확도/브레인+마우스 운동)

charge

to impose or ask as a price or fee

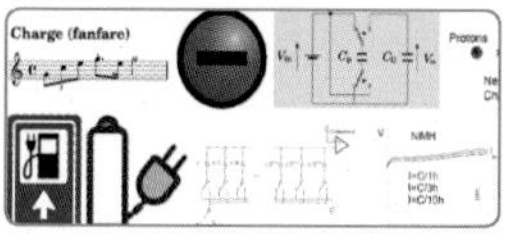

ask for, bill, impose, invoice

청구하다, 부담지우다

She charged me ten dollars for a haircut.

check

to inspect or verify, or bill

examine, test, confirm, investigate

확인하다, 조사하다, 수표, 계산서

You have to check your writing for misspellings.

choose, chose, chosen

to select something from a number of alternatives

take, pick, select

고르다, 선택하다

She always chooses what she wants to choose.

command

to give orders, require, compel, direct with specific authority

direct, instruct, order

명령하다, 지휘하다

He is a general who commands an army.

* 이미지는 구글에서 찾은 것으로, 단어와 이미지가 다를 수 있습니다. 'Test 3'에서 나만의 이미지를 그려볼 수 있습니다.

Test 1 Connecting Exercise

Score(　　/16)
Self-Evaluation

➢ 서로 맞는 것을 연결하시오.

Ⓐ 1~4 영어 단어와 우리말 뜻 연결하기

1	charge	청구하다, 부담지우다
2	command	확인하다, 조사하다, 수표, 계산서
3	choose, chose, chosen	명령하다, 지휘하다
4	check	고르다, 선택하다

Ⓑ 5~8 영어 단어와 영어 설명 연결하기

5	command	to select something from a number of alternatives
6	charge	to inspect or verify, or bill
7	choose, chose, chosen	to impose or ask as a price or fee
8	check	to give orders, require, compel, direct with specific authority

Ⓒ 9~12 영어 단어와 동의어 연결하기

9	choose, chose, chosen	direct, instruct, order
10	command	ask for, bill, impose, invoice
11	charge	take, pick, select
12	check	examine, test, confirm, investigate

Ⓓ 13~16 우리말 뜻과 영어 단어 연결하기

13	청구하다, 부담지우다	charge
14	확인하다, 조사하다, 수표, 계산서	check
15	고르다, 선택하다	command
16	명령하다, 지휘하다	choose, chose, chosen

Test 2 Writing Exercise

Score(/12)
Self-Evaluation

Ⓐ 1~4 다음 단어에 맞는 뜻을 쓰시오.

1 charge ______________________

2 check ______________________

3 command ______________________

4 choose, chose, chosen ______________________

Ⓑ 5~8 다음 뜻에 맞는 영어 단어와 영어 동의어, 영어 설명을 쓰시오.

5 고르다, 선택하다

______________ ______________________

____

6 청구하다, 부담지우다

______________ ______________________

____

7 확인하다, 조사하다, 수표, 계산서

______________ ______________________

____

8 명령하다, 지휘하다

______________ ______________________

____

Ⓒ 9~12 다음 영어 문장을 의미가 떠오를 때까지 소리 내어 읽어보시오. 2초 이내

9 She charged me ten dollars for a haircut.

____

10 You have to check your writing for misspellings.

____

11 She always chooses what she wants to choose.

____

12 He is a general who commands an army.

____

Test 3 Imaging Exercise

➢ 다음 단어에 맞는 나만의 짧은 영어 설명을 써보자. (또는 그림을 그려보자.)

charge
[ʧaːrdʒ]

check
[ʧek]

choose, chose, chosen
[ʧuːz, tʃouz, ʧóuzn]

command
[kəmǽnd]

➢ Month 04-DAY 18 영어 문장과 우리말

She charged me ten dollars for a haircut.
그녀는 나에게 헤어커트 비용으로 10달러를 청구했습니다.

You have to check your writing for misspellings.
당신은 당신의 글쓰기에 오타가 없는지 확인해야 합니다.

She always chooses what she wants to choose.
그녀는 항상 자신이 선택하고 싶은 것을 선택합니다.

He is a general who commands an army.
그는 군대를 지휘하는 장군입니다.

Vocabulary

➢ 음원을 들으면서 소리를 무조건 따라해 보시오. (빠르기 & 정확도/브레인 + 마우스 운동)

communicate

to impart or exchange (thoughts, feelings, or ideas)

talk, speak, transmit

의사소통하다

Animals communicate by using a variety of signs.

construct

to build or form by putting together parts

build, make, form, establish

건설하다, 세우다, 만들다

They are planning to construct a new bridge.

count

to check over one by one to determine the total number

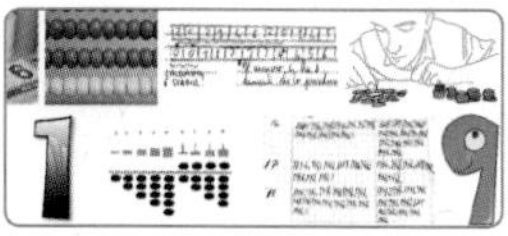

enumerate, reckon, calculate, compute

세다

You have to count to three before firing.

create

to cause to exist, bring into being as something unique

make, form, produce

만들어내다, 창조하다

They created a new city in the desert.

* 이미지는 구글에서 찾은 것으로, 단어와 이미지가 다를 수 있습니다. 'Test 3'에서 나만의 이미지를 그려볼 수 있습니다.

Test 1 Connecting Exercise

Score(　　/16)
Self-Evaluation

➢ 서로 맞는 것을 연결하시오.

Ⓐ 1~4 영어 단어와 우리말 뜻 연결하기

1 count	•	• 의사소통하다
2 communicate	•	• 건설하다, 세우다, 만들다
3 create	•	• 만들어내다, 창조하다
4 construct	•	• 세다

Ⓑ 5~8 영어 단어와 영어 설명 연결하기

5 construct	•	• to check over one by one to determine the total number
6 count	•	• to impart or exchange (thoughts, feelings, or ideas)
7 create	•	• to cause to exist, bring into being as something unique
8 communicate	•	• to build or form by putting together parts

Ⓒ 9~12 영어 단어와 동의어 연결하기

9 construct	•	• make, form, produce
10 communicate	•	• build, make, form, establish
11 create	•	• talk, speak, transmit
12 count	•	• enumerate, reckon, calculate, compute

Ⓓ 13~16 우리말 뜻과 영어 단어 연결하기

13 건설하다, 세우다, 만들다	•	• count
14 만들어내다, 창조하다	•	• construct
15 세다	•	• create
16 의사소통하다	•	• communicate

Test 2 Writing Exercise

Score(/12)
Self-Evaluation

A 1~4 다음 단어에 맞는 뜻을 쓰시오.

1 count ______________________

2 communicate ______________________

3 create ______________________

4 construct ______________________

B 5~8 다음 뜻에 맞는 영어 단어와 영어 동의어, 영어 설명을 쓰시오.

5 건설하다, 세우다, 만들다

______________ ______________________

____

6 의사소통하다

______________ ______________________

____

7 세다

______________ ______________________

____

8 만들어내다, 창조하다

______________ ______________________

____

C 9~12 다음 영어 문장을 의미가 떠오를 때까지 소리 내어 읽어보시오. 2초 이내

9 Animals communicate by using a variety of signs.

____

10 They are planning to construct a new bridge.

____

11 You have to count to three before firing.

____

12 They created a new city in the desert.

____

Test 3 Imaging Exercise

➢ 다음 단어에 맞는 나만의 짧은 영어 설명을 써보자. (또는 그림을 그려보자.)

communicate
[kəmjúːnəkèit]

construct
[kənstrʌkt]

count
[kaunt]

create
[kriéit]

➢ Month 04-DAY 19 영어 문장과 우리말

Animals communicate by using a variety of signs.
동물들은 다양한 신호를 써서 의사소통을 합니다.

They are planning to construct a new bridge.
그들은 새로운 다리를 건설할 것을 계획하고 있다.

You have to count to three before firing.
당신은 발사 전에 셋을 세어야 합니다.

They created a new city in the desert.
그들은 사막에 새로운 도시를 만들었습니다.

Vocabulary

➢ 음원을 들으면서 소리를 무조건 따라해 보시오. (빠르기 & 정확도/브레인 + 마우스 운동)

deal, dealt, dealt

to be occupied or concerned, trade or do business

handle, treat, trade, distribute

취급하다, 다루다, 거래하다, 나눠주다

This shop deals in women's clothing and cosmetics.

decorate

to furnish or design the interior of

adorn, beautify, embellish, ornament

장식하다

She decorated the box with glitter and ribbons.

deliver

to bring or transport to the proper place

distribute, hand over, turn over

배달하다

The pizza will be delivered in 30 minutes.

dial

to make a telephone call to

call, ring, telephone

전화 걸다, 다이얼을 돌리다

He dialed 911 when he saw the fire.

* 이미지는 구글에서 찾은 것으로, 단어와 이미지가 다를 수 있습니다. 'Test 3'에서 나만의 이미지를 그려볼 수 있습니다.

Test 1 Connecting Exercise

Score(　　/16)
Self-Evaluation

➢ 서로 맞는 것을 연결하시오.

Ⓐ 1~4 영어 단어와 우리말 뜻 연결하기

1 deliver	•	•	취급하다, 다루다, 거래하다, 나눠주다
2 dial	•	•	장식하다
3 decorate	•	•	배달하다
4 deal, dealt, dealt	•	•	전화 걸다, 다이얼을 돌리다

Ⓑ 5~8 영어 단어와 영어 설명 연결하기

5 decorate	•	•	to be occupied or concerned, trade or do business
6 deliver	•	•	to bring or transport to the proper place
7 dial	•	•	to furnish or design the interior of
8 deal,dealt,dealt	•	•	to make a telephone call to

Ⓒ 9~12 영어 단어와 동의어 연결하기

9 deal, dealt, dealt	•	•	handle, treat, trade, distribute
10 dial	•	•	adorn, beautify, embellish, ornament
11 deliver	•	•	distribute, hand over, turn over
12 decorate	•	•	call, ring, telephone

Ⓓ 13~16 우리말 뜻과 영어 단어 연결하기

13 배달하다	•	•	deal,dealt,dealt
14 장식하다	•	•	dial
15 취급하다, 다루다, 거래하다, 나눠주다	•	•	decorate
16 전화 걸다, 다이얼을 돌리다	•	•	deliver

Test 2 Writing Exercise

Score(　　/12)
Self-Evaluation

Ⓐ 1~4 다음 단어에 맞는 뜻을 쓰시오.

1 deliver ______________________

2 deal, dealt, dealt ______________________

3 decorate ______________________

4 dial ______________________

Ⓑ 5~8 다음 뜻에 맞는 영어 단어와 영어 동의어, 영어 설명을 쓰시오.

5 장식하다

______________ ______________________

____

6 배달하다

______________ ______________________

____

7 취급하다, 다루다, 거래하다, 나눠주다

______________ ______________________

____

8 전화 걸다, 다이얼을 돌리다

______________ ______________________

____

Ⓒ 9~12 다음 영어 문장을 의미가 떠오를 때까지 소리 내어 읽어보시오. 2초 이내

9 The pizza will be delivered in 30 minutes.

____

10 This shop deals in women's clothing and cosmetics.

____

11 She decorated the box with glitter and ribbons.

____

12 He dialed 911 when he saw the fire.

____

Test 3 Imaging Exercise

➢ 다음 단어에 맞는 나만의 짧은 영어 설명을 써보자. (또는 그림을 그려보자.)

deal, dealt, dealt
[diːl, delt, delt]

decorate
[dékərèit]

deliver
[dilívər]

dial
[dáiəl]

➢ Month 04-DAY 20 영어 문장과 우리말

This shop deals in women's clothing and cosmetics.
이 가게는 여성용 의류와 화장품을 취급합니다.

She decorated the box with glitter and ribbons.
그녀는 반짝이와 리본으로 상자를 장식했습니다.

The pizza will be delivered in 30 minutes.
피자는 30분 안에 배달됩니다.

He dialed 911 when he saw the fire.
그는 화재를 봤을 때 119에 전화를 걸었습니다.

Month **05** Verbs

Day 01	disguise, drown, dry, ease
Day 02	fear, figure, float, gather
Day 03	hang, hang, interview, itch
Day 04	jet, kill, lean, lick
Day 05	mention, oppose, overturn, plant
Day 06	press, publish, quit, remove
Day 07	rule, shuffle, spare, stain
Day 08	stay, strike, touch, wait
Day 09	wave, whine, worsen, wrinkle
Day 10	yield, add, afford, amuse
Day 11	angle, answer, apply, attract
Day 12	awake, batter, bend, bind
Day 13	compete, contribute, control, convince
Day 14	defeat, dip, examine, explode
Day 15	flash, flip, generate, hope
Day 16	imprison, include, increase, interpret
Day 17	invent, maintain, mend, multiply
Day 18	number, outwit, overhear, overview
Day 19	parade, perform, plead, promise
Day 20	purr, quicken, rely, respond

DAY 01 Vocabulary

➢ 음원을 들으면서 소리를 무조건 따라해 보시오. (빠르기&정확도/브레인+마우스 운동)

disguise

to modify the appearance or manner in order to conceal the identity of

hide, cover, conceal, mask

변장하다, 위장하다

He disguised himself as a guard and escaped.

drown

to die or kill under water

submerge, drench

익사시키다, 물에 빠뜨리다,
익사하다, 물에 빠지다

They jumped in the river and were drowned.

dry

to remove the moisture from or to become dry

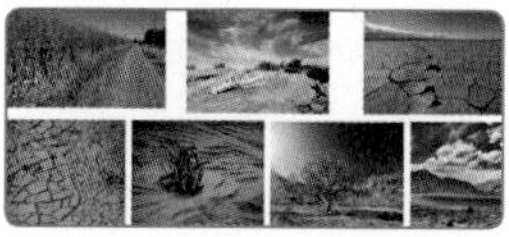

dehydrate, dehumidify, dried-up

건조시키다, 건조하다, 마르다,
마른, 건조한

The wet sheets dried quickly in the sun.

ease

to make or become less burdensome, less discomfort or pain of

relieve, calm, soothe, tranquilize

완화하다, 진정시키다, 가벼워지다,
편함, 쉬움

The government eased various regulations in this field.

* 이미지는 구글에서 찾은 것으로, 단어와 이미지가 다를 수 있습니다. 'Test 3'에서 나만의 이미지를 그려볼 수 있습니다.

Test 1 Connecting Exercise

Score(/16)
Self-Evaluation

➢ 서로 맞는 것을 연결하시오.

Ⓐ 1~4 영어 단어와 우리말 뜻 연결하기

1 drown	•	• 건조시키다, 건조하다, 마르다, 마른, 건조한
2 dry	•	• 변장하다, 위장하다
3 ease	•	• 완화하다, 진정시키다, 가벼워지다, 편함, 쉬움
4 disguise	•	• 익사시키다, 물에 빠뜨리다, 익사하다, 물에 빠지다

Ⓑ 5~8 영어 단어와 영어 설명 연결하기

5 disguise	•	• to make or become less burdensome, less discomfort or pain of
6 ease	•	• to remove the moisture from or to become dry
7 dry	•	• to modify the appearance or manner in order to conceal the identity of
8 drown	•	• to die or kill under water

Ⓒ 9~12 영어 단어와 동의어 연결하기

9 disguise	•	• submerge, drench
10 dry	•	• dehydrate, dehumidify, dried-up
11 ease	•	• hide, cover, conceal, mask
12 drown	•	• relieve, calm, soothe, tranquilize

Ⓓ 13~16 우리말 뜻과 영어 단어 연결하기

13 건조시키다, 건조하다, 마르다, 마른, 건조한	•	• dry
14 변장하다, 위장하다	•	• drown
15 익사시키다, 물에 빠뜨리다, 익사하다, 물에 빠지다	•	• disguise
16 완화하다, 진정시키다, 가벼워지다, 편함, 쉬움	•	• ease

Test 2 Writing Exercise

Score(　　/12)
Self-Evaluation

A 1~4 다음 단어에 맞는 뜻을 쓰시오.

1 drown ______

2 ease ______

3 dry ______

4 disguise ______

B 5~8 다음 뜻에 맞는 영어 단어와 영어 동의어, 영어 설명을 쓰시오.

5 건조시키다, 건조하다, 마르다, 마른, 건조한

______ ______

______

6 변장하다, 위장하다

______ ______

______

7 완화하다, 진정시키다, 가벼워지다, 편함, 쉬움

______ ______

______

8 익사시키다, 물에 빠뜨리다, 익사하다, 물에 빠지다

______ ______

______

C 9~12 다음 영어 문장을 의미가 떠오를 때까지 소리 내어 읽어보시오. 2초 이내

9 He disguised himself as a guard and escaped.

______

10 The government eased various regulations in this field.

______

11 They jumped in the river and were drowned.

______

12 The wet sheets dried quickly in the sun.

______

Test 3 Imaging Exercise

➢ 다음 단어에 맞는 나만의 짧은 영어 설명을 써보자. (또는 그림을 그려보자.)

disguise
[disgáiz]

drown
[draun]

dry
[drai]

ease
[i:z]

➢ Month 05-DAY 01 영어 문장과 우리말

He disguised himself as a guard and escaped.
그는 경비원으로 변장하고 도망쳤습니다.

They jumped in the river and were drowned.
그들은 강물에 뛰어들었고 익사하였습니다.

The wet sheets dried quickly in the sun.
젖은 시트는(천이불은) 햇볕에 빨리 말랐습니다.

The government eased various regulations in this field.
정부는 이 분야에서 여러 규정들을 완화하였습니다.

Vocabulary

➢ 음원을 들으면서 소리를 무조건 따라해 보시오. (빠르기&정확도/브레인+마우스 운동)

fear

to be afraid or to be worried

worry, be afraid of,
be scared of

두려워하다, 두려움, 걱정

Most girls fear insects like spiders or cockroaches.

figure

to make a likeness of

depict, understand, calculate

그려내다, 파악해 내다,
계산하다, 그림

I want to figure out what that is.

float

to rest or remain on the surface of a liquid

glide, sail, drift

뜨다, 가라앉지 않고 떠다니다

A small boat is floating on the river.

gather

to collect or to come together around a central point

collect, assemble,
congregate, accumulate

모으다, 모이다

Supporters of President Trump gathered near Trump Tower.

* 이미지는 구글에서 찾은 것으로, 단어와 이미지가 다를 수 있습니다. 'Test 3'에서 나만의 이미지를 그려볼 수 있습니다.

Connecting Exercise

Test 1

Score(/16)
Self-Evaluation

➢ 서로 맞는 것을 연결하시오.

Ⓐ 1~4 영어 단어와 우리말 뜻 연결하기

1 gather	•	• 뜨다, 가라앉지 않고 떠다니다
2 fear	•	• 두려워하다, 두려움, 걱정
3 float	•	• 그려내다, 파악해 내다, 계산하다, 그림
4 figure	•	• 모으다, 모이다

Ⓑ 5~8 영어 단어와 영어 설명 연결하기

5 float	•	• to make a likeness of
6 fear	•	• to rest or remain on the surface of a liquid
7 figure	•	• to be afraid or to be worried
8 gather	•	• to collect or to come together around a central point

Ⓒ 9~12 영어 단어와 동의어 연결하기

9 figure	•	• depict, understand, calculate
10 fear	•	• collect, assemble, congregate, accumulate
11 float	•	• glide, sail, drift
12 gather	•	• worry, be afraid of, be scared of

Ⓓ 13~16 우리말 뜻과 영어 단어 연결하기

13 그려내다, 파악해 내다, 계산하다, 그림	•	• gather
14 뜨다, 가라앉지 않고 떠다니다	•	• fear
15 모으다, 모이다	•	• figure
16 두려워하다, 두려움, 걱정	•	• float

Test 2 Writing Exercise

Score(/12)
Self-Evaluation

A 1~4 다음 단어에 맞는 뜻을 쓰시오.

1 figure ____________________

2 gather ____________________

3 fear ____________________

4 float ____________________

B 5~8 다음 뜻에 맞는 영어 단어와 영어 동의어, 영어 설명을 쓰시오.

5 그려내다, 파악해 내다, 계산하다, 그림

____________ ____________________

____

6 두려워하다, 두려움, 걱정

____________ ____________________

____

7 뜨다, 가라앉지 않고 떠다니다

____________ ____________________

____

8 모으다, 모이다

____________ ____________________

____

C 9~12 다음 영어 문장을 의미가 떠오를 때까지 소리 내어 읽어보시오. 2초 이내

9 I want to figure out what that is.

____

10 A small boat is floating on the river.

____

11 Supporters of President Trump gathered near Trump Tower.

____

12 Most girls fear insects like spiders or cockroaches.

____

Test 3 Imaging Exercise

➢ 다음 단어에 맞는 나만의 짧은 영어 설명을 써보자. (또는 그림을 그려보자.)

fear
[fiər]

figure
[fígjər]

float
[flout]

gather
[gæðər]

➢ Month 05-DAY 02 영어 문장과 우리말

Most girls fear insects like spiders or cockroaches.
대부분의 소녀는 거미나 바퀴벌레 같은 곤충을 두려워합니다.

I want to figure out what that is.
나는 저것이 무엇인지 알아내고 싶다.

A small boat is floating on the river.
작은 배가 강에 떠 있습니다.

Supporters of President Trump gathered near Trump Tower.
트럼프 대통령 지지자들이 트럼프타워 근처에 모여들었습니다.

DAY 03 Vocabulary

➢ 음원을 들으면서 소리를 무조건 따라해 보시오. (빠르기 & 정확도/브레인 + 마우스 운동)

hang, hung, hung

to fasten from above with no support from below

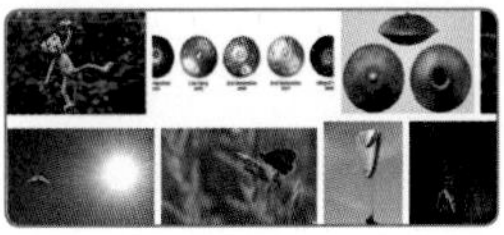

suspend, cling, sling, dangle

걸다, 매달다

He hung the hat on a wall peg.

hang, hanged, hanged

to kill a person by tying a rope around his neck

gibbet

교수형에 처하다, 목매달아 죽이다

They hanged the prisoner at dawn in 1849.

interview

to have an interview with

question, interrogate

직접 만나 이야기를 나누다, 인터뷰

He interviewed very famous people for various subjects.

itch

to feel, have, or produce an itch

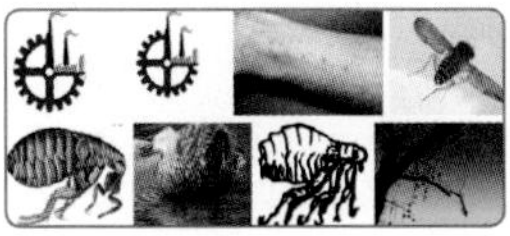

itching, itchiness

가렵다, 가려워 긁다, 가려움

I've got an itch, scratch my back.

* 이미지는 구글에서 찾은 것으로, 단어와 이미지가 다를 수 있습니다. 'Test 3'에서 나만의 이미지를 그려볼 수 있습니다.

Test 1 Connecting Exercise

Score(/16)
Self-Evaluation

➢ 서로 맞는 것을 연결하시오.

Ⓐ 1~4 영어 단어와 우리말 뜻 연결하기

1	hang, hanged, hanged	교수형에 처하다, 목매달아 죽이다
2	interview	걸다, 매달다
3	hang, hung, hung	가렵다, 가려워 긁다, 가려움
4	itch	직접 만나 이야기를 나누다, 인터뷰

Ⓑ 5~8 영어 단어와 영어 설명 연결하기

5	hang, hung, hung	to fasten from above with no support from below
6	hang, hanged, hanged	to kill a person by tying a rope around his neck
7	interview	to feel, have, or produce an itch
8	itch	to have an interview with

Ⓒ 9~12 영어 단어와 동의어 연결하기

9	itch	suspend, cling, sling, dangle
10	interview	question, interrogate
11	hang, hanged, hanged	gibbet
12	hang, hung, hung	itching, itchiness

Ⓓ 13~16 우리말 뜻과 영어 단어 연결하기

13	직접 만나 이야기를 나누다, 인터뷰	hang, hung, hung
14	걸다, 매달다	itch
15	가렵다, 가려워 긁다, 가려움	hang, hanged, hanged
16	교수형에 처하다, 목매달아 죽이다	interview

Test 2 Writing Exercise

Score(/12)
Self-Evaluation

Ⓐ 1~4 다음 단어에 맞는 뜻을 쓰시오.

1 itch ______

2 hang, hung, hung ______

3 interview ______

4 hang, hanged, hanged ______

Ⓑ 5~8 다음 뜻에 맞는 영어 단어와 영어 동의어, 영어 설명을 쓰시오.

5 가렵다, 가려워 긁다, 가려움

______ ______

______

6 직접 만나 이야기를 나누다, 인터뷰

______ ______

______

7 걸다, 매달다

______ ______

______

8 교수형에 처하다, 목매달아 죽이다

______ ______

______

Ⓒ 9~12 다음 영어 문장을 의미가 떠오를 때까지 소리 내어 읽어보시오. 2초 이내

9 He hung the hat on a wall peg.

______

10 He interviewed very famous people for various subjects.

______

11 I've got an itch, scratch my back.

______

12 They hanged the prisoner at dawn in 1849.

______

Test 3 Imaging Exercise

➢ 다음 단어에 맞는 나만의 짧은 영어 설명을 써보자. (또는 그림을 그려보자.)

hang, hung, hung
[hæŋ, hʌŋ, hʌŋ]

hang, hanged, hanged
[hæŋ, hæŋd, hæŋd]

interview
[íntərvjùː]

itch
[itʃ]

➢ Month 05-DAY 03 영어 문장과 우리말

He hung the hat on a wall peg.
그는 모자를 벽(벽걸이)에 걸었습니다.

They hanged the prisoner at dawn in 1849.
그들은 죄수를 1849년 새벽 교수형에 처했습니다.

He interviewed very famous people for various subjects.
그는 다양한 주제에 대해 매우 유명한 사람들과 인터뷰했습니다.

I've got an itch, scratch my back.
가려우니 등 좀 긁어줘.

DAY 04 Vocabulary

➢ 음원을 들으면서 소리를 무조건 따라해 보시오. (빠르기&정확도/브레인+마우스 운동)

jet

to shoot (something) forth in a stream, or jet plane or jet engine

stream, shoot, flow, rush

분사하다, 분사, 제트비행기

A jet plane is a jet-propelled airplane.

kill

to put to death

murder, killing

죽이다, 죽임, 살인

The armed forces killed more than 1,000 people.

lean

to incline the body so as to be supported

bend, slope, incline

기대다, 기대게 하다

He leaned his golf clubs against the wall.

lick

to pass the tongue over or along

lap up

핥다, 날름거리다

The cat licked the milk from the bowl.

* 이미지는 구글에서 찾은 것으로, 단어와 이미지가 다를 수 있습니다. 'Test 3'에서 나만의 이미지를 그려볼 수 있습니다.

Test 1 Connecting Exercise

Score(/16)
Self-Evaluation

≫ 서로 맞는 것을 연결하시오.

Ⓐ 1~4 영어 단어와 우리말 뜻 연결하기

1 lean	•	• 핥다, 날름거리다
2 lick	•	• 죽이다, 죽임, 살인
3 kill	•	• 분사하다, 분사, 제트비행기
4 jet	•	• 기대다, 기대게 하다

Ⓑ 5~8 영어 단어와 영어 설명 연결하기

5 lean	•	• to pass the tongue over or along
6 jet	•	• to incline the body so as to be supported
7 lick	•	• to shoot (something) forth in a stream, or jet plane or jet engine
8 kill	•	• to put to death

Ⓒ 9~12 영어 단어와 동의어 연결하기

9 jet	•	• murder, killing
10 kill	•	• bend, slope, incline
11 lean	•	• lap up
12 lick	•	• stream, shoot, flow, rush

Ⓓ 13~16 우리말 뜻과 영어 단어 연결하기

13 핥다, 날름거리다	•	• kill
14 죽이다, 죽임, 살인	•	• lick
15 분사하다, 분사, 제트비행기	•	• lean
16 기대다, 기대게 하다	•	• jet

Test 2 Writing Exercise

Score(/12)
Self-Evaluation

Ⓐ 1~4 다음 단어에 맞는 뜻을 쓰시오.

1 kill ______

2 lean ______

3 lick ______

4 jet ______

Ⓑ 5~8 다음 뜻에 맞는 영어 단어와 영어 동의어, 영어 설명을 쓰시오.

5 분사하다, 분사, 제트비행기

______ ______

______

6 기대다, 기대게 하다

______ ______

______

7 핥다, 날름거리다

______ ______

______

8 죽이다, 죽임, 살인

______ ______

______

Ⓒ 9~12 다음 영어 문장을 의미가 떠오를 때까지 소리 내어 읽어보시오. 2초 이내

9 The armed forces killed more than 1,000 people.

______

10 He leaned his golf clubs against the wall.

______

11 A jet plane is a jet-propelled airplane.

______

12 The cat licked the milk from the bowl.

______

Test 3

➤ 다음 단어에 맞는 나만의 짧은 영어 설명을 써보자. (또는 그림을 그려보자.)

jet
[dʒet]

kill
[kil]

lean
[liːn]

lick
[lik]

➤ Month 05-DAY 04 영어 문장과 우리말

A jet plane is a jet-propelled airplane.
제트 비행기는 제트 추진 비행기입니다.

The armed forces killed more than 1,000 people.
무장한 군인들이 천명이 넘는 사람들을 죽였습니다.

He leaned his golf clubs against the wall.
그는 그의 골프채를 벽에 기대어 놓았습니다.

The cat licked the milk from the bowl.
고양이가 그릇에 우유를 핥아 먹었습니다.

Vocabulary

➢ **음원을 들으면서 소리를 무조건 따라해 보시오.** (빠르기&정확도/브레인+마우스 운동)

mention

to refer to or speak about briefly

comment, remark

짧게 말하다, 언급하다, 언급

He mentioned that he might go to Seoul.

oppose

to fight against

counter, object, resist

반대하다, 대항하다

70% oppose the government on this matter.

overturn

to cause to turn over

capsize, reverse, overthrow, defeat

뒤집다

Their boat overturned near New York Bay on Sunday.

plant

to put or set in the ground for growth, as seeds or young trees

transplant, implant

심다, 재배하다, 식물

He planted fruit and vegetables in the garden.

* 이미지는 구글에서 찾은 것으로, 단어와 이미지가 다를 수 있습니다. 'Test 3'에서 나만의 이미지를 그려볼 수 있습니다.

Test 1 Connecting Exercise

Score(/16)
Self-Evaluation

➢ 서로 맞는 것을 연결하시오.

A 1~4 영어 단어와 우리말 뜻 연결하기

1 plant	•	•	심다, 재배하다, 식물
2 overturn	•	•	뒤집다
3 oppose	•	•	반대하다, 대항하다
4 mention	•	•	짧게 말하다, 언급하다, 언급

B 5~8 영어 단어와 영어 설명 연결하기

5 plant	•	•	to fight against
6 mention	•	•	to put or set in the ground for growth, as seeds or young trees
7 oppose	•	•	to cause to turn over
8 overturn	•	•	to refer to or speak about briefly

C 9~12 영어 단어와 동의어 연결하기

9 overturn	•	•	capsize, reverse, overthrow, defeat
10 plant	•	•	transplant, implant
11 mention	•	•	comment, remark
12 oppose	•	•	counter, object, resist

D 13~16 우리말 뜻과 영어 단어 연결하기

13 반대하다, 대항하다	•	•	mention
14 심다, 재배하다, 식물	•	•	overturn
15 짧게 말하다, 언급하다, 언급	•	•	plant
16 뒤집다	•	•	oppose

Test 2 Writing Exercise

Score(/12)
Self-Evaluation

A 1~4 다음 단어에 맞는 뜻을 쓰시오.

1 mention ______________________

2 plant ______________________

3 overturn ______________________

4 oppose ______________________

B 5~8 다음 뜻에 맞는 영어 단어와 영어 동의어, 영어 설명을 쓰시오.

5 심다, 재배하다, 식물

______________ ______________________

____

6 짧게 말하다, 언급하다, 언급

______________ ______________________

____

7 반대하다, 대항하다

______________ ______________________

____

8 뒤집다

______________ ______________________

____

C 9~12 다음 영어 문장을 의미가 떠오를 때까지 소리 내어 읽어보시오. 2초 이내

9 He planted fruit and vegetables in the garden.

____

10 He mentioned that he might go to Seoul.

____

11 70% oppose the government on this matter.

____

12 Their boat overturned near New York Bay on Sunday.

____

Test 3 Imaging Exercise

➢ 다음 단어에 맞는 나만의 짧은 영어 설명을 써보자. (또는 그림을 그려보자.)

mention
[ménʃən]

oppose
[əpóuz]

overturn
[ou'vərtər,n]

plant
[plænt]

➢ Month 05-DAY 05 영어 문장과 우리말

He mentioned that he might go to Seoul.
그는 그가 서울에 갈지도 모른다고 말했습니다.

70% oppose the government on this matter.
70퍼센트가 이 문제에 대하여 정부를 반대하고 있습니다.

Their boat overturned near New York Bay on Sunday.
그들의 보트가 일요일 뉴욕만 근처에서 뒤집혔습니다.

He planted fruit and vegetables in the garden.
그는 정원에 과실과 채소를 심었습니다.

DAY 06 Vocabulary

➢ 음원을 들으면서 소리를 무조건 따라해 보시오. (빠르기&정확도/브레인+마우스 운동)

press

to exert steady weight or force against

push down, depress, pressing, pressure

누르다, 압력을 가하다

He pressed a button and the door closed.

publish

to issue a publication

issue, produce, print, put out

출판하다, 발표하다, 발행하다

My book was published in August 31, 2017.

quit

to stop, cease, or discontinue

stop, cease, discontinue

그만두다, 중단하다

After he quitted his job, he quitted smoking.

remove

to move from a place

erase, eliminate, get rid of

제거하다, 없애다

I can't remove this stain from my shirt.

* 이미지는 구글에서 찾은 것으로, 단어와 이미지가 다를 수 있습니다. 'Test 3'에서 나만의 이미지를 그려볼 수 있습니다.

Test 1 Connecting Exercise

Score(/16)
Self-Evaluation

➢ 서로 맞는 것을 연결하시오.

Ⓐ 1~4 영어 단어와 우리말 뜻 연결하기

1 publish •	• 그만두다, 중단하다
2 remove •	• 누르다, 압력을 가하다
3 quit •	• 제거하다, 없애다
4 press •	• 출판하다, 발표하다, 발행하다

Ⓑ 5~8 영어 단어와 영어 설명 연결하기

5 publish •	• to issue a publication
6 remove •	• to exert steady weight or force against
7 press •	• to move from a place
8 quit •	• to stop, cease, or discontinue

Ⓒ 9~12 영어 단어와 동의어 연결하기

9 press •	• push down, depress, pressing, pressure
10 quit •	• stop, cease, discontinue
11 publish •	• erase, eliminate, get rid of
12 remove •	• issue, produce, print, put out

Ⓓ 13~16 우리말 뜻과 영어 단어 연결하기

13 그만두다, 중단하다 •	• press
14 출판하다, 발표하다, 발행하다 •	• remove
15 누르다, 압력을 가하다 •	• publish
16 제거하다, 없애다 •	• quit

Test 2 Writing Exercise

Score(/12)
Self-Evaluation

A 1~4 다음 단어에 맞는 뜻을 쓰시오.

1 quit ______________________

2 remove ______________________

3 press ______________________

4 publish ______________________

B 5~8 다음 뜻에 맞는 영어 단어와 영어 동의어, 영어 설명을 쓰시오.

5 누르다, 압력을 가하다

______________ ______________________

____

6 그만두다, 중단하다

______________ ______________________

____

7 제거하다, 없애다

______________ ______________________

____

8 출판하다, 발표하다, 발행하다

______________ ______________________

____

C 9~12 다음 영어 문장을 의미가 떠오를 때까지 소리 내어 읽어보시오. 2초 이내

9 I can't remove this stain from my shirt.

____

10 He pressed a button and the door closed.

____

11 After he quitted his job, he quitted smoking.

____

12 My book was published in August 31, 2017.

____

Test 3 Imaging Exercise

➢ 다음 단어에 맞는 나만의 짧은 영어 설명을 써보자. (또는 그림을 그려보자.)

press
[pres]

publish
[pʌbliʃ]

quit
[kwit]

remove
[rimúːv]

➢ Month 05-DAY 06 영어 문장과 우리말

He pressed a button and the door closed.
그가 버튼을 눌렀고, 그리고 문이 닫혔습니다.

My book was published in August 31, 2017.
내 책은 2017년 8월 31일에 출판되었습니다.

After he quitted his job, he quitted smoking.
그는 직장을 그만둔 뒤, 담배를 끊었습니다.

I can't remove this stain from my shirt.
나는 셔츠에서 이 얼룩을 지울 수 없습니다.

DAY 07 Vocabulary

➢ 음원을 들으면서 소리를 무조건 따라해 보시오. (빠르기&정확도/브레인+마우스 운동)

rule

to exercise control, dominion, or direction over

govern, lead, control, manage

지배하다, 다스리다, 규정, 규칙

The king ruled his kingdom for ten years.

shuffle

to walk without lifting the feet, or to mix together

shamble, drag, mix

발을 질질 끌며 걷다, 뒤섞다, 얼버무리다

It's your turn to shuffle the cards.

spare

to refrain from killing, or punishing

save, use, back-up, reserve

살려두다, 남겨두다, 할애하다, 아껴쓰다, 예비의, 여분

The oldest temple was spared from the fire.

stain

to discolor, soil, or spot

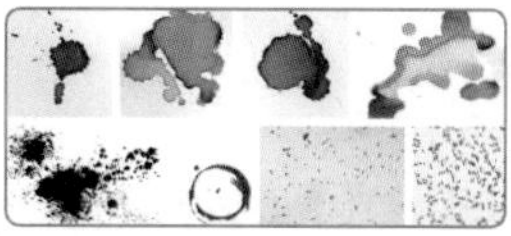

soil, discolor, dirty

얼룩지다, 더럽히다, 얼룩지게 하다, 얼룩, 오점

My dress has been stained with spilled coffee.

* 이미지는 구글에서 찾은 것으로, 단어와 이미지가 다를 수 있습니다. 'Test 3'에서 나만의 이미지를 그려볼 수 있습니다.

Test 1 Connecting Exercise

Score(/16)
Self-Evaluation

➢ 서로 맞는 것을 연결하시오.

Ⓐ 1~4 영어 단어와 우리말 뜻 연결하기

1 spare	지배하다, 다스리다, 규정, 규칙
2 rule	발을 질질 끌며 걷다, 뒤섞다, 얼버무리다
3 shuffle	살려두다, 남겨두다, 할애하다, 아껴쓰다, 예비의, 여분
4 stain	얼룩지다, 더럽히다, 얼룩지게 하다, 얼룩, 오점

Ⓑ 5~8 영어 단어와 영어 설명 연결하기

5 spare	to walk without lifting the feet, or to mix together
6 rule	to refrain from killing, or punishing
7 stain	to exercise control, dominion, or direction over
8 shuffle	to discolor, soil, or spot

Ⓒ 9~12 영어 단어와 동의어 연결하기

9 shuffle	save, use, back-up, reserve
10 spare	govern, lead, control, manage
11 stain	soil, discolor, dirty
12 rule	shamble, drag, mix

Ⓓ 13~16 우리말 뜻과 영어 단어 연결하기

13 지배하다, 다스리다, 규정, 규칙	rule
14 발을 질질 끌며 걷다, 뒤섞다, 얼버무리다	shuffle
15 살려두다, 남겨두다, 할애하다, 아껴쓰다, 예비의, 여분	stain
16 얼룩지다, 더럽히다, 얼룩지게 하다, 얼룩, 오점	spare

Test 2 Writing Exercise

Score(/12)
Self-Evaluation

A 1~4 다음 단어에 맞는 뜻을 쓰시오.

1 spare ____________________

2 rule ____________________

3 shuffle ____________________

4 stain ____________________

B 5~8 다음 뜻에 맞는 영어 단어와 영어 동의어, 영어 설명을 쓰시오.

5 지배하다, 다스리다, 규정, 규칙

____________ ____________________

____

6 발을 질질 끌며 걷다, 뒤섞다, 얼버무리다

____________ ____________________

____

7 얼룩지다, 더럽히다, 얼룩지게 하다, 얼룩, 오점

____________ ____________________

____

8 살려두다, 남겨두다, 할애하다, 아껴쓰다, 예비의, 여분

____________ ____________________

____

C 9~12 다음 영어 문장을 의미가 떠오를 때까지 소리 내어 읽어보시오. 2초 이내

9 My dress has been stained with spilled coffee.

____

10 The oldest temple was spared from the fire.

____

11 The king ruled his kingdom for ten years.

____

12 It's your turn to shuffle the cards.

____

Test 3 Imaging Exercise

➢ 다음 단어에 맞는 나만의 짧은 영어 설명을 써보자. (또는 그림을 그려보자.)

rule
[ruːl]

shuffle
[ʃʌfl]

spare
[spɛər]

stain
[stein]

➢ Month 05-DAY 07 영어 문장과 우리말

The king ruled his kingdom for ten years.
왕은 10년 동안 그의 왕국을 다스렸습니다.

It's your turn to shuffle the cards.
당신이 카드를 섞을 차례입니다.

The oldest temple was spared from the fire.
가장 오래된 사찰은 화재에서 살아남았습니다.

My dress has been stained with spilled coffee.
나의 드레스가 엎질러진 커피로 얼룩졌습니다.

➢ 음원을 들으면서 소리를 무조건 따라해 보시오. (빠르기&정확도/브레인+마우스 운동)

stay

to continue to be in a place or condition

remain, linger, stand

(어떤 장소나 상태에) 머물다, 남다

I want to stay home and stay calm.

strike, struck, struck

to hit sharply, as with a hand, fist, weapon, or implement

hit, smack, thump

(손, 주먹, 무기, 도구 등으로) 때리다, 강타하다, 부딪치다

He was striking his horse with his whip.

touch

to be in contact

feel, hit, contact

만지다, 대다

I said "Don't touch any of my things!"

wait

to remain or rest in expectation of

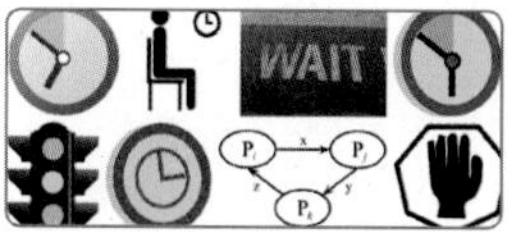

await, anticipate

기다리다

I stayed at home, waiting for her call.

* 이미지는 구글에서 찾은 것으로, 단어와 이미지가 다를 수 있습니다. 'Test 3'에서 나만의 이미지를 그려볼 수 있습니다.

Test 1 Connecting Exercise

Score(/16)
Self-Evaluation

➢ 서로 맞는 것을 연결하시오.

Ⓐ 1~4 영어 단어와 우리말 뜻 연결하기

1 strike, struck, struck	•	• (어떤 장소나 상태에) 머물다, 남다
2 wait	•	• 만지다, 대다
3 touch	•	• 기다리다
4 stay	•	• (손, 주먹, 무기, 도구 등으로) 때리다, 강타하다, 부딪치다

Ⓑ 5~8 영어 단어와 영어 설명 연결하기

5 stay	•	• to hit sharply, as with a hand, fist, weapon, or implement
6 strike, struck, struck	•	• to remain or rest in expectation of
7 touch	•	• to continue to be in a place or condition
8 wait	•	• to be in contact

Ⓒ 9~12 영어 단어와 동의어 연결하기

9 strike, struck, struck	•	• feel, hit, contact
10 touch	•	• remain, linger, stand
11 wait	•	• hit, smack, thump
12 stay	•	• await, anticipate

Ⓓ 13~16 우리말 뜻과 영어 단어 연결하기

13 (어떤 장소나 상태에) 머물다, 남다	•	• strike, struck, struck
14 (손, 주먹, 무기, 도구 등으로) 때리다, 강타하다, 부딪치다	•	• touch
15 만지다, 대다	•	• wait
16 기다리다	•	• stay

Test 2 Writing Exercise

Score(/12)
Self-Evaluation

Ⓐ 1~4 다음 단어에 맞는 뜻을 쓰시오.

1 wait ______________________

2 stay ______________________

3 touch ______________________

4 strike, struck, struck ______________________

Ⓑ 5~8 다음 뜻에 맞는 영어 단어와 영어 동의어, 영어 설명을 쓰시오.

5 (손, 주먹, 무기, 도구 등으로) 때리다, 강타하다, 부딪치다

______________ ______________________

____

6 기다리다

______________ ______________________

____

7 (어떤 장소나 상태에) 머물다, 남다

______________ ______________________

____

8 만지다, 대다

______________ ______________________

____

Ⓒ 9~12 다음 영어 문장을 의미가 떠오를 때까지 소리 내어 읽어보시오. 2초 이내

9 I said "Don't touch any of my things!"

____

10 I want to stay home and stay calm.

____

11 I stayed at home, waiting for her call.

____

12 He was striking his horse with his whip.

____

> 다음 단어에 맞는 나만의 짧은 영어 설명을 써보자. (또는 그림을 그려보자.)

stay
[stei]

strike, struck, struck
[straik, strʌk, strʌk]

touch
[tʌʧ]

wait
[weit]

> Month 05-DAY 08 영어 문장과 우리말

I want to stay home and stay calm.
나는 집에 있고 싶고 그리고 조용히 있고 싶습니다.

He was striking his horse with his whip.
그는 말을 채찍으로 치고 있었습니다.

I said "Don't touch any of my things!"
나는 "내 물건에 손대지 마세요"라고 말했습니다.

I stayed at home, waiting for her call.
나는 그녀의 전화를 기다리면서 집에 있었습니다.

Vocabulary

➢ **음원을 들으면서 소리를 무조건 따라해 보시오.** (빠르기&정확도/브레인+마우스 운동)

wave

to move freely back and forth or up and down in the air

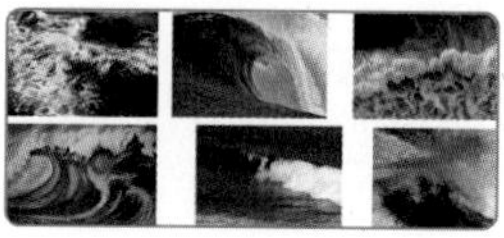

swing, wield, flutter

앞뒤 상하로 자유롭게 움직이다, 손을 흔들다, 물결치다, 파동

She waved to me from across the street.

whine

to utter with a whine

cry, sob, pule, whimper

징징대다, 칭얼대다

I heard a child whining in the background.

worsen

to make or become worse

deteriorate, decline, decay, get worse

더 나빠지다, 악화되다

Conditions in the water supply have further worsened.

wrinkle

to form wrinkles in or to become wrinkled

crease, crinkle, furrow

주름잡다, 구기다, 주름지다, 구겨지다, 주름, 구김살

She wrinkled her dress by sitting on it.

* 이미지는 구글에서 찾은 것으로, 단어와 이미지가 다를 수 있습니다. 'Test 3'에서 나만의 이미지를 그려볼 수 있습니다.

Test 1 Connecting Exercise

Score(/16)
Self-Evaluation

➢ 서로 맞는 것을 연결하시오.

Ⓐ 1~4 영어 단어와 우리말 뜻 연결하기

1 worsen	•	• 앞뒤 상하로 자유롭게 움직이다, 손을 흔들다, 물결치다, 파동
2 whine	•	• 주름잡다, 구기다, 주름지다, 구겨지다, 주름, 구김살
3 wave	•	• 더 나빠지다, 악화되다
4 wrinkle	•	• 징징대다, 칭얼대다

Ⓑ 5~8 영어 단어와 영어 설명 연결하기

5 wrinkle	•	• to make or become worse
6 worsen	•	• to utter with a whine
7 whine	•	• to form wrinkles in or to become wrinkled
8 wave	•	• to move freely back and forth or up and down in the air

Ⓒ 9~12 영어 단어와 동의어 연결하기

9 wrinkle	•	• deteriorate, decline, decay, get worse
10 whine	•	• swing, wield, flutter
11 worsen	•	• cry, sob, pule, whimper
12 wave	•	• crease, crinkle, furrow

Ⓓ 13~16 우리말 뜻과 영어 단어 연결하기

13 더 나빠지다, 악화되다	•	• worsen
14 앞뒤 상하로 자유롭게 움직이다, 손을 흔들다, 물결치다, 파동	•	• whine
15 주름잡다, 구기다, 주름지다, 구겨지다, 주름, 구김살	•	• wave
16 징징대다, 칭얼대다	•	• wrinkle

Test 2 Writing Exercise

Score(/12)
Self-Evaluation

Ⓐ 1~4 다음 단어에 맞는 뜻을 쓰시오.

1 wave ______

2 wrinkle ______

3 worsen ______

4 whine ______

Ⓑ 5~8 다음 뜻에 맞는 영어 단어와 영어 동의어, 영어 설명을 쓰시오.

5 주름잡다, 구기다, 주름지다, 구겨지다, 주름, 구김살

______ ______

______

6 더 나빠지다, 악화되다

______ ______

______

7 앞뒤 상하로 자유롭게 움직이다, 손을 흔들다, 물결치다, 파동

______ ______

______

8 징징대다, 칭얼대다

______ ______

______

Ⓒ 9~12 다음 영어 문장을 의미가 떠오를 때까지 소리 내어 읽어보시오. 2초 이내

9 Conditions in the water supply have further worsened.

______

10 I heard a child whining in the background.

______

11 She wrinkled her dress by sitting on it.

______

12 She waved to me from across the street.

______

Test 3

➢ 다음 단어에 맞는 나만의 짧은 영어 설명을 써보자. (또는 그림을 그려보자.)

wave
[weiv]

whine
[hwain]

worsen
[wə́ːrsn]

wrinkle
[ríŋkl]

➢ Month 05-DAY 09 영어 문장과 우리말

She waved to me from across the street.
그녀는 길 건너에서 나에게 손을 흔들었습니다.

I heard a child whining in the background.
나는 등 뒤에서 아이의 칭얼거리며 우는 소리를 들었습니다.

Conditions in the water supply have further worsened.
물공급 상황이 더욱 악화되었습니다.

She wrinkled her dress by sitting on it.
그녀는 드레스를 깔고 앉는 바람에 드레스에 주름이 갔습니다.

DAY 10 Vocabulary

➢ 음원을 들으면서 소리를 무조건 따라해 보시오. (빠르기&정확도/브레인+마우스 운동)

yield

to give forth by a natural process, or to surrender to superior power

produce, provide, surrender, give up

산출하다, 낳다, 굴복하다

This land yields a crop worth $1.75 billion.

add

to unite or join

count up, sum up, join

더하다

If you add 5 to 10, you get 15.

afford

to be able to undergo or to supply

bear, stand, or furnish, give

할 여유가 있다, 할 수 있다, 제공하다

It's too expensive, therefore we can't afford it.

amuse

to cause to laugh or smile by being funny

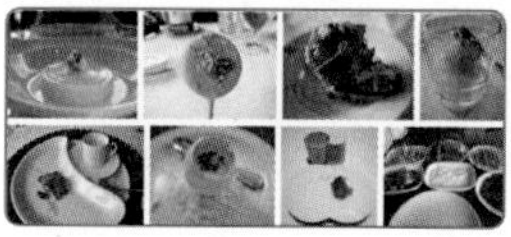

entertain, please, delight

즐겁게 하다

He amused the crowd with jokes.

* 이미지는 구글에서 찾은 것으로, 단어와 이미지가 다를 수 있습니다. 'Test 3'에서 나만의 이미지를 그려볼 수 있습니다.

Test 1 Connecting Exercise

Score(/16)
Self-Evaluation

➢ 서로 맞는 것을 연결하시오.

Ⓐ 1~4 영어 단어와 우리말 뜻 연결하기

1 afford	•	• 즐겁게 하다
2 add	•	• 더하다
3 yield	•	• 할 여유가 있다, 할 수 있다, 제공하다
4 amuse	•	• 산출하다, 낳다, 굴복하다

Ⓑ 5~8 영어 단어와 영어 설명 연결하기

5 amuse	•	• to give forth by a natural process, or to surrender to superior power
6 add	•	• to cause to laugh or smile by being funny
7 yield	•	• to unite or join
8 afford	•	• to be able to undergo or to supply

Ⓒ 9~12 영어 단어와 동의어 연결하기

9 add	•	• bear, stand, or furnish, give
10 yield	•	• produce, provide, surrender, give up
11 amuse	•	• count up, sum up, join
12 afford	•	• entertain, please, delight

Ⓓ 13~16 우리말 뜻과 영어 단어 연결하기

13 더하다	•	• amuse
14 산출하다, 낳다, 굴복하다	•	• afford
15 할 여유가 있다, 할 수 있다, 제공하다	•	• add
16 즐겁게 하다	•	• yield

Test 2 Writing Exercise

Score(/12)
Self-Evaluation

Ⓐ 1~4 다음 단어에 맞는 뜻을 쓰시오.

1 yield ______

2 amuse ______

3 add ______

4 afford ______

Ⓑ 5~8 다음 뜻에 맞는 영어 단어와 영어 동의어, 영어 설명을 쓰시오.

5 더하다

______ ______

______

6 즐겁게 하다

______ ______

______

7 산출하다, 낳다, 굴복하다

______ ______

______

8 할 여유가 있다, 할 수 있다, 제공하다

______ ______

______

Ⓒ 9~12 다음 영어 문장을 의미가 떠오를 때까지 소리 내어 읽어보시오. 2.5초 이내

9 He amused the crowd with jokes.

______

10 This land yields a crop worth $1.75 billion.

______

11 If you add 5 to 10, you get 15.

______

12 It's too expensive, therefore we can't afford it.

______

Test 3 Imaging Exercise

➢ 다음 단어에 맞는 나만의 짧은 영어 설명을 써보자. (또는 그림을 그려보자.)

yield
[jiːld]

add
[æd]

afford
[əfɔ́ːrd]

amuse
[əmjúːz]

➢ Month 05-DAY 10 영어 문장과 우리말

This land yields a crop worth $1.75 billion.
이 땅은 십칠억 오천달러에 달하는 농작물을 생산합니다.

If you add 5 to 10, you get 15.
10에 5를 더하면 15가 됩니다.

It's too expensive, therefore we can't afford it.
너무 비싸서 우리는 그것을 감당할 수 없습니다.

He amused the crowd with jokes.
그는 농담으로 사람들을 즐겁게 했다.

Vocabulary

➢ **음원을 들으면서 소리를 무조건 따라해 보시오.** (빠르기&정확도/브레인+마우스 운동)

angle

to fish with a hook and line

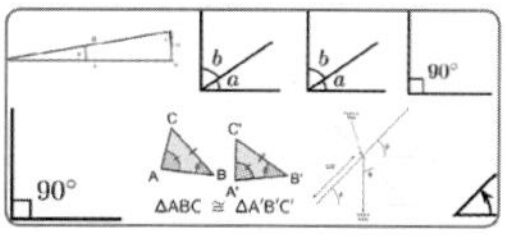

fish, troll, bend

낚시, 낚시하다, 얻으려 하다,
각도, 각, 꺾어지다

The road angles to the right at right angle.

answer

to say or write in reply

reply, respond, response, reaction

대답하다, 대답, 응답

She answered that she was unable to join us.

apply

to put to practical use

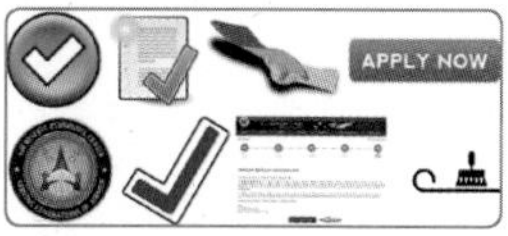

utilize, employ, use

지원하다, 적용하다

Scientists can apply a theory to a practical problem.

attract

to draw by a physical force

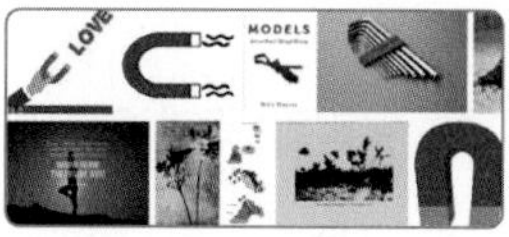

allure, draw, charm, fascinate

끌다, 당기다

The gravitational force of the earth attracts all objects.

* 이미지는 구글에서 찾은 것으로, 단어와 이미지가 다를 수 있습니다. 'Test 3'에서 나만의 이미지를 그려볼 수 있습니다.

Test 1 Connecting Exercise

Score(　　/16)
Self-Evaluation

≫ 서로 맞는 것을 연결하시오.

A 1~4 영어 단어와 우리말 뜻 연결하기

1 apply	•	• 대답하다, 대답, 응답
2 attract	•	• 끌다, 당기다
3 angle	•	• 낚시, 낚시하다, 얻으려 하다, 각도, 각, 꺾어지다
4 answer	•	• 지원하다, 적용하다

B 5~8 영어 단어와 영어 설명 연결하기

5 apply	•	• to fish with a hook and line
6 attract	•	• to draw by a physical force
7 angle	•	• to say or write in reply
8 answer	•	• to put to practical use

C 9~12 영어 단어와 동의어 연결하기

9 attract	•	• allure, draw, charm, fascinate
10 apply	•	• reply, respond, response, reaction
11 angle	•	• utilize, employ, use
12 answer	•	• fish, troll, bend

D 13~16 우리말 뜻과 영어 단어 연결하기

13 대답하다, 대답, 응답	•	• apply
14 낚시, 낚시하다, 얻으려 하다, 각도, 각, 꺾어지다	•	• answer
15 지원하다, 적용하다	•	• angle
16 끌다, 당기다	•	• attract

Test 2 Writing Exercise

Score(　　/12)
Self-Evaluation

Ⓐ 1~4 다음 단어에 맞는 뜻을 쓰시오.

1 answer ______________________

2 attract ______________________

3 angle ______________________

4 apply ______________________

Ⓑ 5~8 다음 뜻에 맞는 영어 단어와 영어 동의어, 영어 설명을 쓰시오.

5 낚시, 낚시하다, 얻으려 하다, 각도, 각, 꺾어지다

______________ ______________________

____

6 끌다, 당기다

______________ ______________________

____

7 대답하다, 대답, 응답

______________ ______________________

____

8 지원하다, 적용하다

______________ ______________________

____

Ⓒ 9~12 다음 영어 문장을 의미가 떠오를 때까지 소리 내어 읽어보시오. 2.5초 이내

9 The road angles to the right at right angle.

____

10 Scientists can apply a theory to a practical problem.

____

11 She answered that she was unable to join us.

____

12 The gravitational force of the earth attracts all objects.

____

Test 3 Imaging Exercise

➢ 다음 단어에 맞는 나만의 짧은 영어 설명을 써보자. (또는 그림을 그려보자.)

angle
[æŋgl]

answer
[ænsər]

apply
[əplái]

attract
[ətrǽkt]

➢ Month 05-DAY 11 영어 문장과 우리말

The road angles to the right at right angle.
길이 오른쪽으로 90도 직각으로 꺾어졌다.

She answered that she was unable to join us.
그녀는 우리와 함께할 수 없다고 대답했다.

Scientists can apply a theory to a practical problem.
과학자들은 실제 문제에 이론을 적용할 수 있습니다.

The gravitational force of the earth attracts all objects.
지구 중력은 모든 물체를 끌어당깁니다.

Vocabulary

➢ 음원을 들으면서 소리를 무조건 따라해 보시오. (빠르기 & 정확도/브레인 + 마우스 운동)

awake, awoke, awaken

to rouse from sleep

waken, wake up

깨우다, 깨어나다

The sound of birds awoke her in the morning.

batter

to hit heavily

beat, strike, knock, assault

난타하다, 강타하다

He was battered to death with a large stick.

bend

to form a curve, as by pushing or pulling

twist, bow, curve

구부리다

The lane bends to the right at the end.

bind, bound, bound

to tie or hold, as with a rope or cord

tie, hold, fasten, fix

묶다, 잡아매다

You have to bind your hair with a ribbon.

* 이미지는 구글에서 찾은 것으로, 단어와 이미지가 다를 수 있습니다. 'Test 3'에서 나만의 이미지를 그려볼 수 있습니다.

Test 1 Connecting Exercise

Score(/16)
Self-Evaluation

➢ 서로 맞는 것을 연결하시오.

A 1~4 영어 단어와 우리말 뜻 연결하기

1	bind, bound, bound	●	● 구부리다
2	awake, awoke, awaken	●	● 묶다, 잡아매다
3	bend	●	● 난타하다, 강타하다
4	batter	●	● 깨우다, 깨어나다

B 5~8 영어 단어와 영어 설명 연결하기

5	awake, awoke, awaken	●	● to tie or hold, as with a rope or cord
6	bend	●	● to hit heavily
7	batter	●	● to rouse from sleep
8	bind, bound, bound	●	● to form a curve, as by pushing or pulling

C 9~12 영어 단어와 동의어 연결하기

9	batter	●	● twist, bow, curve
10	bend	●	● beat, strike, knock, assault
11	bind, bound, bound	●	● tie, hold, fasten, fix
12	awake, awoke, awaken	●	● waken, wake up

D 13~16 우리말 뜻과 영어 단어 연결하기

13	구부리다	●	● batter
14	난타하다, 강타하다	●	● awake, awoke, awaken
15	묶다, 잡아매다	●	● bind, bound, bound
16	깨우다, 깨어나다	●	● bend

Test 2 Writing Exercise

Score(　　/12)
Self-Evaluation

Ⓐ 1~4 다음 단어에 맞는 뜻을 쓰시오.

1 bind, bound, bound ______

2 bend ______

3 batter ______

4 awake, awoke, awaken ______

Ⓑ 5~8 다음 뜻에 맞는 영어 단어와 영어 동의어, 영어 설명을 쓰시오.

5 깨우다, 깨어나다

______ ______

______

6 구부리다

______ ______

______

7 묶다, 잡아매다

______ ______

______

8 난타하다, 강타하다

______ ______

______

Ⓒ 9~12 다음 영어 문장을 의미가 떠오를 때까지 소리 내어 읽어보시오. 2.5초 이내

9 You have to bind your hair with a ribbon.

______

10 The sound of birds awoke her in the morning.

______

11 He was battered to death with a large stick.

______

12 The lane bends to the right at the end.

______

Test 3

➢ 다음 단어에 맞는 나만의 짧은 영어 설명을 써보자. (또는 그림을 그려보자.)

awake, awoke, awaken
[əwéik, əwóuk, əwóukən]

batter
[bǽtər]

bend
[bend]

bind, bound, bound
[baind, baund, baund]

➢ Month 05-DAY 12 영어 문장과 우리말

The sound of birds awoke her in the morning.
아침에 새 소리가 그녀를 깨웠습니다.

He was battered to death with a large stick.
그는 큰 막대기로 죽도록 맞았다.

The lane bends to the right at the end.
차선이 끝에서 오른쪽으로 구부러집니다.

You have to bind your hair with a ribbon.
당신의 머리카락을 리본으로 묶어야 합니다.

DAY 13 # Vocabulary

➢ **음원을 들으면서 소리를 무조건 따라해 보시오.** (빠르기&정확도/브레인+마우스 운동)

compete

to try to beat others in a contest

contend, fight, challenge, struggle

경쟁하다, 겨루다

We are competing against them in the next round.

contribute

to give (money, support, assistance, etc.)

give, help, serve, provide, supply

기여하다, 기부하다

Design faults in the airplane contributed to the tragedy.

control

to regulate or operate (a machine)

command, direct, rule, regulate

조종하다, 지배, 조정

She tried to control her husband in every way.

convince

to make (someone) agree, understand, or realize the truth of something

assure, persuade

확신시키다, 납득시키다

These experiences convinced me that it would be possible.

* 이미지는 구글에서 찾은 것으로, 단어와 이미지가 다를 수 있습니다. 'Test 3'에서 나만의 이미지를 그려볼 수 있습니다.

Test 1 Connecting Exercise

Score(　　/16)
Self-Evaluation

➢ 서로 맞는 것을 연결하시오.

Ⓐ 1~4 영어 단어와 우리말 뜻 연결하기

1 compete	•	• 조종하다, 지배, 조정
2 contribute	•	• 기여하다, 기부하다
3 control	•	• 경쟁하다, 겨루다
4 convince	•	• 확신시키다, 납득시키다

Ⓑ 5~8 영어 단어와 영어 설명 연결하기

5 control	•	• to try to beat others in a contest
6 contribute	•	• to make (someone) agree, understand, or realize the truth of something
7 compete	•	• to regulate or operate (a machine)
8 convince	•	• to give (money, support, assistance, etc.)

Ⓒ 9~12 영어 단어와 동의어 연결하기

9 control	•	• command, direct, rule, regulate
10 convince	•	• give, help, serve, provide, supply
11 compete	•	• assure, persuade
12 contribute	•	• contend, fight, challenge, struggle

Ⓓ 13~16 우리말 뜻과 영어 단어 연결하기

13 경쟁하다, 겨루다	•	• convince
14 기여하다, 기부하다	•	• compete
15 조종하다, 지배, 조정	•	• contribute
16 확신시키다, 납득시키다	•	• control

Test 2 Writing Exercise

Score(/12)
Self-Evaluation

A 1~4 다음 단어에 맞는 뜻을 쓰시오.

1 convince ______________________

2 compete ______________________

3 contribute ______________________

4 control ______________________

B 5~8 다음 뜻에 맞는 영어 단어와 영어 동의어, 영어 설명을 쓰시오.

5 확신시키다, 납득시키다

______________ ______________________

____

6 경쟁하다, 겨루다

______________ ______________________

____

7 조종하다, 지배, 조정

______________ ______________________

____

8 기여하다, 기부하다

______________ ______________________

____

C 9~12 다음 영어 문장을 의미가 떠오를 때까지 소리 내어 읽어보시오. 2.5초 이내

9 Design faults in the airplane contributed to the tragedy.

____

10 We are competing against them in the next round.

____

11 She tried to control her husband in every way.

____

12 These experiences convinced me that it would be possible.

____

Test 3 Imaging Exercise

➢ 다음 단어에 맞는 나만의 짧은 영어 설명을 써보자. (또는 그림을 그려보자.)

compete
[kəmpíːt]

contribute
[kəntríbjuːt]

control
[kəntróul]

convince
[kənvíns]

➢ Month 05-DAY 13 영어 문장과 우리말

We are competing against them in the next round.
다음 라운드에 우리는 그들과 겨루게 됩니다.

Design faults in the airplane contributed to the tragedy.
비행기의 설계 결함이 비극에 일조(기여)했습니다.

She tried to control her husband in every way.
그녀는 모든 면에서 남편을 통제하려고 했습니다.

These experiences convinced me that it would be possible.
이러한 경험들이 나에게 그것이 가능할 것이라는 확신을 주었습니다.

DAY 14 Vocabulary

➢ **음원을 들으면서 소리를 무조건 따라해 보시오.** (빠르기&정확도/브레인+마우스 운동)

defeat

to overcome in a contest

vanquish, beat, conquer

이기다, 물리치다

General Yi Sun-sin defeated the enemy everytime in every battle.

dip

to plunge briefly into a liquid, as in order to wet, coat, or saturate

plunge, immerse, bathe, rinse

담그다, 잠기다, 퍼내다, 떠내다, 연루시키다

She dips the beef into the sauce before cooking.

examine

to observe carefully

analyse, analyze, study, inspect

시험하다, 검사하다, 조사하다

The immigration officer examined her passport and stamped it.

explode

to burst or cause to burst

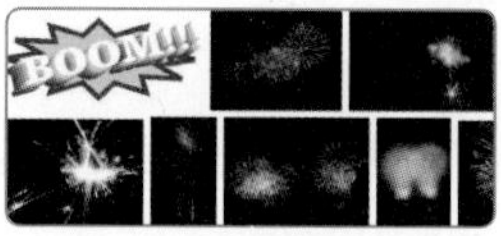

blast, burst, fire

터지다, 폭발하다

The bomb exploded as soon as they had left.

* 이미지는 구글에서 찾은 것으로, 단어와 이미지가 다를 수 있습니다. 'Test 3'에서 나만의 이미지를 그려볼 수 있습니다.

Test 1 Connecting Exercise

Score(　　/16)
Self-Evaluation

➢ 서로 맞는 것을 연결하시오.

Ⓐ 1~4 영어 단어와 우리말 뜻 연결하기

1 defeat	•	• 이기다, 물리치다
2 explode	•	• 터지다, 폭발하다
3 dip	•	• 담그다, 잠기다, 퍼내다, 떠내다, 연루시키다
4 examine	•	• 시험하다, 검사하다, 조사하다

Ⓑ 5~8 영어 단어와 영어 설명 연결하기

5 explode	•	• to burst or cause to burst
6 dip	•	• to plunge briefly into a liquid, as in order to wet, coat, or saturate
7 examine	•	• to overcome in a contest
8 defeat	•	• to observe carefully

Ⓒ 9~12 영어 단어와 동의어 연결하기

9 examine	•	• analyse, analyze, study, inspect
10 explode	•	• blast, burst, fire
11 dip	•	• plunge, immerse, bathe, rinse
12 defeat	•	• vanquish, beat, conquer

Ⓓ 13~16 우리말 뜻과 영어 단어 연결하기

13 터지다, 폭발하다	•	• explode
14 이기다, 물리치다	•	• defeat
15 시험하다, 검사하다, 조사하다	•	• dip
16 담그다, 잠기다, 퍼내다, 떠내다, 연루시키다	•	• examine

Test 2 Writing Exercise

Score(/12)
Self-Evaluation

A 1~4 다음 단어에 맞는 뜻을 쓰시오.

1 defeat ______________________

2 dip ______________________

3 explode ______________________

4 examine ______________________

B 5~8 다음 뜻에 맞는 영어 단어와 영어 동의어, 영어 설명을 쓰시오.

5 이기다, 물리치다

______________ ______________________

____

6 시험하다, 검사하다, 조사하다

______________ ______________________

____

7 담그다, 잠기다, 퍼내다, 떠내다, 연루시키다

______________ ______________________

____

8 터지다, 폭발하다

______________ ______________________

____

C 9~12 다음 영어 문장을 의미가 떠오를 때까지 소리 내어 읽어보시오. 2.5초 이내

9 She dips the beef into the sauce before cooking.

____

10 General Yi Sun-sin defeated the enemy everytime in every battle.

____

11 The bomb exploded as soon as they had left.

____

12 The immigration officer examined her passport and stamped it.

____

Test 3 Imaging Exercise

➢ 다음 단어에 맞는 나만의 짧은 영어 설명을 써보자. (또는 그림을 그려보자.)

defeat
[difíːt]

dip
[dip]

examine
[igzǽmin]

explode
[iksplóud]

➢ Month 05-DAY 14 영어 문장과 우리말

General Yi Sun-sin defeated the enemy everytime in every battle.
이순신 장군은 모든 전투에서 매번 적을 물리쳤습니다.

She dips the beef into the sauce before cooking.
그녀는 요리하기 전에 소고기를 소스에 담급니다.

The immigration officer examined her passport and stamped it.
입국 심사관이 그녀의 여권을 검사하고 스탬프를 찍어주었습니다.

The bomb exploded as soon as they had left.
그들이 떠나자마자 폭탄이 터졌습니다.

DAY 15 Vocabulary

➢ 음원을 들으면서 소리를 무조건 따라해 보시오. (빠르기 & 정확도/브레인 + 마우스 운동)

flash

to cause to burst into flame

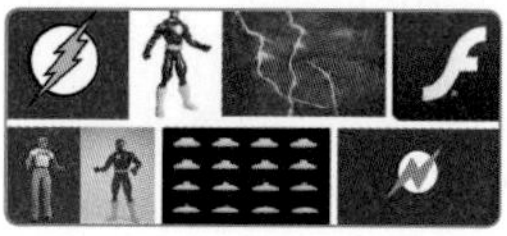

sparkle, glint, glitter, glisten

번쩍이다, 깜박이다, 섬광, 플래시

The LEDs lights are flashing as a warning sign.

flip

to toss, as with a snap of a finger and thumb

flick, cast, throw, tumble

가볍게 던지다, 손가락으로 튀기다, 뒤집다, 뒤집히다

I flipped a cigarette butt out of the window.

generate

to produce or bring into being

produce, create, make, form

일으키다, 발생시키다, 만들어 내다

The minister said the reforms would generate new jobs.

hope

to have a wish

wish, believe, expect, anticipate

바라다, 희망, 희망하다

I hope you will enjoy your stay in Seoul.

* 이미지는 구글에서 찾은 것으로, 단어와 이미지가 다를 수 있습니다. 'Test 3'에서 나만의 이미지를 그려볼 수 있습니다.

Test 1 Connecting Exercise

Score(/16)
Self-Evaluation

➢ 서로 맞는 것을 연결하시오.

Ⓐ 1~4 영어 단어와 우리말 뜻 연결하기

1 generate	•	• 바라다, 희망, 희망하다
2 flip	•	• 가볍게 던지다, 손가락으로 튀기다, 뒤집다, 뒤집히다
3 flash	•	• 번쩍이다, 깜박이다, 섬광, 플래시
4 hope	•	• 일으키다, 발생시키다, 만들어 내다

Ⓑ 5~8 영어 단어와 영어 설명 연결하기

5 flash	•	• to toss, as with a snap of a finger and thumb
6 generate	•	• to cause to burst into flame
7 flip	•	• to produce or bring into being
8 hope	•	• to have a wish

Ⓒ 9~12 영어 단어와 동의어 연결하기

9 generate	•	• wish, believe, expect, anticipate
10 flip	•	• sparkle, glint, glitter, glisten
11 hope	•	• produce, create, make, form
12 flash	•	• flick, cast, throw, tumble

Ⓓ 13~16 우리말 뜻과 영어 단어 연결하기

13 가볍게 던지다, 손가락으로 튀기다, 뒤집다, 뒤집히다	•	• generate
14 바라다, 희망, 희망하다	•	• flip
15 번쩍이다, 깜박이다, 섬광, 플래시	•	• flash
16 일으키다, 발생시키다, 만들어 내다	•	• hope

Test 2 Writing Exercise

Score(/12)
Self-Evaluation

Ⓐ 1~4 다음 단어에 맞는 뜻을 쓰시오.

1 hope ______________________

2 flash ______________________

3 flip ______________________

4 generate ______________________

Ⓑ 5~8 다음 뜻에 맞는 영어 단어와 영어 동의어, 영어 설명을 쓰시오.

5 가볍게 던지다, 손가락으로 튀기다, 뒤집다, 뒤집히다

______________ ______________________

____

6 번쩍이다, 깜박이다, 섬광, 플래시

______________ ______________________

____

7 일으키다, 발생시키다, 만들어 내다

______________ ______________________

____

8 바라다, 희망, 희망하다

______________ ______________________

____

Ⓒ 9~12 다음 영어 문장을 의미가 떠오를 때까지 소리 내어 읽어보시오. 2.5초 이내

9 I hope you will enjoy your stay in Seoul.

____

10 I flipped a cigarette butt out of the window.

____

11 The minister said the reforms would generate new jobs.

____

12 The LEDs lights are flashing as a warning sign.

____

Test 3 Imaging Exercise

➢ 다음 단어에 맞는 나만의 짧은 영어 설명을 써보자. (또는 그림을 그려보자.)

flash
[flæʃ]

flip
[flip]

generate
[dʒénərèit]

hope
[houp]

➢ Month 05-DAY 15 영어 문장과 우리말

The LEDs lights are flashing as a warning sign.
경고의 표시로 LED 빛이 깜빡이고 있습니다.

I flipped a cigarette butt out of the window.
나는 창문 밖으로 담배꽁초를 툭 튕겨 버렸다.

The minister said the reforms would generate new jobs.
장관은 개혁이 새로운 일자리를 창출할 것이라고 말했습니다.

I hope you will enjoy your stay in Seoul.
서울에서 즐거운 시간이 되시길 바랍니다.

DAY 16 Vocabulary

➢ 음원을 들으면서 소리를 무조건 따라해 보시오. (빠르기&정확도/브레인+마우스 운동)

imprison

to put in prison or to put in jail

confine, detain, constrain, incarcerate

감옥에 갇히다, 투옥되다

He was imprisoned for twenty years for his crimes.

include

to contain or take in as a part

contain, involve, comprise

포함하다

The list includes the names of many famous writers.

increase

to become greater or larger

raise, extend, boost, expand

올리다, 늘리다, 증가시키다, 증가하다, 증가, 늘림

The company has increased the price of its products.

interpret

to explain the meaning of

translate, convert, paraphrase

해석하다, 통역하다

Robots can not interpret natural languages better than humans.

* 이미지는 구글에서 찾은 것으로, 단어와 이미지가 다를 수 있습니다. 'Test 3'에서 나만의 이미지를 그려볼 수 있습니다.

Test 1 Connecting Exercise

Score(/16)
Self-Evaluation

➢ 서로 맞는 것을 연결하시오.

Ⓐ 1~4 영어 단어와 우리말 뜻 연결하기

1 include	•	• 감옥에 갇히다, 투옥되다
2 increase	•	• 올리다, 늘리다, 증가시키다, 증가하다, 증가, 늘림
3 interpret	•	• 포함하다
4 imprison	•	• 해석하다, 통역하다

Ⓑ 5~8 영어 단어와 영어 설명 연결하기

5 include	•	• to explain the meaning of
6 imprison	•	• to become greater or larger
7 increase	•	• to put in prison or to put in jail
8 interpret	•	• to contain or take in as a part

Ⓒ 9~12 영어 단어와 동의어 연결하기

9 interpret	•	• raise, extend, boost, expand
10 increase	•	• confine, detain, constrain, incarcerate
11 imprison	•	• contain, involve, comprise
12 include	•	• translate, convert, paraphrase

Ⓓ 13~16 우리말 뜻과 영어 단어 연결하기

13 포함하다	•	• include
14 해석하다, 통역하다	•	• increase
15 올리다, 늘리다, 증가시키다, 증가하다, 증가, 늘림	•	• imprison
16 감옥에 갇히다, 투옥되다	•	• interpret

Test 2 Writing Exercise

Score(/12)
Self-Evaluation

Ⓐ 1~4 다음 단어에 맞는 뜻을 쓰시오.

1 include ____________________

2 interpret ____________________

3 imprison ____________________

4 increase ____________________

Ⓑ 5~8 다음 뜻에 맞는 영어 단어와 영어 동의어, 영어 설명을 쓰시오.

5 올리다, 늘리다, 증가시키다, 증가하다, 증가, 늘림

__________ ____________________

____

6 포함하다

__________ ____________________

____

7 해석하다, 통역하다

__________ ____________________

____

8 감옥에 갇히다, 투옥되다

__________ ____________________

____

Ⓒ 9~12 다음 영어 문장을 의미가 떠오를 때까지 소리 내어 읽어보시오. 2.5초 이내

9 He was imprisoned for twenty years for his crimes.

____

10 The list includes the names of many famous writers.

____

11 The company has increased the price of its products.

____

12 Robots can not interpret natural languages better than humans.

____

Test 3 Imaging Exercise

➤ 다음 단어에 맞는 나만의 짧은 영어 설명을 써보자. (또는 그림을 그려보자.)

imprison
[imprízn]

include
[inklú:d]

increase
[inkrí:s]

interpret
[intə́:rprit]

➤ Month 05-DAY 16 영어 문장과 우리말

He was imprisoned for twenty years for his crimes.
그는 그의 범죄로 인해 20년 동안 감옥에 갇혔습니다.

The list includes the names of many famous writers.
그 명단은(리스트는) 많은 유명한 작가들을 싣고 있습니다.

The company has increased the price of its products.
그 회사는 제품의 값을 올렸습니다.

Robots can not interpret natural languages better than humans.
로봇은 자연언어를 사람들보다 더 잘 해석할 수 없습니다.

Vocabulary

➢ **음원을 들으면서 소리를 무조건 따라해 보시오.** (빠르기&정확도/브레인+마우스 운동)

invent

to create or devise (new ideas, machines, etc)

create, devise, design, produce

발명하다, 고안하다, 개발하다, 꾸며내다

Apple Inc. invented the first smartphone in early 2007.

maintain

to continue or retain

continue, keep, retain, sustain

유지하다, 지속하다, 주장하다

To maintain good health, we need to exercise regularly.

mend

to make repairs

repair, fix, reform, correct

수선하다, 고치다, 수선, 고침

She mended clothes by needlework with needle and thread.

multiply

to combine (two numbers or quantities) by multiplication

multiplication, increase

곱하다, 증가시키다

If you multiply 4 by 5, you get 20.

* 이미지는 구글에서 찾은 것으로, 단어와 이미지가 다를 수 있습니다. 'Test 3'에서 나만의 이미지를 그려볼 수 있습니다.

Test 1 Connecting Exercise

Score(/16)
Self-Evaluation

➢ 서로 맞는 것을 연결하시오.

Ⓐ 1~4 영어 단어와 우리말 뜻 연결하기

1 multiply	•	• 발명하다, 고안하다, 개발하다, 꾸며내다
2 invent	•	• 유지하다, 지속하다, 주장하다
3 mend	•	• 곱하다, 증가시키다
4 maintain	•	• 수선하다, 고치다, 수선, 고침

Ⓑ 5~8 영어 단어와 영어 설명 연결하기

5 invent	•	• to combine (two numbers or quantities) by multiplication
6 maintain	•	• to make repairs
7 multiply	•	• to continue or retain
8 mend	•	• to create or devise (new ideas, machines, etc)

Ⓒ 9~12 영어 단어와 동의어 연결하기

9 invent	•	• multiplication, increase
10 mend	•	• create, devise, design, produce
11 multiply	•	• continue, keep, retain, sustain
12 maintain	•	• repair, fix, reform, correct

Ⓓ 13~16 우리말 뜻과 영어 단어 연결하기

13 수선하다, 고치다, 수선, 고침	•	• invent
14 곱하다, 증가시키다	•	• multiply
15 발명하다, 고안하다, 개발하다, 꾸며내다	•	• mend
16 유지하다, 지속하다, 주장하다	•	• maintain

Test 2 Writing Exercise

Score(/12)
Self-Evaluation

A 1~4 다음 단어에 맞는 뜻을 쓰시오.

1 maintain ______

2 multiply ______

3 mend ______

4 invent ______

B 5~8 다음 뜻에 맞는 영어 단어와 영어 동의어, 영어 설명을 쓰시오.

5 발명하다, 고안하다, 개발하다, 꾸며내다

______ ______

______

6 유지하다, 지속하다, 주장하다

______ ______

______

7 수선하다, 고치다, 수선, 고침

______ ______

______

8 곱하다, 증가시키다

______ ______

______

C 9~12 다음 영어 문장을 의미가 떠오를 때까지 소리 내어 읽어보시오. 2.5초 이내

9 She mended clothes by needlework with needle and thread.

______

10 To maintain good health, we need to exercise regularly.

______

11 If you multiply 4 by 5, you get 20.

______

12 Apple Inc. invented the first smartphone in early 2007.

______

Test 3 Imaging Exercise

➢ 다음 단어에 맞는 나만의 짧은 영어 설명을 써보자. (또는 그림을 그려보자.)

invent
[invént]

maintain
[meintéin]

mend
[mend]

multiply
[mʌltəplài]

➢ Month 05-DAY 17 영어 문장과 우리말

Apple Inc. invented the first smartphone in early 2007.
애플사가 2007년에 최초의 스마트폰을 개발했습니다.

To maintain good health, we need to exercise regularly.
건강을 유지하기 위하여 우리는 규칙적으로 운동을 해야 합니다.

She mended clothes by needlework with needle and thread.
그녀는 바늘과 실로 바느질하여 옷을 수선하였습니다.

If you multiply 4 by 5, you get 20.
4에 5를 곱하면 20이 됩니다.

DAY 18 Vocabulary

➢ 음원을 들으면서 소리를 무조건 따라해 보시오. (빠르기&정확도/브레인+마우스 운동)

number

to call off numbers

count, numerate, enumerate

수를 세다, 수, 숫자

I can number from one to trillion in english.

outwit

to get the better of by cunning or ingenuity

outsmart, get the better of

한술 더 떠 속이다, 한 수 위다

You must outwit your opponent to win at chess.

overhear

to hear something without the speaker's awareness or intent

hear, listen to

우연히 듣다

I overheard two people talking in the next room.

overview

A broad, comprehensive view

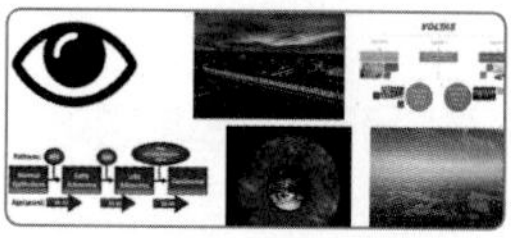

survey, summary, review

개관, 전체를 봄, 요약하여 봄

This book provides a broad overview of American history.

* 이미지는 구글에서 찾은 것으로, 단어와 이미지가 다를 수 있습니다. 'Test 3'에서 나만의 이미지를 그려볼 수 있습니다.

Test 1 Connecting Exercise

Score(　　/16)
Self-Evaluation

≫ 서로 맞는 것을 연결하시오.

Ⓐ 1~4 영어 단어와 우리말 뜻 연결하기

1 number	●	● 우연히 듣다
2 overview	●	● 개관, 전체를 봄, 요약하여 봄
3 overhear	●	● 한술 더 떠 속이다, 한 수 위다
4 outwit	●	● 수를 세다, 수, 숫자

Ⓑ 5~8 영어 단어와 영어 설명 연결하기

5 number	●	● A broad, comprehensive view
6 outwit	●	● to hear something without the speaker's awareness or intent
7 overhear	●	● to call off numbers
8 overview	●	● to get the better of by cunning or ingenuity

Ⓒ 9~12 영어 단어와 동의어 연결하기

9 number	●	● count, numerate, enumerate
10 outwit	●	● survey, summary, review
11 overhear	●	● hear, listen to
12 overview	●	● outsmart, get the better of

Ⓓ 13~16 우리말 뜻과 영어 단어 연결하기

13 개관, 전체를 봄, 요약하여 봄	●	● outwit
14 한술 더 떠 속이다, 한 수 위다	●	● overview
15 우연히 듣다	●	● overhear
16 수를 세다, 수, 숫자	●	● number

Test 2 Writing Exercise

Score(　　/12)
Self-Evaluation

Ⓐ 1~4 다음 단어에 맞는 뜻을 쓰시오.

1 overview ____________________

2 overhear ____________________

3 outwit ____________________

4 number ____________________

Ⓑ 5~8 다음 뜻에 맞는 영어 단어와 영어 동의어, 영어 설명을 쓰시오.

5 우연히 듣다

__________ ____________________

____

6 수를 세다, 수, 숫자

__________ ____________________

____

7 한술 더 떠 속이다, 한 수 위다

__________ ____________________

____

8 개관, 전체를 봄, 요약하여 봄

__________ ____________________

____

Ⓒ 9~12 다음 영어 문장을 의미가 떠오를 때까지 소리 내어 읽어보시오. 2.5초 이내

9 You must outwit your opponent to win at chess.

____

10 This book provides a broad overview of American history.

____

11 I overheard two people talking in the next room.

____

12 I can number from one to trillion in english.

____

Test 3 Imaging Exercise

➢ 다음 단어에 맞는 나만의 짧은 영어 설명을 써보자. (또는 그림을 그려보자.)

number
[nʌmbər]

outwit
[àutwít]

overhear
[ou'vərhi'r]

overview
[ou'vərvju,]

➢ Month 05-DAY 18 영어 문장과 우리말

I can number from one to trillion in english.
나는 일부터 조까지 영어로 셀 수 있습니다.

You must outwit your opponent to win at chess.
체스에서 이기려면 상대방보다 한 수 위로 속여야 합니다.

I overheard two people talking in the next room.
나는 옆방에서 두 사람이 나누는 얘기를 우연히 들었습니다.

This book provides a broad overview of American history.
이 책은 미국 역사를 개괄적으로 보여주는 책입니다.

Vocabulary

➢ 음원을 들으면서 소리를 무조건 따라해 보시오. (빠르기 & 정확도/브레인 + 마우스 운동)

parade

to take part in a parade

march, process

행진하다, 과시하다, 행렬, 행진

More than five thousand people paraded down the street.

perform

to begin and do

do, enact, carry out

하다, 행하다, 공연하다

Each part of the engine performs a different function.

plead

to appeal earnestly

beg, appeal, solicit

탄원하다, 호소하다, 간청하다

I pleaded and pleaded but it was no use.

promise

to make a promise of or to give an assurance of

guarantee, pledge, swear

약속하다, 약속

If you make a promise, you should keep it.

* 이미지는 구글에서 찾은 것으로, 단어와 이미지가 다를 수 있습니다. 'Test 3'에서 나만의 이미지를 그려볼 수 있습니다.

Test 1 Connecting Exercise

Score(/16)
Self-Evaluation

➢ 서로 맞는 것을 연결하시오.

Ⓐ 1~4 영어 단어와 우리말 뜻 연결하기

1 promise •	• 약속하다, 약속
2 parade •	• 행진하다, 과시하다, 행렬, 행진
3 perform •	• 하다, 행하다, 공연하다
4 plead •	• 탄원하다, 호소하다, 간청하다

Ⓑ 5~8 영어 단어와 영어 설명 연결하기

5 promise •	• to take part in a parade
6 perform •	• to make a promise of or to give an assurance of
7 parade •	• to begin and do
8 plead •	• to appeal earnestly

Ⓒ 9~12 영어 단어와 동의어 연결하기

9 promise •	• beg, appeal, solicit
10 parade •	• do, enact, carry out
11 perform •	• march, process
12 plead •	• guarantee, pledge, swear

Ⓓ 13~16 우리말 뜻과 영어 단어 연결하기

13 하다, 행하다, 공연하다 •	• plead
14 약속하다, 약속 •	• promise
15 탄원하다, 호소하다, 간청하다 •	• parade
16 행진하다, 과시하다, 행렬, 행진 •	• perform

Test 2 Writing Exercise

Score(/12)
Self-Evaluation

Ⓐ 1~4 다음 단어에 맞는 뜻을 쓰시오.

1 promise ______

2 perform ______

3 parade ______

4 plead ______

Ⓑ 5~8 다음 뜻에 맞는 영어 단어와 영어 동의어, 영어 설명을 쓰시오.

5 탄원하다, 호소하다, 간청하다

______ ______

______

6 약속하다, 약속

______ ______

______

7 하다, 행하다, 공연하다

______ ______

______

8 행진하다, 과시하다, 행렬, 행진

______ ______

______

Ⓒ 9~12 다음 영어 문장을 의미가 떠오를 때까지 소리 내어 읽어보시오. 2.5초 이내

9 Each part of the engine performs a different function.

______

10 More than five thousand people paraded down the street.

______

11 I pleaded and pleaded but it was no use.

______

12 If you make a promise, you should keep it.

______

Test 3 Imaging Exercise

➢ 다음 단어에 맞는 나만의 짧은 영어 설명을 써보자. (또는 그림을 그려보자.)

parade
[pəréid]

perform
[pərfɔ́ːrm]

plead
[pliːd]

promise
[prámis]

➢ Month 05-DAY 19 영어 문장과 우리말

More than five thousand people paraded down the street.
오천 명이 넘는 사람들이 거리를 행진했습니다.

Each part of the engine performs a different function.
각 파트의 엔진이 다른 기능을 수행합니다.

I pleaded and pleaded but it was no use.
나는 빌고 또 빌었지만 소용없었습니다.

If you make a promise, you should keep it.
약속하면 지켜야 합니다.

DAY 20 Vocabulary

➢ **음원을 들으면서 소리를 무조건 따라해 보시오.** (빠르기 & 정확도/브레인 + 마우스 운동)

purr

to make or utter a soft vibrant sound

whir, whiz

가볍게 떠는 소리가 나다,
(동물들의) 카르르 하는 소리

This motor fan purred as if a cat purred.

quicken

to make more rapid

speed, accelerate, vitalize

빠르게 하다, 빨라지다,
활기 띠게 하다, 활기차지다

She quickened her pace, and then her heartbeat quickened.

rely

to be dependent (on)

depend, trust

의지하다, 믿다

You should only rely on your belief and wisdom.

respond

to make a reply, or to act in return

answer, reply, react

응답하다, 반응하다

He always responds to my email by phone call.

* 이미지는 구글에서 찾은 것으로, 단어와 이미지가 다를 수 있습니다. 'Test 3'에서 나만의 이미지를 그려볼 수 있습니다.

Test 1 Connecting Exercise

Score(　　/16)
Self-Evaluation

➢ 서로 맞는 것을 연결하시오.

Ⓐ 1~4 영어 단어와 우리말 뜻 연결하기

1 purr	•	• 빠르게 하다, 빨라지다, 활기 띠게 하다, 활기차지다
2 rely	•	• 의지하다, 믿다
3 quicken	•	• 가볍게 떠는 소리가 나다, (동물들의) 카르르 하는 소리
4 respond	•	• 응답하다, 반응하다

Ⓑ 5~8 영어 단어와 영어 설명 연결하기

5 rely	•	• to make a reply, or to act in return
6 quicken	•	• to make more rapid
7 respond	•	• to make or utter a soft vibrant sound
8 purr	•	• to be dependent (on)

Ⓒ 9~12 영어 단어와 동의어 연결하기

9 quicken	•	• speed, accelerate, vitalize
10 respond	•	• depend, trust
11 rely	•	• whir, whiz
12 purr	•	• answer, reply, react

Ⓓ 13~16 우리말 뜻과 영어 단어 연결하기

13 응답하다, 반응하다	•	• purr
14 의지하다, 믿다	•	• rely
15 빠르게 하다, 빨라지다, 활기 띠게 하다, 활기차지다	•	• quicken
16 가볍게 떠는 소리가 나다, (동물들의) 카르르 하는 소리	•	• respond

Test 2 Writing Exercise

Score(/12)
Self-Evaluation

Ⓐ 1~4 다음 단어에 맞는 뜻을 쓰시오.

1 quicken ____________________

2 purr ____________________

3 respond ____________________

4 rely ____________________

Ⓑ 5~8 다음 뜻에 맞는 영어 단어와 영어 동의어, 영어 설명을 쓰시오.

5 응답하다, 반응하다

__________ ____________________

____

6 의지하다, 믿다

__________ ____________________

____

7 빠르게 하다, 빨라지다, 활기 띠게 하다, 활기차지다

__________ ____________________

____

8 가볍게 떠는 소리가 나다, (동물들의) 카르르 하는 소리

__________ ____________________

____

Ⓒ 9~12 다음 영어 문장을 의미가 떠오를 때까지 소리 내어 읽어보시오. 2.5초 이내

9 This motor fan purred as if a cat purred.

____

10 You should only rely on your belief and wisdom.

____

11 He always responds to my email by phone call.

____

12 She quickened her pace, and then her heartbeat quickened.

____

Test 3 Imaging Exercise

➢ 다음 단어에 맞는 나만의 짧은 영어 설명을 써보자. (또는 그림을 그려보자.)

purr
[pəːr]

quicken
[kwíkən]

rely
[rilái]

respond
[rispánd]

➢ Month 05-DAY 20 영어 문장과 우리말

This motor fan purred as if a cat purred.
이 선풍기는 마치 고양이가 우는 것 같이 카르르 하는 진동소리를 낸다.

She quickened her pace, and then her heartbeat quickened.
그녀는 발걸음을 빨리했고, 심장박동이 빨라졌습니다.

You should only rely on your belief and wisdom.
당신은 오직 당신의 믿음과 지혜만을 의지해야 합니다.

He always responds to my email by phone call.
그는 나의 이메일에 항상 전화로 응답합니다.

Month 06 Verbs

- Day 01 save, scold, search, shrug
- Day 02 stampede, starve, tie, waste
- Day 03 whistle, wish, advertise, burst
- Day 04 clap, dig, equip, fade
- Day 05 flee, frown, gasp, groan
- Day 06 guard, guide, hesitate, log
- Day 07 mean, measure, necessitate, obtain
- Day 08 overcome, peek, raise, rob
- Day 09 scoop, scribble, shine, sort
- Day 10 stamp, wake, bite, bray
- Day 11 cure, describe, devote, discriminate
- Day 12 display, drop, fold, freeze
- Day 13 graduate, hit, intimate, knit
- Day 14 land, lie, match, overthrow
- Day 15 protect, provide, retain, saw
- Day 16 sell, sign, spy, stammer
- Day 17 start, step, threaten, belong
- Day 18 compose, crow, direct, dissolve
- Day 19 enlist, fix, foretell, hide
- Day 20 immigrate, leap, load, murder

DAY 01 Vocabulary

➢ 음원을 들으면서 소리를 무조건 따라해 보시오. (빠르기&정확도/브레인+마우스 운동)

save

to rescue from harm, danger, or loss

rescue, extricate, protect, guard

(위험으로부터) 구하다, 살리다, (돈을) 저축하다

The rescuer saved the victims of a railroad accident.

scold

to express harsh or angry disapproval to someone

reprimand, rebuke, blame

꾸짖다

She scolded the child for coming home so late.

search

to look through thoroughly in order to find someone or something

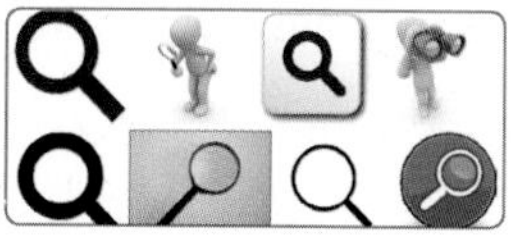

inspect, investigate, explore, probe

찾다, 수색하다, 수색, 탐색

I was searching for the right words to say.

shrug

to raise the shoulders, especially as a gesture of doubt, disdain, or indifference

gesticulate, gesture

어깨를 으쓱하다

When I asked him, he just shrugged his shoulders.

* 이미지는 구글에서 찾은 것으로, 단어와 이미지가 다를 수 있습니다. 'Test 3'에서 나만의 이미지를 그려볼 수 있습니다.

Test 1 Connecting Exercise

Score(/16)
Self-Evaluation

➢ 서로 맞는 것을 연결하시오.

A 1~4 영어 단어와 우리말 뜻 연결하기

1 scold	●	● 꾸짖다
2 save	●	● (위험으로부터) 구하다, 살리다, (돈을) 저축하다
3 search	●	● 찾다, 수색하다, 수색, 탐색
4 shrug	●	● 어깨를 으쓱하다

B 5~8 영어 단어와 영어 설명 연결하기

5 save	●	● to express harsh or angry disapproval to someone
6 search	●	● to look through thoroughly in order to find someone or something
7 scold	●	● to raise the shoulders, especially as a gesture of doubt, disdain, or indifference
8 shrug	●	● to rescue from harm, danger, or loss

C 9~12 영어 단어와 동의어 연결하기

9 scold	●	● reprimand, rebuke, blame
10 save	●	● inspect, investigate, explore, probe
11 shrug	●	● rescue, extricate, protect, guard
12 search	●	● gesticulate, gesture

D 13~16 우리말 뜻과 영어 단어 연결하기

13 찾다, 수색하다, 수색, 탐색	●	● save
14 (위험으로부터) 구하다, 살리다, (돈을) 저축하다	●	● shrug
15 어깨를 으쓱하다	●	● search
16 꾸짖다	●	● scold

Test 2 Writing Exercise

Score(/12)
Self-Evaluation

Ⓐ 1~4 다음 단어에 맞는 뜻을 쓰시오.

1 scold ______

2 search ______

3 save ______

4 shrug ______

Ⓑ 5~8 다음 뜻에 맞는 영어 단어와 영어 동의어, 영어 설명을 쓰시오.

5 어깨를 으쓱하다

______ ______

______

6 (위험으로부터) 구하다, 살리다, (돈을) 저축하다

______ ______

______

7 찾다, 수색하다, 수색, 탐색

______ ______

______

8 꾸짖다

______ ______

______

Ⓒ 9~12 다음 영어 문장을 의미가 떠오를 때까지 소리 내어 읽어보시오. 2.5초 이내

9 The rescuer saved the victims of a railroad accident.

______

10 She scolded the child for coming home so late.

______

11 I was searching for the right words to say.

______

12 When I asked him, he just shrugged his shoulders.

______

Test 3 Imaging Exercise

➢ 다음 단어에 맞는 나만의 짧은 영어 설명을 써보자. (또는 그림을 그려보자.)

save
[seiv]

scold
[skould]

search
[səːrʧ]

shrug
[ʃrʌg]

➢ Month 06-DAY 01 영어 문장과 우리말

The rescuer saved the victims of a railroad accident.
구조 대원이 철도 사고의 희생자들을 구해 냈습니다.

She scolded the child for coming home so late.
그녀는 아이가 너무 늦게 왔다고 꾸짖었습니다.

I was searching for the right words to say.
나는 해야 할 적절한 말을 찾고 있었습니다.

When I asked him, he just shrugged his shoulders.
내가 그에게 물었을 때 그는 단지 어깨를 으쓱했습니다.

➢ 음원을 들으면서 소리를 무조건 따라해 보시오. (빠르기&정확도/브레인+마우스 운동)

stampede

to flee or rush in a stampede

rush, dash

우르르 달아나다,
앞을 다투어 달아나다

The crowd stampeded and many were crushed or trampled.

starve

to suffer or die from extreme lack of food

famish, hunger

굶주리다, 굶어 죽다

Many people are starving to death in the world.

tie

to fasten or be fastened with string, thread, etc

bind, fasten, join, unite

묶다, 잡아매다, 넥타이

I tied the ends of the plastic bag together.

waste

to use, consume, spend, or expend thoughtlessly or carelessly

lavish, squander, dissipate

(조심 없이, 생각 없이) 소비하다,
낭비하다, 써버리다

To waste natural resources is a waste of energy.

* 이미지는 구글에서 찾은 것으로, 단어와 이미지가 다를 수 있습니다. 'Test 3'에서 나만의 이미지를 그려볼 수 있습니다.

Test 1 Connecting Exercise

Score(/16)
Self-Evaluation

➢ 서로 맞는 것을 연결하시오.

A 1~4 영어 단어와 우리말 뜻 연결하기

1 waste	•	• 굶주리다, 굶어 죽다
2 starve	•	• 묶다, 잡아매다, 넥타이
3 tie	•	• (조심 없이, 생각 없이) 소비하다, 낭비하다, 써버리다
4 stampede	•	• 우르르 달아나다, 앞을 다투어 달아나다

B 5~8 영어 단어와 영어 설명 연결하기

5 stampede	•	• to suffer or die from extreme lack of food
6 waste	•	• to flee or rush in a stampede
7 starve	•	• to use, consume, spend, or expend thoughtlessly or carelessly
8 tie	•	• to fasten or be fastened with string, thread, etc

C 9~12 영어 단어와 동의어 연결하기

9 stampede	•	• famish, hunger
10 waste	•	• rush, dash
11 starve	•	• bind, fasten, join, unite
12 tie	•	• lavish, squander, dissipate

D 13~16 우리말 뜻과 영어 단어 연결하기

13 굶주리다, 굶어 죽다	•	• waste
14 묶다, 잡아매다, 넥타이	•	• tie
15 우르르 달아나다, 앞을 다투어 달아나다	•	• starve
16 (조심 없이, 생각 없이) 소비하다, 낭비하다, 써버리다	•	• stampede

Test 2 Writing Exercise

Score(/12)
Self-Evaluation

A 1~4 다음 단어에 맞는 뜻을 쓰시오.

1 tie ______
2 stampede ______
3 starve ______
4 waste ______

B 5~8 다음 뜻에 맞는 영어 단어와 영어 동의어, 영어 설명을 쓰시오.

5 (조심 없이, 생각 없이) 소비하다, 낭비하다, 써버리다

______ ______

______

6 우르르 달아나다, 앞을 다투어 달아나다

______ ______

______

7 묶다, 잡아매다, 넥타이

______ ______

______

8 굶주리다, 굶어 죽다

______ ______

______

C 9~12 다음 영어 문장을 의미가 떠오를 때까지 소리 내어 읽어보시오. 2.5초 이내

9 To waste natural resources is a waste of energy.

______

10 I tied the ends of the plastic bag together.

______

11 The crowd stampeded and many were crushed or trampled.

______

12 Many people are starving to death in the world.

______

Test 3 Imaging Exercise

➢ 다음 단어에 맞는 나만의 짧은 영어 설명을 써보자. (또는 그림을 그려보자.)

stampede
[stæmpíːd]

starve
[staːrv]

tie
[tai]

waste
[weist]

➢ Month 06-DAY 02 영어 문장과 우리말

The crowd stampeded and many were crushed or trampled.
군중들이 우르르 몰려 달려 많은 사람들이 넘어지고 짓밟혔습니다.

Many people are starving to death in the world.
전세계적으로 많은 사람들이 굶주림에 죽어가고 있습니다.

I tied the ends of the plastic bag together.
나는 비닐봉지를 묶었습니다.

To waste natural resources is a waste of energy.
천연자원을 낭비하는 것은 에너지의 낭비입니다.

➢ 음원을 들으면서 소리를 무조건 따라해 보시오. (빠르기&정확도/브레인+마우스 운동)

whistle

to make a high clear musical sound by whistling

make whistling sounds

호각을 불다, 휘파람을 불다, 호각, 휘파람

Can you whistle? Yes, I can whistle a melody.

wish

to want or to long for

want, desire, long for

원하다, 바라다(목적절은 반드시 과거시제로 쓰여짐)

I wish I could help you, but I can't.

advertise

to make public announcement of

announce, broadcast, proclaim

광고하다

This company is advertising a new brand of electric car.

burst, burst, burst

to explode

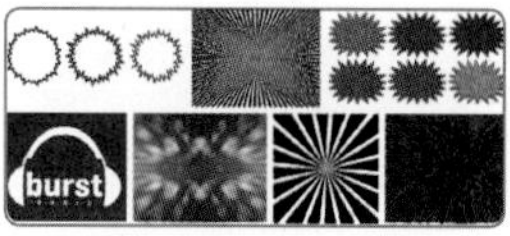

explode, blow up

폭발하다, 터뜨리다

If you burst into tears, you suddenly begin to cry.

* 이미지는 구글에서 찾은 것으로, 단어와 이미지가 다를 수 있습니다. 'Test 3'에서 나만의 이미지를 그려볼 수 있습니다.

Test 1 Connecting Exercise

Score(/16)
Self-Evaluation

➢ 서로 맞는 것을 연결하시오.

Ⓐ 1~4 영어 단어와 우리말 뜻 연결하기

1 advertise	•	• 호각을 불다, 휘파람을 불다, 호각, 휘파람
2 whistle	•	• 폭발하다, 터뜨리다
3 burst, burst, burst	•	• 원하다, 바라다(목적절은 반드시 과거시제로 쓰여짐)
4 wish	•	• 광고하다

Ⓑ 5~8 영어 단어와 영어 설명 연결하기

5 wish	•	• to make a high clear musical sound by whistling
6 whistle	•	• to explode
7 advertise	•	• to want or to long for
8 burst, burst, burst	•	• to make public announcement of

Ⓒ 9~12 영어 단어와 동의어 연결하기

9 whistle	•	• make whistling sounds
10 advertise	•	• explode, blow up
11 burst, burst, burst	•	• want, desire, long for
12 wish	•	• announce, broadcast, proclaim

Ⓓ 13~16 우리말 뜻과 영어 단어 연결하기

13 원하다, 바라다(목적절은 반드시 과거시제로 쓰여짐)	•	• wish
14 호각을 불다, 휘파람을 불다, 호각, 휘파람	•	• advertise
15 폭발하다, 터뜨리다	•	• whistle
16 광고하다	•	• burst, burst, burst

Test 2 Writing Exercise

Score(/12)
Self-Evaluation

Ⓐ 1~4 다음 단어에 맞는 뜻을 쓰시오.

1 advertise ______

2 wish ______

3 whistle ______

4 burst, burst, burst ______

Ⓑ 5~8 다음 뜻에 맞는 영어 단어와 영어 동의어, 영어 설명을 쓰시오.

5 원하다, 바라다(목적절은 반드시 과거시제로 쓰여짐)

______ ______

______

6 호각을 불다, 휘파람을 불다, 호각, 휘파람

______ ______

______

7 폭발하다, 터뜨리다

______ ______

______

8 광고하다

______ ______

______

Ⓒ 9~12 다음 영어 문장을 의미가 떠오를 때까지 소리 내어 읽어보시오. 2.5초 이내

9 This company is advertising a new brand of electric car.

______

10 If you burst into tears, you suddenly begin to cry.

______

11 I wish I could help you, but I can't.

______

12 Can you whistle? Yes, I can whistle a melody.

______

Test 3 Imaging Exercise

➢ 다음 단어에 맞는 나만의 짧은 영어 설명을 써보자. (또는 그림을 그려보자.)

whistle
[hwísl]

wish
[wiʃ]

advertise
[ǽdvərtàiz]

burst, burst, burst
[bəːrst, bəːrst, bəːrst]

➢ Month 06-DAY 03 영어 문장과 우리말

Can you whistle? Yes, I can whistle a melody.
휘파람을 불 수 있습니까? 예, 나는 휘파람으로 멜로디를 낼 수 있습니다.

I wish I could help you, but I can't.
당신을 돕기를 원합니다만 그렇게 할 수 없습니다.

This company is advertising a new brand of electric car.
이 회사는 새로운 브랜드의 전기차를 광고하고 있습니다.

If you burst into tears, you suddenly begin to cry.
당신의 눈물이 쏟아진다면 당신이 갑자기 울기 시작한다는 것이다.

Vocabulary

➢ 음원을 들으면서 소리를 무조건 따라해 보시오. (빠르기 & 정확도/브레인 + 마우스 운동)

clap

to strike the palms of one's hands together

clapping, cheer

탁 치다, 손뼉치다, 박수치다

The audience started to clap loudly before the singer appeared.

dig, dug, dug

to break up, turn over, or remove earth, sand, etc.

mine, bore, unearth, excavate

파다, 파내다

The prisoners dug a tunnel to escape from the jail.

equip

to supply and provide with necessities such as tools

furnish, supply, provide

갖추다, 채비하다, 갖추게 하다

A good education will equip you to handle such problems.

fade

to lose brightness and to become dim

dim, grow dim, disappear

희미해지다, 사라지다

All colour fades, especially under the impact of direct sunlight.

* 이미지는 구글에서 찾은 것으로, 단어와 이미지가 다를 수 있습니다. 'Test 3'에서 나만의 이미지를 그려볼 수 있습니다.

Test 1 Connecting Exercise

Score(　　/16)
Self-Evaluation

➢ 서로 맞는 것을 연결하시오.

Ⓐ 1~4 영어 단어와 우리말 뜻 연결하기

1 fade	•	• 갖추다, 채비하다, 갖추게 하다
2 dig, dug, dug	•	• 희미해지다, 사라지다
3 equip	•	• 파다, 파내다
4 clap	•	• 탁 치다, 손뼉치다, 박수치다

Ⓑ 5~8 영어 단어와 영어 설명 연결하기

5 clap	•	• to supply and provide with necessities such as tools
6 equip	•	• to break up, turn over, or remove earth, sand, etc.
7 fade	•	• to strike the palms of one's hands together
8 dig, dug, dug	•	• to lose brightness and to become dim

Ⓒ 9~12 영어 단어와 동의어 연결하기

9 equip	•	• clapping, cheer
10 fade	•	• dim, grow dim, disappear
11 dig, dug, dug	•	• mine, bore, unearth, excavate
12 clap	•	• furnish, supply, provide

Ⓓ 13~16 우리말 뜻과 영어 단어 연결하기

13 파다, 파내다	•	• clap
14 탁 치다, 손뼉치다, 박수치다	•	• dig, dug, dug
15 희미해지다, 사라지다	•	• equip
16 갖추다, 채비하다, 갖추게 하다	•	• fade

Test 2 Writing Exercise

Score(　　/12)
Self-Evaluation

Ⓐ 1~4 다음 단어에 맞는 뜻을 쓰시오.

1 clap ______________________

2 dig, dug, dug ______________________

3 fade ______________________

4 equip ______________________

Ⓑ 5~8 다음 뜻에 맞는 영어 단어와 영어 동의어, 영어 설명을 쓰시오.

5 희미해지다, 사라지다

__________ ______________________

____

6 파다, 파내다

__________ ______________________

____

7 갖추다, 채비하다, 갖추게 하다

__________ ______________________

____

8 탁 치다, 손뼉치다, 박수치다

__________ ______________________

____

Ⓒ 9~12 다음 영어 문장을 의미가 떠오를 때까지 소리 내어 읽어보시오. 2.5초 이내

9 The audience started to clap loudly before the singer appeared.

____

10 A good education will equip you to handle such problems.

____

11 All colour fades, especially under the impact of direct sunlight.

____

12 The prisoners dug a tunnel to escape from the jail.

____

Test 3 Imaging Exercise

➤ 다음 단어에 맞는 나만의 짧은 영어 설명을 써보자. (또는 그림을 그려보자.)

clap
[klæp]

dig, dug, dug
[dig, dʌg, dʌg]

equip
[ikwíp]

fade
[feid]

➤ Month 06-DAY 04 영어 문장과 우리말

The audience started to clap loudly before the singer appeared.
가수가 나타나기 전에 청중들은 박수를 치기 시작했습니다.

The prisoners dug a tunnel to escape from the jail.
죄수들은 감옥에서 탈출하기 위하여 터널을 팠다.

A good education will equip you to handle such problems.
좋은 교육은 그런 문제를 해결할 수 있도록 당신을 준비시킬 것입니다.

All colour fades, especially under the impact of direct sunlight.
특히, 직사광선의 영향으로 모든 색상이 희미해집니다.

DAY 05 Vocabulary

➢ 음원을 들으면서 소리를 무조건 따라해 보시오. (빠르기&정확도/브레인+마우스 운동)

flee, fled, fled

to run away, as from trouble or danger

run away, escape

도망치다, 달아나다

After fleeing the North Korea, he fled to South Korea.

frown

to wrinkle the brow, as in thought or displeasure

scowl, glower

눈살을 찌푸리다

She frowned at me but I didn't know the reason.

gasp

to draw in the breath sharply, as from shock

huff, puff, pant

급하게 숨을 몰아쉬다,
헐떡거리다, 숨 막힘

He gasped for breath and sweat dropped from his forehead.

groan

to utter a deep, mournful sound expressive of pain or grief

moan, complain, sigh

신음하다, 신음소리 내다, 불평하다

The man on the floor began to groan with pain.

* 이미지는 구글에서 찾은 것으로, 단어와 이미지가 다를 수 있습니다. 'Test 3'에서 나만의 이미지를 그려볼 수 있습니다.

Test 1 Connecting Exercise

Score(/16)
Self-Evaluation

➢ 서로 맞는 것을 연결하시오.

Ⓐ 1~4 영어 단어와 우리말 뜻 연결하기

1 gasp	●	● 급하게 숨을 몰아쉬다, 헐떡거리다, 숨막힘
2 flee, fled, fled	●	● 눈살을 찌푸리다
3 groan	●	● 도망치다, 달아나다
4 frown	●	● 신음하다, 신음소리 내다, 불평하다

Ⓑ 5~8 영어 단어와 영어 설명 연결하기

5 frown	●	● to utter a deep, mournful sound expressive of pain or grief
6 gasp	●	● to draw in the breath sharply, as from shock
7 groan	●	● to run away, as from trouble or danger
8 flee, fled, fled	●	● to wrinkle the brow, as in thought or displeasure

Ⓒ 9~12 영어 단어와 동의어 연결하기

9 gasp	●	● run away, escape
10 flee, fled, fled	●	● scowl, glower
11 frown	●	● huff, puff, pant
12 groan	●	● moan, complain, sigh

Ⓓ 13~16 우리말 뜻과 영어 단어 연결하기

13 급하게 숨을 몰아쉬다, 헐떡거리다, 숨막힘	●	● groan
14 도망치다, 달아나다	●	● gasp
15 신음하다, 신음소리 내다, 불평하다	●	● flee, fled, fled
16 눈살을 찌푸리다	●	● frown

Test 2 Writing Exercise

Score(/12)
Self-Evaluation

Ⓐ 1~4 다음 단어에 맞는 뜻을 쓰시오.

1 gasp ______

2 groan ______

3 flee, fled, fled ______

4 frown ______

Ⓑ 5~8 다음 뜻에 맞는 영어 단어와 영어 동의어, 영어 설명을 쓰시오.

5 신음하다, 신음소리 내다, 불평하다

______ ______

______

6 도망치다, 달아나다

______ ______

______

7 급하게 숨을 몰아쉬다, 헐떡거리다, 숨막힘

______ ______

______

8 눈살을 찌푸리다

______ ______

______

Ⓒ 9~12 다음 영어 문장을 의미가 떠오를 때까지 소리 내어 읽어보시오. 2.5초 이내

9 After fleeing the North Korea, he fled to South Korea.

______

10 The man on the floor began to groan with pain.

______

11 She frowned at me but I didn't know the reason.

______

12 He gasped for breath and sweat dropped from his forehead.

______

Test 3 Imaging Exercise

➢ 다음 단어에 맞는 나만의 짧은 영어 설명을 써보자. (또는 그림을 그려보자.)

flee, fled, fled
[fliː, fled, fled]

frown
[fraun]

gasp
[gæsp]

groan
[groun]

➢ Month 06-DAY 05 영어 문장과 우리말

After fleeing the North Korea, he fled to South Korea.
북한을 탈출한 후 그는 한국으로 망명했습니다.

She frowned at me but I didn't know the reason.
그녀는 내게 눈살을 찌푸렸지만 나는 그 이유를 알지 못했습니다.

He gasped for breath and sweat dropped from his forehead.
그는 숨을 헐떡거렸고 이마에서 땀을 흘렸습니다.

The man on the floor began to groan with pain.
바닥에 있는 남자가 고통으로 신음하기 시작했습니다.

DAY 06 Vocabulary

➢ 음원을 들으면서 소리를 무조건 따라해 보시오. (빠르기&정확도/브레인+마우스 운동)

guard

to watch over or shield (a person or thing) from danger or harm

protect, shield, defend, secure

지키다, 지키는 사람, 경비원

A guard is a person who guards persons or things.

guide

to show and lead the way for (a person)

lead, direct, escort

안내하다, 안내자

I need someone to guide me because I don't know.

hesitate

to pause or wait in acting or doing

temporize, hum and haw

망설이다, 주저하다

She hesitated for a second before receiving the cell phone.

log

enter into a log, as on ships and planes

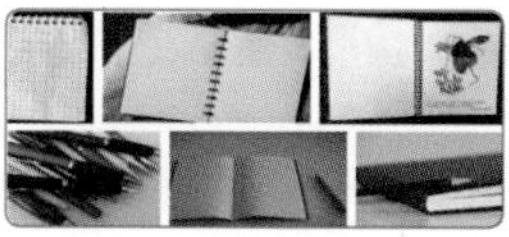

record, book, note, register

기록하다, 접속하다, 기록일지, 벌채하다, 통나무

All details of the work are logged in the computer.

* 이미지는 구글에서 찾은 것으로, 단어와 이미지가 다를 수 있습니다. 'Test 3'에서 나만의 이미지를 그려볼 수 있습니다.

Test 1 Connecting Exercise

Score(　/16)
Self-Evaluation

➢ 서로 맞는 것을 연결하시오.

Ⓐ 1~4 영어 단어와 우리말 뜻 연결하기

1	guide	•	• 지키다, 지키는 사람, 경비원
2	log	•	• 기록하다, 접속하다, 기록일지, 벌채하다, 통나무
3	hesitate	•	• 망설이다, 주저하다
4	guard	•	• 안내하다, 안내자

Ⓑ 5~8 영어 단어와 영어 설명 연결하기

5	guard	•	• to pause or wait in acting or doing
6	hesitate	•	• enter into a log, as on ships and planes
7	log	•	• to watch over or shield (a person or thing) from danger or harm
8	guide	•	• to show and lead the way for (a person)

Ⓒ 9~12 영어 단어와 동의어 연결하기

9	hesitate	•	• record, book, note, register
10	log	•	• temporize, hum and haw
11	guide	•	• protect, shield, defend, secure
12	guard	•	• lead, direct, escort

Ⓓ 13~16 우리말 뜻과 영어 단어 연결하기

13	지키다, 지키는 사람, 경비원	•	• guard
14	망설이다, 주저하다	•	• log
15	안내하다, 안내자	•	• guide
16	기록하다, 접속하다, 기록일지, 벌채하다, 통나무	•	• hesitate

Test 2 Writing Exercise

Score(　　/12)
Self-Evaluation

A 1~4 다음 단어에 맞는 뜻을 쓰시오.

1 log ____________________

2 guide ____________________

3 hesitate ____________________

4 guard ____________________

B 5~8 다음 뜻에 맞는 영어 단어와 영어 동의어, 영어 설명을 쓰시오.

5 기록하다, 접속하다, 기록일지, 벌채하다, 통나무

__________ ____________________

____

6 안내하다, 안내자

__________ ____________________

____

7 지키다, 지키는 사람, 경비원

__________ ____________________

____

8 망설이다, 주저하다

__________ ____________________

____

C 9~12 다음 영어 문장을 의미가 떠오를 때까지 소리 내어 읽어보시오. 2.5초 이내

9 I need someone to guide me because I don't know.

____

10 All details of the work are logged in the computer.

____

11 She hesitated for a second before receiving the cell phone.

____

12 A guard is a person who guards persons or things.

____

Test 3 Imaging Exercise

➤ 다음 단어에 맞는 나만의 짧은 영어 설명을 써보자. (또는 그림을 그려보자.)

guard
[gaːrd]

guide
[gaid]

hesitate
[hézətèit]

log
[lɔːg]

➤ Month 06-DAY 06 영어 문장과 우리말

A guard is a person who guards persons or things.
경비원은 사람이나 물건을 경비하는 사람입니다.

I need someone to guide me because I don't know.
내가 모르기 때문에 나를 안내할 사람이 필요합니다.

She hesitated for a second before receiving the cell phone.
그녀는 휴대폰을 받기 전에 잠시 주저했습니다.

All details of the work are logged in the computer.
작업의 모든 세부사항이 컴퓨터에 기록됩니다.

➢ 음원을 들으면서 소리를 무조건 따라해 보시오. (빠르기 & 정확도/브레인 + 마우스 운동)

mean, meant, meant

to intend to convey or indicate

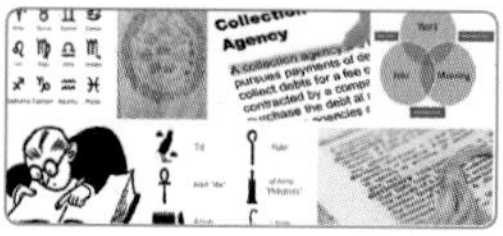

connote, denote, intend

의미하다, 나타내다, 뜻하다, 뜻, 평균, 하찮은, 사소한

What does it mean? I don't know what you mean.

measure

to determine the size, amount, etc

quantify, size, estimate, weigh

측정하다

I measured the length, width and height of the box.

necessitate

to make necessary, or to require or compel

require, compel

필요하게 만들다, 요구하다, 강요하다

The increased traffic jams necessitate the widening of the road.

obtain

to come into possession of

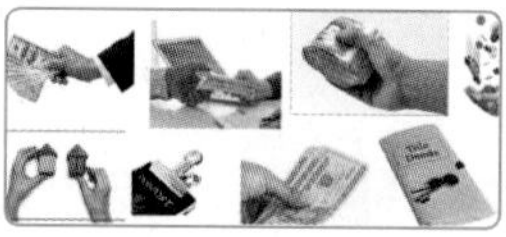

get, acquire, procure

얻다

This kind of information can be obtained from the Internet.

* 이미지는 구글에서 찾은 것으로, 단어와 이미지가 다를 수 있습니다. 'Test 3'에서 나만의 이미지를 그려볼 수 있습니다.

Test 1 Connecting Exercise

Score(　/16)
Self-Evaluation

➢ 서로 맞는 것을 연결하시오.

Ⓐ 1~4 영어 단어와 우리말 뜻 연결하기

1 necessitate •	• 얻다
2 measure •	• 필요하게 만들다, 요구하다, 강요하다
3 mean, meant, meant •	• 측정하다
4 obtain •	• 의미하다, 나타내다, 뜻하다, 뜻, 평균, 하찮은, 사소한

Ⓑ 5~8 영어 단어와 영어 설명 연결하기

5 mean, meant, meant •	• to determine the size, amount, etc
6 obtain •	• to intend to convey or indicate
7 necessitate •	• to make necessary, or to require or compel
8 measure •	• to come into possession of

Ⓒ 9~12 영어 단어와 동의어 연결하기

9 measure •	• connote, denote, intend
10 mean, meant, meant •	• quantify, size, estimate, weigh
11 necessitate •	• require, compel
12 obtain •	• get, acquire, procure

Ⓓ 13~16 우리말 뜻과 영어 단어 연결하기

13 얻다 •	• necessitate
14 측정하다 •	• measure
15 의미하다, 나타내다, 뜻하다, 뜻, 평균, 하찮은, 사소한 •	• mean, meant, meant
16 필요하게 만들다, 요구하다, 강요하다 •	• obtain

Test 2 Writing Exercise

Score(/12)
Self-Evaluation

Ⓐ 1~4 다음 단어에 맞는 뜻을 쓰시오.

1 necessitate ____________

2 mean, meant, meant ____________

3 measure ____________

4 obtain ____________

Ⓑ 5~8 다음 뜻에 맞는 영어 단어와 영어 동의어, 영어 설명을 쓰시오.

5 필요하게 만들다, 요구하다, 강요하다

____________ ____________

____

6 얻다

____________ ____________

____

7 측정하다

____________ ____________

____

8 의미하다, 나타내다, 뜻하다, 뜻, 평균, 하찮은, 사소한

____________ ____________

____

Ⓒ 9~12 다음 영어 문장을 의미가 떠오를 때까지 소리 내어 읽어보시오. 2.5초 이내

9 The increased traffic jams necessitate the widening of the road.

____

10 This kind of information can be obtained from the Internet.

____

11 What does it mean? I don't know what you mean.

____

12 I measured the length, width and height of the box.

____

Test 3 Imaging Exercise

➢ 다음 단어에 맞는 나만의 짧은 영어 설명을 써보자. (또는 그림을 그려보자.)

mean, meant, meant
[miːn, ment, ment]

measure
[méʒər]

necessitate
[nəsésətèit]

obtain
[əbtéin]

➢ Month 06-DAY 07 영어 문장과 우리말

What does it mean? I don't know what you mean.
그것이 무슨 뜻(말)입니까? 당신이 무엇을 뜻(말)하는지 모르겠습니다.

I measured the length, width and height of the box.
나는 상자의 길이와 폭과 높이를 재었습니다.

The increased traffic jams necessitate the widening of the road.
교통체증의 증가가 도로확장을 필요로 하게 만듭니다.

This kind of information can be obtained from the Internet.
이런 종류의 정보는 인터넷에서 얻을 수 있습니다.

DAY 08 Vocabulary

➢ 음원을 들으면서 소리를 무조건 따라해 보시오. (빠르기 & 정확도 / 브레인 + 마우스 운동)

overcome, overcame, overcome

to get the better of in a struggle or conflict

defeat, beat, conquer

극복하다

I fought to overcome my fear and finally overcame it.

peek

to glance quickly

glance, peer, spy

엿보다

She peeked at him through a crack in the wall.

raise

to move to a higher position

elevate, lift, rear, bring up

올리다, 높이다, 기르다

He always raises his hand when he asks a question.

rob

to steal something from

dispossess, deprive, steal from

빼앗다, 훔치다, 강탈하다

I've been robbed by burglars who robbed a bank.

* 이미지는 구글에서 찾은 것으로, 단어와 이미지가 다를 수 있습니다. 'Test 3'에서 나만의 이미지를 그려볼 수 있습니다.

Test 1 Connecting Exercise

Score(/16)
Self-Evaluation

➢ 서로 맞는 것을 연결하시오.

Ⓐ 1~4 영어 단어와 우리말 뜻 연결하기

1	overcome, overcame, overcome	극복하다
2	rob	빼앗다, 훔치다, 강탈하다
3	raise	올리다, 높이다, 기르다
4	peek	엿보다

Ⓑ 5~8 영어 단어와 영어 설명 연결하기

5	rob	to steal something from
6	peek	to glance quickly
7	overcome, overcame, overcome	to move to a higher position
8	raise	to get the better of in a struggle or conflict

Ⓒ 9~12 영어 단어와 동의어 연결하기

9	rob	defeat, beat, conquer
10	peek	elevate, lift, rear, bring up
11	overcome, overcame, overcome	dispossess, deprive, steal from
12	raise	glance, peer, spy

Ⓓ 13~16 우리말 뜻과 영어 단어 연결하기

13	빼앗다, 훔치다, 강탈하다	overcome, overcame, overcome
14	엿보다	peek
15	올리다, 높이다, 기르다	raise
16	극복하다	rob

Test 2 Writing Exercise

Score(　　/12)
Self-Evaluation

Ⓐ 1~4 다음 단어에 맞는 뜻을 쓰시오.

1 peek ______
2 raise ______
3 rob ______
4 overcome, overcame, overcome ______

Ⓑ 5~8 다음 뜻에 맞는 영어 단어와 영어 동의어, 영어 설명을 쓰시오.

5 극복하다
______ ______
______

6 빼앗다, 훔치다, 강탈하다
______ ______
______

7 엿보다
______ ______
______

8 올리다, 높이다, 기르다
______ ______
______

Ⓒ 9~12 다음 영어 문장을 의미가 떠오를 때까지 소리 내어 읽어보시오. 2.5초 이내

9 I've been robbed by burglars who robbed a bank.
______

10 I fought to overcome my fear and finally overcame it.
______

11 She peeked at him through a crack in the wall.
______

12 He always raises his hand when he asks a question.
______

Test 3 Imaging Exercise

➢ 다음 단어에 맞는 나만의 짧은 영어 설명을 써보자. (또는 그림을 그려보자.)

overcome, overcame, overcome
[ouˈvərkəˌm, òuvərkéim, ouˈvərkəˌm]

peek
[pi:k]

raise
[reiz]

rob
[rab]

➢ Month 06-DAY 08 영어 문장과 우리말

I fought to overcome my fear and finally overcame it.
나는 두려움을 극복하기 위해 싸웠고 마침내 그것을 극복했습니다.

She peeked at him through a crack in the wall.
그녀는 벽에 난 틈새로 그를 엿보았습니다.

He always raises his hand when he asks a question.
그는 질문할 때 항상 손을 듭니다.

I've been robbed by burglars who robbed a bank.
나는 은행을 털은 도둑들에게 다 털렸습니다.

➢ 음원을 들으면서 소리를 무조건 따라해 보시오. (빠르기&정확도/브레인+마우스 운동)

scoop

to take up or out with or as if with a scoop

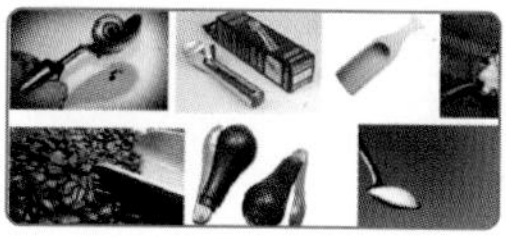

shovel, spade, excavate, spoon

국자로 푸다, 삽으로 푸다, 국자, 삽

She scooped popcorn out of the container into a bag.

scribble

to write or draw in a hasty or illegible manner

scrabble, scrawl, doodle

휘갈겨 쓰다, 그리다, 낙서를 하다

My child has scribbled all over the wall with crayons.

shine

to reflect light

glow, sparkle, glitter, polish

빛나다, 반짝이다, 반짝이게 하다

The sun is shining and it is a good morning.

sort

to separate from others

arrange, group, class, separate

분류하다, 종류

She sorted the books into new ones and old ones.

* 이미지는 구글에서 찾은 것으로, 단어와 이미지가 다를 수 있습니다. 'Test 3'에서 나만의 이미지를 그려볼 수 있습니다.

Test 1 Connecting Exercise

Score(/16)
Self-Evaluation

➢ 서로 맞는 것을 연결하시오.

Ⓐ 1~4 영어 단어와 우리말 뜻 연결하기

1 shine	•	• 국자로 푸다, 삽으로 푸다, 국자, 삽
2 scribble	•	• 분류하다, 종류
3 sort	•	• 빛나다, 반짝이다, 반짝이게 하다
4 scoop	•	• 휘갈겨 쓰다, 그리다, 낙서를 하다

Ⓑ 5~8 영어 단어와 영어 설명 연결하기

5 sort	•	• to reflect light
6 shine	•	• to take up or out with or as if with a scoop
7 scribble	•	• to write or draw in a hasty or illegible manner
8 scoop	•	• to separate from others

Ⓒ 9~12 영어 단어와 동의어 연결하기

9 scribble	•	• glow, sparkle, glitter, polish
10 sort	•	• shovel, spade, excavate, spoon
11 scoop	•	• arrange, group, class, separate
12 shine	•	• scrabble, scrawl, doodle

Ⓓ 13~16 우리말 뜻과 영어 단어 연결하기

13 빛나다, 반짝이다, 반짝이게 하다	•	• scribble
14 국자로 푸다, 삽으로 푸다, 국자, 삽	•	• shine
15 휘갈겨 쓰다, 그리다, 낙서를 하다	•	• sort
16 분류하다, 종류	•	• scoop

Test 2 Writing Exercise

Score(/12)
Self-Evaluation

A 1~4 다음 단어에 맞는 뜻을 쓰시오.

1 scoop

2 scribble

3 shine

4 sort

B 5~8 다음 뜻에 맞는 영어 단어와 영어 동의어, 영어 설명을 쓰시오.

5 국자로 푸다, 삽으로 푸다, 국자, 삽

6 빛나다, 반짝이다, 반짝이게 하다

7 분류하다, 종류

8 휘갈겨 쓰다, 그리다, 낙서를 하다

C 9~12 다음 영어 문장을 의미가 떠오를 때까지 소리 내어 읽어보시오. 2.5초 이내

9 She sorted the books into new ones and old ones.

10 She scooped popcorn out of the container into a bag.

11 The sun is shining and it is a good morning.

12 My child has scribbled all over the wall with crayons.

Test 3

➢ 다음 단어에 맞는 나만의 짧은 영어 설명을 써보자. (또는 그림을 그려보자.)

scoop
[sku:p]

scribble
[skríbl]

shine
[ʃain]

sort
[sɔ:rt]

➢ Month 06-DAY 09 영어 문장과 우리말

She scooped popcorn out of the container into a bag.
그녀는 팝콘을 통에서 퍼내 봉지에 담았습니다.

My child has scribbled all over the wall with crayons.
우리 애가 벽에 온통 낙서를 해놓았습니다.

The sun is shining and it is a good morning.
태양은 빛나고 좋은 아침입니다.

She sorted the books into new ones and old ones.
그녀는 책을 오래된 책과 새 책으로 분류하였습니다.

Vocabulary

➢ 음원을 들으면서 소리를 무조건 따라해 보시오. (빠르기&정확도/브레인+마우스 운동)

stamp

to bring down (the foot) forcibly

print, mark, imprint

(강하게 발로) 팍팍 밟다, 찍다, 표시하다, 우표

I stamped the date at the top of the letter.

wake, woke, woken

to cease to sleep or to become awake

awaken, awake, arouse

깨다, 깨우다

It was still bright when I woke from my daydreams.

bite, bit, bitten

to grip or cut off as if with the teeth or jaws

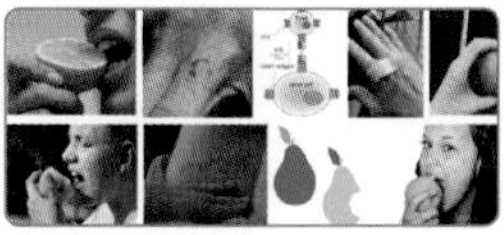

grip, cut off, tear with

물다, 깨물다, 물어뜯다

The past tense of bite is bit. My dog bit me.

bray

to utter the loud, harsh cry of a donkey

heehaw

당나귀가 울다, 당나귀 울음

The donkey brayed and the bray of a donkey awoked me.

* 이미지는 구글에서 찾은 것으로, 단어와 이미지가 다를 수 있습니다. 'Test 3'에서 나만의 이미지를 그려볼 수 있습니다.

Test 1 Connecting Exercise

Score(/16)
Self-Evaluation

➢ 서로 맞는 것을 연결하시오.

Ⓐ 1~4 영어 단어와 우리말 뜻 연결하기

1	bite, bit, bitten	•	• (강하게 발로) 팍팍 밟다, 찍다, 표시하다, 우표
2	bray	•	• 물다, 깨물다, 물어뜯다
3	wake, woke, woken	•	• 당나귀가 울다, 당나귀 울음
4	stamp	•	• 깨다, 깨우다

Ⓑ 5~8 영어 단어와 영어 설명 연결하기

5	bite, bit, bitten	•	• to utter the loud, harsh cry of a donkey
6	bray	•	• to grip or cut off as if with the teeth or jaws
7	stamp	•	• to bring down (the foot) forcibly
8	wake, woke, woken	•	• to cease to sleep or to become awake

Ⓒ 9~12 영어 단어와 동의어 연결하기

9	bite, bit, bitten	•	• grip, cut off, tear with
10	wake, woke, woken	•	• heehaw
11	stamp	•	• print, mark, imprint
12	bray	•	• awaken, awake, arouse

Ⓓ 13~16 우리말 뜻과 영어 단어 연결하기

13	깨다, 깨우다	•	• stamp
14	당나귀가 울다, 당나귀 울음	•	• wake, woke, woken
15	(강하게 발로) 팍팍 밟다, 찍다, 표시하다, 우표	•	• bite, bit, bitten
16	물다, 깨물다, 물어뜯다	•	• bray

Test 2 Writing Exercise

Score(　　/12)
Self-Evaluation

Ⓐ 1~4 다음 단어에 맞는 뜻을 쓰시오.

1 bray ____________________

2 bite, bit, bitten ____________________

3 wake, woke, woken ____________________

4 stamp ____________________

Ⓑ 5~8 다음 뜻에 맞는 영어 단어와 영어 동의어, 영어 설명을 쓰시오.

5 깨다, 깨우다

__________ ____________________

____

6 물다, 깨물다, 물어뜯다

__________ ____________________

____

7 (강하게 발로) 팍팍 밟다, 찍다, 표시하다, 우표

__________ ____________________

____

8 당나귀가 울다, 당나귀 울음

__________ ____________________

____

Ⓒ 9~12 다음 영어 문장을 의미가 떠오를 때까지 소리 내어 읽어보시오. 2.5초 이내

9 The donkey brayed and the bray of a donkey awoked me.

____

10 The past tense of bite is bit. My dog bit me.

____

11 I stamped the date at the top of the letter.

____

12 It was still bright when I woke from my daydreams.

____

Test 3 Imaging Exercise

➢ 다음 단어에 맞는 나만의 짧은 영어 설명을 써보자. (또는 그림을 그려보자.)

stamp
[stæmp]

wake, woke, woken
[weik, wouk, wóukən]

bite, bit, bitten
[bait, bit, bítn]

bray
[brei]

➢ Month 06-DAY 10 영어 문장과 우리말

I stamped the date at the top of the letter.
나는 날짜를 편지의 상단에 표시했습니다.

It was still bright when I woke from my daydreams.
내가 백일몽에서 깨어났을 때 여전히 날이 밝았습니다.

The past tense of bite is bit. My dog bit me.
bite의 과거시제는 bit이다. 우리 개가 나를 물었다.

The donkey brayed and the bray of a donkey awoked me.
당나귀가 울었고, 당나귀 울음소리가 나를 깨웠다.

Vocabulary

➢ 음원을 들으면서 소리를 무조건 따라해 보시오. (빠르기&정확도/브레인+마우스 운동)

cure

to eliminate a disease from the body by medical or other treatment

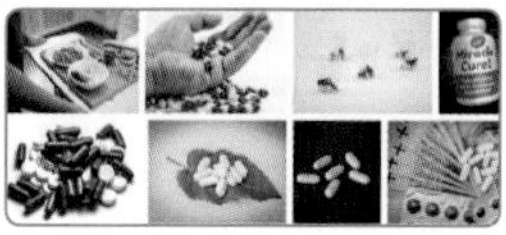

heal, remedy, mend

치료하다, 치료

This new medicine cures the patient of cancer without side effects.

describe

to tell or depict in words

depict, explain, represent

묘사하다, 설명하다

He described the traffic accident in detail to the police officer.

devote

to apply or dedicate (oneself, time, money, etc) to some pursuit

dedicate, give, use, apply

헌신하다, 바치다, 전념하다

He decided to devote the rest of his life to music.

discriminate

to make a clear distinction

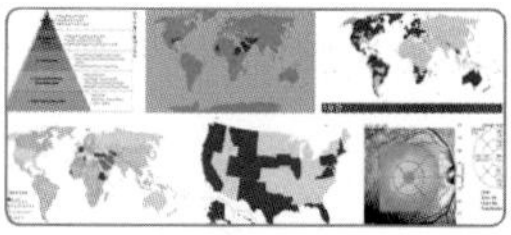

distinguish, differentiate

차별하다, 구별하다

Discriminating against people because of their skin color was very wrong.

* 이미지는 구글에서 찾은 것으로, 단어와 이미지가 다를 수 있습니다. 'Test 3'에서 나만의 이미지를 그려볼 수 있습니다.

Test 1 Connecting Exercise

Score(/16)
Self-Evaluation

➢ 서로 맞는 것을 연결하시오.

Ⓐ 1~4 영어 단어와 우리말 뜻 연결하기

1 devote	•	• 묘사하다, 설명하다
2 cure	•	• 차별하다, 구별하다
3 discriminate	•	• 치료하다, 치료
4 describe	•	• 헌신하다, 바치다, 전념하다

Ⓑ 5~8 영어 단어와 영어 설명 연결하기

5 discriminate	•	• to make a clear distinction
6 cure	•	• to tell or depict in words
7 describe	•	• to eliminate a disease from the body by medical or other treatment
8 devote	•	• to apply or dedicate (oneself, time, money, etc) to some pursuit

Ⓒ 9~12 영어 단어와 동의어 연결하기

9 devote	•	• distinguish, differentiate
10 cure	•	• dedicate, give, use, apply
11 describe	•	• heal, remedy, mend
12 discriminate	•	• depict, explain, represent

Ⓓ 13~16 우리말 뜻과 영어 단어 연결하기

13 치료하다, 치료	•	• discriminate
14 헌신하다, 바치다, 전념하다	•	• cure
15 차별하다, 구별하다	•	• describe
16 묘사하다, 설명하다	•	• devote

Test 2 Writing Exercise

Score(/12)
Self-Evaluation

A 1~4 다음 단어에 맞는 뜻을 쓰시오.

1 devote ______

2 cure ______

3 describe ______

4 discriminate ______

B 5~8 다음 뜻에 맞는 영어 단어와 영어 동의어, 영어 설명을 쓰시오.

5 묘사하다, 설명하다

______ ______

______

6 헌신하다, 바치다, 전념하다

______ ______

______

7 차별하다, 구별하다

______ ______

______

8 치료하다, 치료

______ ______

______

C 9~12 다음 영어 문장을 의미가 떠오를 때까지 소리 내어 읽어보시오. 3초 이내

9 He described the traffic accident in detail to the police officer.

______

10 This new medicine cures the patient of cancer without side effects.

______

11 Discriminating against people because of their skin color was very wrong.

______

12 He decided to devote the rest of his life to music.

______

Imaging Exercise

Test 3

➤ 다음 단어에 맞는 나만의 짧은 영어 설명을 써보자. (또는 그림을 그려보자.)

cure
[kjuər]

describe
[diskráib]

devote
[divóut]

discriminate
[diskrímənèit]

➤ Month 06-DAY 11 영어 문장과 우리말

This new medicine cures the patient of cancer without side effects.
이 새로운 약은 암환자를 부작용 없이 치료합니다.

He described the traffic accident in detail to the police officer.
그는 경찰관에게 그 교통사고를 자세히 설명하였습니다.

He decided to devote the rest of his life to music.
그는 남은 인생을 음악에 바치기로 결심하였습니다.

Discriminating against people because of their skin color was very wrong.
피부색으로 사람을 차별하는 것은 매우 나쁩니다.

➢ 음원을 들으면서 소리를 무조건 따라해 보시오. (빠르기 & 정확도/브레인 + 마우스 운동)

display

to show or make visible

show, exhibit, expose, disclose

전시하다, 진열하다, 보여주다,
드러내다, 전시, 진열

They are displaying many kinds of new products in this exhibition.

drop

to let fall

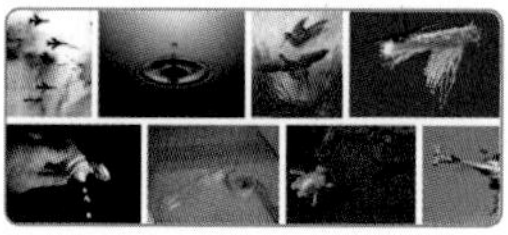

plunge, fall, dive

떨어뜨리다, 떨어지다,
물방울, 방울

I'll drop you at the corner nearest to the station.

fold

to bend over or double up so that one part lies on another part

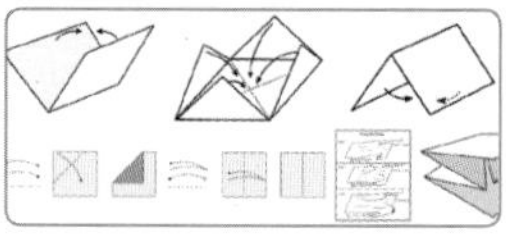

bend, double

접다, (두 겹, 세 겹으로) 접다

You can't fold a paper in half more than eight times.

freeze, froze, frozen

to pass from the liquid to the solid state by loss of heat

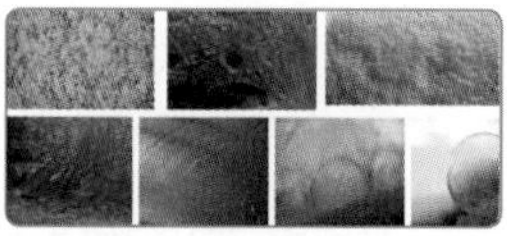

ice, chill, refrigerate, harden

얼다, 얼음이 얼다,
냉각되다, 고체가 되다

If the water pipes freeze, you should thaw the frozen pipes.

* 이미지는 구글에서 찾은 것으로, 단어와 이미지가 다를 수 있습니다. 'Test 3'에서 나만의 이미지를 그려볼 수 있습니다.

Test 1 Connecting Exercise

Score(/16)
Self-Evaluation

➢ 서로 맞는 것을 연결하시오.

Ⓐ 1~4 영어 단어와 우리말 뜻 연결하기

1	display	•	• 접다, (두 겹, 세 겹으로) 접다
2	freeze, froze, frozen	•	• 전시하다, 진열하다, 보여주다, 드러내다, 전시, 진열
3	drop	•	• 얼다, 얼음이 얼다, 냉각되다, 고체가 되다
4	fold	•	• 떨어뜨리다, 떨어지다, 물방울, 방울

Ⓑ 5~8 영어 단어와 영어 설명 연결하기

5	drop	•	• to pass from the liquid to the solid state by loss of heat
6	freeze, froze, frozen	•	• to bend over or double up so that one part lies on another part
7	fold	•	• to let fall
8	display	•	• to show or make visible

Ⓒ 9~12 영어 단어와 동의어 연결하기

9	freeze, froze, frozen	•	• ice, chill, refrigerate, harden
10	fold	•	• bend, double
11	display	•	• plunge, fall, dive
12	drop	•	• show, exhibit, expose, disclose

Ⓓ 13~16 우리말 뜻과 영어 단어 연결하기

13	얼다, 얼음이 얼다, 냉각되다, 고체가 되다	•	• fold
14	접다, (두 겹, 세 겹으로) 접다	•	• display
15	전시하다, 진열하다, 보여주다, 드러내다, 전시, 진열	•	• freeze, froze, frozen
16	떨어뜨리다, 떨어지다, 물방울, 방울	•	• drop

Test 2 Writing Exercise

Score(　　/12)
Self-Evaluation

Ⓐ 1~4 다음 단어에 맞는 뜻을 쓰시오.

1 fold ____________________

2 display ____________________

3 freeze, froze, frozen ____________________

4 drop ____________________

Ⓑ 5~8 다음 뜻에 맞는 영어 단어와 영어 동의어, 영어 설명을 쓰시오.

5 접다, (두 겹, 세 겹으로) 접다

____________ ____________________

____

6 전시하다, 진열하다, 보여주다, 드러내다, 전시, 진열

____________ ____________________

____

7 떨어뜨리다, 떨어지다, 물방울, 방울

____________ ____________________

____

8 얼다, 얼음이 얼다, 냉각되다, 고체가 되다

____________ ____________________

____

Ⓒ 9~12 다음 영어 문장을 의미가 떠오를 때까지 소리 내어 읽어보시오. 3초 이내

9 I'll drop you at the corner nearest to the station.

____

10 You can't fold a paper in half more than eight times.

____

11 They are displaying many kinds of new products in this exhibition.

____

12 If the water pipes freeze, you should thaw the frozen pipes.

____

Test 3 Imaging Exercise

➢ 다음 단어에 맞는 나만의 짧은 영어 설명을 써보자. (또는 그림을 그려보자.)

display
[dispéi]

drop
[drap]

fold
[fould]

freeze, froze, frozen
[friːz, frouz, fróuzn]

➢ Month 06-DAY 12 영어 문장과 우리말

They are displaying many kinds of new products in this exhibition.
그들은 이번 전시회에서 많은 종류의 신제품을 전시하고 있습니다.

I'll drop you at the corner nearest to the station.
역에서 가장 가까운 길모퉁이에서 당신을 내려주겠습니다.

You can't fold a paper in half more than eight times.
당신은 종이 한장을 반으로 계속하여 8번 이상 접을 수 없습니다.

If the water pipes freeze, you should thaw the frozen pipes.
수도관이 얼면 당신은 얼은 수도관을 녹여야 합니다.

DAY 13 Vocabulary

➢ 음원을 들으면서 소리를 무조건 따라해 보시오. (빠르기 & 정확도/브레인 + 마우스 운동)

graduate

to receive an academic degree upon completion of one's studies

qualify, pass, receive a degree

졸업하다

I graduated university on Monday, the 17th of July in 2017.

hit, hit, hit

to come into contact with something forcefully

strike, beat, knock, punch

때리다, 부딪히다, 충돌하다

The car hit the guardrail and my head hit the handle.

intimate

to state or express indirectly

hint, suggest, imply, close

암시하다, 친밀한, 친구

She intimated that she did not want him to call back.

knit

to form (yarn or thread) into fabric by intertwining

weave, intertwine, interlace

뜨개질하다, 옷감을 짜다,
실로 옷을 뜨다

She can knit up a sweater in a couple of days.

* 이미지는 구글에서 찾은 것으로, 단어와 이미지가 다를 수 있습니다. 'Test 3'에서 나만의 이미지를 그려볼 수 있습니다.

Connecting Exercise

Test 1

Score(/16)
Self-Evaluation

➢ 서로 맞는 것을 연결하시오.

Ⓐ 1~4 영어 단어와 우리말 뜻 연결하기

1 intimate	•	• 때리다, 부딪히다, 충돌하다
2 graduate	•	• 암시하다, 친밀한, 친구
3 hit, hit, hit	•	• 뜨개질하다, 옷감을 짜다, 실로 옷을 뜨다
4 knit	•	• 졸업하다

Ⓑ 5~8 영어 단어와 영어 설명 연결하기

5 graduate	•	• to receive an academic degree upon completion of one's studies
6 hit, hit, hit	•	• to come into contact with something forcefully
7 knit	•	• to form (yarn or thread) into fabric by intertwining
8 intimate	•	• to state or express indirectly

Ⓒ 9~12 영어 단어와 동의어 연결하기

9 graduate	•	• strike, beat, knock, punch
10 knit	•	• weave, intertwine, interlace
11 intimate	•	• hint, suggest, imply, close
12 hit, hit, hit	•	• qualify, pass, receive a degree

Ⓓ 13~16 우리말 뜻과 영어 단어 연결하기

13 뜨개질하다, 옷감을 짜다, 실로 옷을 뜨다	•	• hit, hit, hit
14 암시하다, 친밀한, 친구	•	• graduate
15 졸업하다	•	• intimate
16 때리다, 부딪히다, 충돌하다	•	• knit

Test 2 Writing Exercise

Score(/12)
Self-Evaluation

A 1~4 다음 단어에 맞는 뜻을 쓰시오.

1 hit, hit, hit ______

2 knit ______

3 intimate ______

4 graduate ______

B 5~8 다음 뜻에 맞는 영어 단어와 영어 동의어, 영어 설명을 쓰시오.

5 때리다, 부딪히다, 충돌하다

______ ______

______

6 뜨개질하다, 옷감을 짜다, 실로 옷을 뜨다

______ ______

______

7 졸업하다

______ ______

______

8 암시하다, 친밀한, 친구

______ ______

______

C 9~12 다음 영어 문장을 의미가 떠오를 때까지 소리 내어 읽어보시오. 3초 이내

9 She can knit up a sweater in a couple of days.

______

10 She intimated that she did not want him to call back.

______

11 I graduated university on Monday, the 17th of July in 2017.

______

12 The car hit the guardrail and my head hit the handle.

______

Test 3

➢ 다음 단어에 맞는 나만의 짧은 영어 설명을 써보자. (또는 그림을 그려보자.)

graduate
[grædʒuət]

hit, hit, hit
[hit, hit, hit]

intimate
[íntəmət]

knit
[nit]

➢ Month 06-DAY 13 영어 문장과 우리말

I graduated university on Monday, the 17th of July in 2017.
나는 2017년 7월 17일 월요일에 대학을 졸업했습니다.

The car hit the guardrail and my head hit the handle.
차가 가드레일(난간)에 부딪쳤고 내 머리는 핸들에 부딪쳤습니다.

She intimated that she did not want him to call back.
그녀는 그가 다시 전화거는 것을 그녀가 원치 않는다는 것을 암시했습니다.

She can knit up a sweater in a couple of days.
그녀는 이틀이면 스웨터 하나를 뜰 수 있습니다.

Vocabulary

➢ 음원을 들으면서 소리를 무조건 따라해 보시오. (빠르기 & 정확도/브레인 + 마우스 운동)

land

to bring to and unload on land

arrive, dock, put down

땅에 내리다, 내려놓다, 착륙하다, 땅, 육지

The jet landed after a flight of just under three hours.

lie, lay, lain

to rest in a horizontal or flat position, as on a bed or the ground

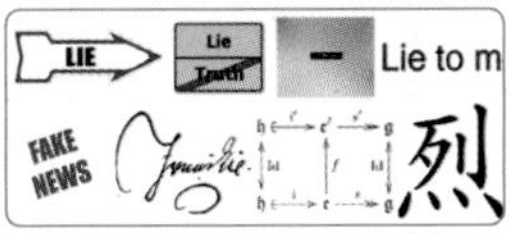

recline, be buried, be placed

눕다, 묻혀있다, 놓여있다

You may lie down on the bed until you feel better.

match

to harmonize with another

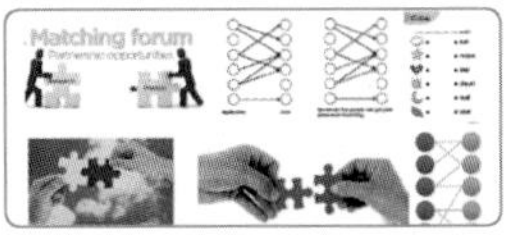

suit, go with, fit with

어울리다, 연결되다, 경기, 시합

This tie matches my shirt and those shoes match your dress.

overthrow

to turn over or to cause the downfall of rulers

overturn, defeat

전복하다, 뒤엎다, 전복, 타도

The government was overthrown in a military coup three years ago.

* 이미지는 구글에서 찾은 것으로, 단어와 이미지가 다를 수 있습니다. 'Test 3'에서 나만의 이미지를 그려볼 수 있습니다.

Test 1 Connecting Exercise

Score(　　/16)
Self-Evaluation

➢ 서로 맞는 것을 연결하시오.

Ⓐ 1~4 영어 단어와 우리말 뜻 연결하기

1 match	•	• 땅에 내리다, 내려놓다, 착륙하다, 땅, 육지
2 overthrow	•	• 어울리다, 연결되다, 경기, 시합
3 lie, lay, lain	•	• 눕다, 묻혀있다, 놓여있다
4 land	•	• 전복하다, 뒤엎다, 전복, 타도

Ⓑ 5~8 영어 단어와 영어 설명 연결하기

5 land	•	• to harmonize with another
6 lie, lay, lain	•	• to rest in a horizontal or flat position, as on a bed or the ground
7 overthrow	•	• to turn over or to cause the downfall of rulers
8 match	•	• to bring to and unload on land

Ⓒ 9~12 영어 단어와 동의어 연결하기

9 overthrow	•	• suit, go with, fit with
10 match	•	• recline, be buried, be placed
11 lie, lay, lain	•	• arrive, dock, put down
12 land	•	• overturn, defeat

Ⓓ 13~16 우리말 뜻과 영어 단어 연결하기

13 전복하다, 뒤엎다, 전복, 타도	•	• overthrow
14 눕다, 묻혀있다, 놓여있다	•	• match
15 어울리다, 연결되다, 경기, 시합	•	• lie, lay, lain
16 땅에 내리다, 내려놓다, 착륙하다, 땅, 육지	•	• land

Test 2 Writing Exercise

Score(/12)
Self-Evaluation

A 1~4 다음 단어에 맞는 뜻을 쓰시오.

1 lie, lay, lain ______

2 match ______

3 land ______

4 overthrow ______

B 5~8 다음 뜻에 맞는 영어 단어와 영어 동의어, 영어 설명을 쓰시오.

5 땅에 내리다, 내려놓다, 착륙하다, 땅, 육지

______ ______

______

6 어울리다, 연결되다, 경기, 시합

______ ______

______

7 눕다, 묻혀있다, 놓여있다

______ ______

______

8 전복하다, 뒤엎다, 전복, 타도

______ ______

______

C 9~12 다음 영어 문장을 의미가 떠오를 때까지 소리 내어 읽어보시오. 3초 이내

9 The jet landed after a flight of just under three hours.

______

10 This tie matches my shirt and those shoes match your dress.

______

11 The government was overthrown in a military coup three years ago.

______

12 You may lie down on the bed until you feel better.

______

Test 3 Imaging Exercise

➢ 다음 단어에 맞는 나만의 짧은 영어 설명을 써보자. (또는 그림을 그려보자.)

land
[lænd]

lie, lay, lain
[lai, lei, lein]

match
[mætʃ]

overthrow
[ouˈvərθrou,]

➢ Month 06-DAY 14 영어 문장과 우리말

The jet landed after a flight of just under three hours.
제트 비행기는 딱 세 시간 비행 끝에 착륙하였습니다.

You may lie down on the bed until you feel better.
기분이 좋아질 때까지 침대에 누워있어도 됩니다.

This tie matches my shirt and those shoes match your dress.
이 넥타이는 내 셔츠와 잘 어울리고 저 구두는 당신 드레스에 잘 어울립니다.

The government was overthrown in a military coup three years ago.
정부가 군사 쿠데타로 3년 전에 전복되었습니다.

➢ 음원을 들으면서 소리를 무조건 따라해 보시오. (빠르기 & 정확도/브레인 + 마우스 운동)

protect

to keep from being damaged, attacked, stolen, or injured

defend, keep, guard, secure

보호하다

He promised to protect her all the days of her life.

provide

to supply something needed, you can use 'with' or 'for' in sentences

supply, give, contribute

주다, 제공하다, 공급하다

I provided him with money, or I provided money for him.

retain

to keep possession of or to continue to have

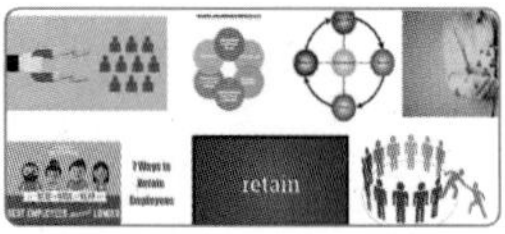

maintain, possess, reserve

유지하다, 지속하다, 보유하다, 계속해서 가지다

This soil retains water as if the sponge retains the water.

saw

to cut or divide with a saw

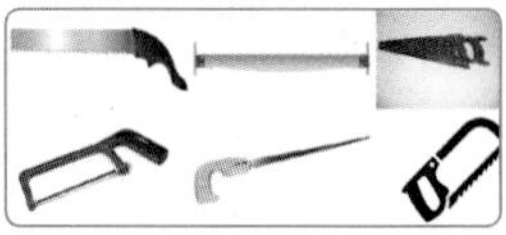

whipsaw, cut

톱질하다, (톱으로) 썰다, 톱

He sawed the log for the fireplace using a sawing machine.

* 이미지는 구글에서 찾은 것으로, 단어와 이미지가 다를 수 있습니다. 'Test 3'에서 나만의 이미지를 그려볼 수 있습니다.

Test 1 Connecting Exercise

Score(/16)
Self-Evaluation

➢ 서로 맞는 것을 연결하시오.

Ⓐ 1~4 영어 단어와 우리말 뜻 연결하기

1 retain	•	• 유지하다, 지속하다, 보유하다, 계속해서 가지다
2 provide	•	• 주다, 제공하다, 공급하다
3 protect	•	• 톱질하다, (톱으로) 썰다, 톱
4 saw	•	• 보호하다

Ⓑ 5~8 영어 단어와 영어 설명 연결하기

5 retain	•	• to keep possession of or to continue to have
6 protect	•	• to supply something needed, you can use 'with' or 'for' in sentences
7 saw	•	• to keep from being damaged, attacked, stolen, or injured
8 provide	•	• to cut or divide with a saw

Ⓒ 9~12 영어 단어와 동의어 연결하기

9 retain	•	• defend, keep, guard, secure
10 provide	•	• supply, give, contribute
11 protect	•	• whipsaw, cut
12 saw	•	• maintain, possess, reserve

Ⓓ 13~16 우리말 뜻과 영어 단어 연결하기

13 톱질하다, (톱으로) 썰다, 톱	•	• saw
14 유지하다, 지속하다, 보유하다, 계속해서 가지다	•	• retain
15 보호하다	•	• provide
16 주다, 제공하다, 공급하다	•	• protect

Test 2 Writing Exercise

Score(　　/12)
Self-Evaluation

Ⓐ 1~4 다음 단어에 맞는 뜻을 쓰시오.

1 protect ____________________

2 retain ____________________

3 provide ____________________

4 saw ____________________

Ⓑ 5~8 다음 뜻에 맞는 영어 단어와 영어 동의어, 영어 설명을 쓰시오.

5 유지하다, 지속하다, 보유하다, 계속해서 가지다

__________ ____________________

____

6 톱질하다, (톱으로) 썰다, 톱

__________ ____________________

____

7 보호하다

__________ ____________________

____

8 주다, 제공하다, 공급하다

__________ ____________________

____

Ⓒ 9~12 다음 영어 문장을 의미가 떠오를 때까지 소리 내어 읽어보시오. 3초 이내

9 He sawed the log for the fireplace using a sawing machine.

____

10 I provided him with money, or I provided money for him.

____

11 This soil retains water as if the sponge retains the water.

____

12 He promised to protect her all the days of her life.

____

Test 3 Imaging Exercise

➢ 다음 단어에 맞는 나만의 짧은 영어 설명을 써보자. (또는 그림을 그려보자.)

protect
[prətékt]

provide
[prəváid]

retain
[ritéin]

saw
[sɔː]

➢ Month 06-DAY 15 영어 문장과 우리말

He promised to protect her all the days of her life.
그는 평생 동안 그녀를 보호하겠다고 약속했습니다.

I provided him with money, or I provided money for him.
나는 그에게 돈을 주었습니다.

This soil retains water as if the sponge retains the water.
이 흙은 스펀지가 물을 보유하고 있는 것처럼 물을 보유합니다.

He sawed the log for the fireplace using a sawing machine.
그는 기계톱을 사용하여 벽난로용으로 통나무를 톱질했습니다.

DAY 16

Vocabulary

➢ 음원을 들으면서 소리를 무조건 따라해 보시오. (빠르기&정확도/브레인+마우스 운동)

sell, sold, sold

to exchange or deliver for money

trade, exchange

~을 팔다

I sold everything I owned except for my car and books.

sign

to write one's signature

mark, gesture, indicate

서명하다, 신호하다, 표지, 기호, 표시

When you sign a document, you write your name on it.

spy

to watch or observe secretly

watch, observe

정탐하다, 조심스럽게 살펴보다, 간첩

The police had been spying on the criminals for several months.

stammer

to speak with involuntary pauses or repetitions

stutter, falter, hem and haw

말을 더듬다, 말더듬

'You m-must m-m-meet m-my m-m-m-mother' is an example of a stammer.

* 이미지는 구글에서 찾은 것으로, 단어와 이미지가 다를 수 있습니다. 'Test 3'에서 나만의 이미지를 그려볼 수 있습니다.

Test 1 Connecting Exercise

Score(　　/16)
Self-Evaluation

➢ 서로 맞는 것을 연결하시오.

Ⓐ 1~4 영어 단어와 우리말 뜻 연결하기

1	sign	•	• 서명하다, 신호하다, 표지, 기호, 표시
2	sell, sold, sold	•	• 정탐하다, 조심스럽게 살펴보다, 간첩
3	spy	•	• 말을 더듬다, 말더듬
4	stammer	•	• ~을 팔다

Ⓑ 5~8 영어 단어와 영어 설명 연결하기

5	spy	•	• to speak with involuntary pauses or repetitions
6	sell, sold, sold	•	• to watch or observe secretly
7	sign	•	• to write one's signature
8	stammer	•	• to exchange or deliver for money

Ⓒ 9~12 영어 단어와 동의어 연결하기

9	sign	•	• stutter, falter, hem and haw
10	spy	•	• mark, gesture, indicate
11	sell, sold, sold	•	• watch, observe
12	stammer	•	• trade, exchange

Ⓓ 13~16 우리말 뜻과 영어 단어 연결하기

13	~을 팔다	•	• stammer
14	정탐하다, 조심스럽게 살펴보다, 간첩	•	• sign
15	말을 더듬다, 말더듬	•	• spy
16	서명하다, 신호하다, 표지, 기호, 표시	•	• sell, sold, sold

Test 2 Writing Exercise

Score(/12)
Self-Evaluation

A 1~4 다음 단어에 맞는 뜻을 쓰시오.

1 sign ______

2 stammer ______

3 sell, sold, sold ______

4 spy ______

B 5~8 다음 뜻에 맞는 영어 단어와 영어 동의어, 영어 설명을 쓰시오.

5 ~을 팔다

______ ______

______

6 서명하다, 신호하다, 표지, 기호, 표시

______ ______

______

7 정탐하다, 조심스럽게 살펴보다, 간첩

______ ______

______

8 말을 더듬다, 말더듬

______ ______

______

C 9~12 다음 영어 문장을 의미가 떠오를 때까지 소리 내어 읽어보시오. 3초 이내

9 The police had been spying on the criminals for several months.

______

10 I sold everything I owned except for my car and books.

______

11 'You m-must m-m-meet m-my m-m-m-mother' is an example of a stammer.

______

12 When you sign a document, you write your name on it.

______

Test 3

➢ 다음 단어에 맞는 나만의 짧은 영어 설명을 써보자. (또는 그림을 그려보자.)

sell, sold, sold
[sel, sould, sould]

sign
[sain]

spy
[spai]

stammer
[stǽmər]

➢ Month 06-DAY 16 영어 문장과 우리말

I sold everything I owned except for my car and books.
나는 책과 자동차를 제외한 내가 가진 모든 것을 팔았다.

When you sign a document, you write your name on it.
당신이 서류에 서명을 할 때, 당신은 거기에 당신의 이름을 씁니다.

The police had been spying on the criminals for several months.
경찰이 여러 달 동안 범죄자들을 감시해 왔습니다.

'You m-must m-m-meet m-my m-m-m-mother' is an example of a stammer.
'당신은 나-나의 ㅇ-어-엄마를 ㅁ-마-만나야 합니다'가 더듬거리는 것의 예다.

DAY 17 Vocabulary

➢ 음원을 들으면서 소리를 무조건 따라해 보시오. (빠르기&정확도/브레인+마우스 운동)

start

to take the first step in doing

initiate, set about, begin, proceed

첫 발걸음을 떼다, 출발하다, 떠나다, 시작하다

A new beginning of english learning has been started from VOCAPOD.

step

to move in steps

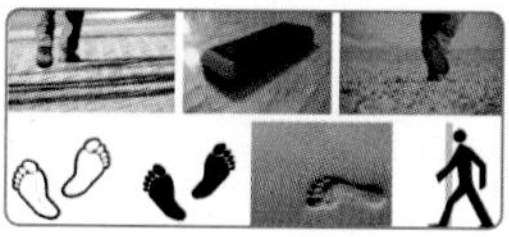

walk, pace, sidestep, footstep

밟다, 내딛다, 발걸음을 옮기다, 스텝, 단계, 걸음, 계단

Neil Armstrong became the first man to step onto the lunar surface.

threaten

to express a threat against

intimidate, menace, warn

위협하다, 협박하다

An armed robber threatened people with a knife at a restaurant.

belong

to be the property or possession of

be part of, relate to

속하다

If something belongs to you, you own it or it is yours.

* 이미지는 구글에서 찾은 것으로, 단어와 이미지가 다를 수 있습니다. 'Test 3'에서 나만의 이미지를 그려볼 수 있습니다.

Test 1 Connecting Exercise

Score(/16)
Self-Evaluation

➢ 서로 맞는 것을 연결하시오.

Ⓐ 1~4 영어 단어와 우리말 뜻 연결하기

1 start	• •	속하다
2 step	• •	밟다, 내딛다, 발걸음을 옮기다, 스텝, 단계, 걸음, 계단
3 threaten	• •	위협하다, 협박하다
4 belong	• •	첫 발걸음을 떼다, 출발하다, 떠나다, 시작하다

Ⓑ 5~8 영어 단어와 영어 설명 연결하기

5 step	• •	to move in steps
6 belong	• •	to express a threat against
7 start	• •	to take the first step in doing
8 threaten	• •	to be the property or possession of

Ⓒ 9~12 영어 단어와 동의어 연결하기

9 start	• •	walk, pace, sidestep, footstep
10 threaten	• •	be part of, relate to
11 step	• •	intimidate, menace, warn
12 belong	• •	initiate, set about, begin, proceed

Ⓓ 13~16 우리말 뜻과 영어 단어 연결하기

13 위협하다, 협박하다	• •	threaten
14 밟다, 내딛다, 발걸음을 옮기다, 스텝, 단계, 걸음, 계단	• •	belong
15 첫 발걸음을 떼다, 출발하다, 떠나다, 시작하다	• •	start
16 속하다	• •	step

Test 2 Writing Exercise

Score(　/12)
Self-Evaluation

A 1~4 다음 단어에 맞는 뜻을 쓰시오.

1 threaten ____________

2 belong ____________

3 start ____________

4 step ____________

B 5~8 다음 뜻에 맞는 영어 단어와 영어 동의어, 영어 설명을 쓰시오.

5 속하다

____________ ____________

____

6 첫 발걸음을 떼다, 출발하다, 떠나다, 시작하다

____________ ____________

____

7 밟다, 내딛다, 발걸음을 옮기다, 스텝, 단계, 걸음, 계단

____________ ____________

____

8 위협하다, 협박하다

____________ ____________

____

C 9~12 다음 영어 문장을 의미가 떠오를 때까지 소리 내어 읽어보시오. 3초 이내

9 An armed robber threatened people with a knife at a restaurant.

____

10 A new beginning of english learning has been started from VOCAPOD.

____

11 Neil Armstrong became the first man to step onto the lunar surface.

____

12 If something belongs to you, you own it or it is yours.

____

Test 3 Imaging Exercise

➢ 다음 단어에 맞는 나만의 짧은 영어 설명을 써보자. (또는 그림을 그려보자.)

start
[staːrt]

step
[step]

threaten
[θrétn]

belong
[bilɔ́ːŋ]

➢ Month 06-DAY 17 영어 문장과 우리말

A new beginning of english learning has been started from VOCAPOD.
보카팟에서부터 영어학습의 새로운 시작이 시작되었습니다.

Neil Armstrong became the first man to step onto the lunar surface.
닐 암스트롱은 달 표면을 밟은 최초의 사람이 되었습니다.

An armed robber threatened people with a knife at a restaurant.
무장 강도가 식당에서 사람들을 칼로 위협하였습니다.

If something belongs to you, you own it or it is yours.
어떤 것이 당신에게 속하게 된다면 당신은 그것을 소유하거나 그것은 당신 것입니다.

DAY 18

Vocabulary

➢ 음원을 들으면서 소리를 무조건 따라해 보시오. (빠르기&정확도/브레인+마우스 운동)

compose

to make or create by putting together parts or elements

constitute, comprise, build, construct

구성하다, 작곡하다

Sugar and water compose syrup. Syrup is composed of sugar and water.

crow

to utter the characteristic cry of a rooster

squawk

수탉의 특징적 울음을 내다, 수탉이 울다, 까마귀

Crows are large black birds that are known for their high intelligence.

direct

to manage or guide by advice, instruction, etc.

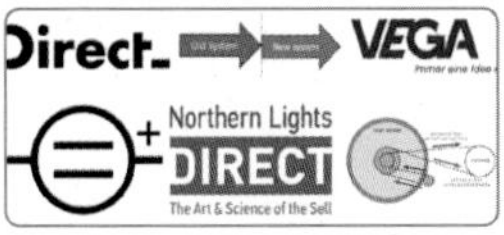

control, run, manage, guide

감독하다, 관리하다, 지시하다, 가리키다, 직접의

A director is a man who directs a play or a film.

dissolve

to make a solution of, as by mixing with a liquid

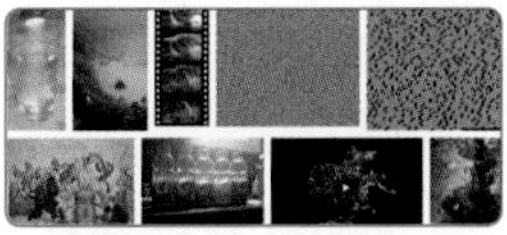

melt, liquefy, disappear, vanish

녹다, 녹이다, 없애다, 소멸시키다, 소멸되다

Salt dissolves in water, and water has the ability to dissolve salt.

* 이미지는 구글에서 찾은 것으로, 단어와 이미지가 다를 수 있습니다. 'Test 3'에서 나만의 이미지를 그려볼 수 있습니다.

Test 1 Connecting Exercise

Score(/16)
Self-Evaluation

➢ 서로 맞는 것을 연결하시오.

Ⓐ 1~4 영어 단어와 우리말 뜻 연결하기

1 dissolve	•	• 녹다, 녹이다, 없애다, 소멸시키다, 소멸되다
2 compose	•	• 감독하다, 관리하다, 지시하다, 가리키다, 직접의
3 direct	•	• 구성하다, 작곡하다
4 crow	•	• 수탉의 특징적 울음을 내다, 수탉이 울다, 까마귀

Ⓑ 5~8 영어 단어와 영어 설명 연결하기

5 dissolve	•	• to make or create by putting together parts or elements
6 compose	•	• to make a solution of, as by mixing with a liquid
7 crow	•	• to utter the characteristic cry of a rooster
8 direct	•	• to manage or guide by advice, instruction, etc.

Ⓒ 9~12 영어 단어와 동의어 연결하기

9 direct	•	• control, run, manage, guide
10 crow	•	• constitute, comprise, build, construct
11 compose	•	• squawk
12 dissolve	•	• melt, liquefy, disappear, vanish

Ⓓ 13~16 우리말 뜻과 영어 단어 연결하기

13 구성하다, 작곡하다	•	• compose
14 수탉의 특징적 울음을 내다, 수탉이 울다, 까마귀	•	• crow
15 감독하다, 관리하다, 지시하다, 가리키다, 직접의	•	• dissolve
16 녹다, 녹이다, 없애다, 소멸시키다, 소멸되다	•	• direct

Test 2 Writing Exercise

Score(　/12)
Self-Evaluation

A 1~4 다음 단어에 맞는 뜻을 쓰시오.

1 direct ______

2 dissolve ______

3 crow ______

4 compose ______

B 5~8 다음 뜻에 맞는 영어 단어와 영어 동의어, 영어 설명을 쓰시오.

5 녹다, 녹이다, 없애다, 소멸시키다, 소멸되다

______ ______

______

6 수탉의 특징적 울음을 내다, 수탉이 울다, 까마귀

______ ______

______

7 감독하다, 관리하다, 지시하다, 가리키다, 직접의

______ ______

______

8 구성하다, 작곡하다

______ ______

______

C 9~12 다음 영어 문장을 의미가 떠오를 때까지 소리 내어 읽어보시오. 3초 이내

9 A director is a man who directs a play or a film.

______

10 Crows are large black birds that are known for their high intelligence.

______

11 Salt dissolves in water, and water has the ability to dissolve salt.

______

12 Sugar and water compose syrup. Syrup is composed of sugar and water.

______

Test 3 Imaging Exercise

➢ 다음 단어에 맞는 나만의 짧은 영어 설명을 써보자. (또는 그림을 그려보자.)

compose
[kəmpóuz]

crow
[krou]

direct
[dirékt]

dissolve
[dizálv]

➢ Month 06-DAY 18 영어 문장과 우리말

Sugar and water compose syrup. Syrup is composed of sugar and water.
설탕과 물이 시럽을 구성합니다. 시럽은 설탕과 물로 이루어져 있습니다.

Crows are large black birds that are known for their high intelligence.
까마귀는 그들의 높은 지능으로 잘 알려진 크고 검은 새입니다.

A director is a man who directs a play or a film.
감독은 연극이나 영화를 감독하는 사람입니다.

Salt dissolves in water, and water has the ability to dissolve salt.
소금은 물에 녹고, 물은 소금을 녹일 수 있습니다.

Vocabulary

➢ 음원을 들으면서 소리를 무조건 따라해 보시오. (빠르기&정확도/브레인+마우스 운동)

enlist

to enter the armed forces, or to engage the support

enroll, enter, register, participate

입대하다, 참가하다, 협력을 약속하다

He enlisted as a soldier for the army in the Korean War.

fix

to correct or set right, or to place permanently

adjust, correct, repair, mend

고치다, 고정시키다, (시간, 장소 등을) 정하다

After fixing a broken machine, I fixed the mirror to the wall.

foretell

to tell about or make known (future events) in advance

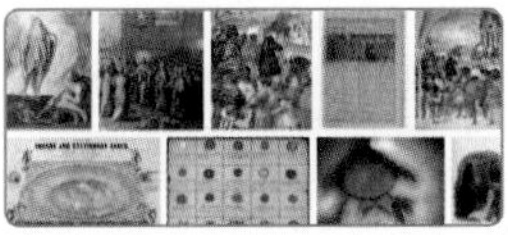

predict, prophesy, forecast

예고하다, 예측하다, 예언하다

An astrologer is a person who foretells the future from the stars.

hide, hid, hidden

to put or keep out of sight

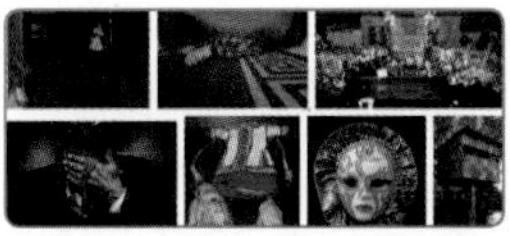

conceal, keep secret

숨기다, 감추다, 가리다, 숨다

After hiding the bicycle in the bushes, we hid behind a tree.

* 이미지는 구글에서 찾은 것으로, 단어와 이미지가 다를 수 있습니다. 'Test 3'에서 나만의 이미지를 그려볼 수 있습니다.

Test 1 Connecting Exercise

Score(　/16)
Self-Evaluation

➢ 서로 맞는 것을 연결하시오.

Ⓐ 1~4 영어 단어와 우리말 뜻 연결하기

1 foretell	●	● 입대하다, 참가하다, 협력을 약속하다
2 hide, hid, hidden	●	● 예고하다, 예측하다, 예언하다
3 fix	●	● 고치다, 고정시키다, (시간, 장소 등을) 정하다
4 enlist	●	● 숨기다, 감추다, 가리다, 숨다

Ⓑ 5~8 영어 단어와 영어 설명 연결하기

5 enlist	●	● to put or keep out of sight
6 fix	●	● to tell about or make known (future events) in advance
7 hide, hid, hidden	●	● to correct or set right, or to place permanently
8 foretell	●	● to enter the armed forces, or to engage the support

Ⓒ 9~12 영어 단어와 동의어 연결하기

9 enlist	●	● conceal, keep secret
10 fix	●	● adjust, correct, repair, mend
11 foretell	●	● predict, prophesy, forecast
12 hide, hid, hidden	●	● enroll, enter, register, participate

Ⓓ 13~16 우리말 뜻과 영어 단어 연결하기

13 예고하다, 예측하다, 예언하다	●	● fix
14 입대하다, 참가하다, 협력을 약속하다	●	● hide, hid, hidden
15 고치다, 고정시키다, (시간, 장소 등을) 정하다	●	● foretell
16 숨기다, 감추다, 가리다, 숨다	●	● enlist

Test 2 Writing Exercise

Score(　　/12)
Self-Evaluation

A 1~4 다음 단어에 맞는 뜻을 쓰시오.

1 hide, hid, hidden ____________

2 foretell ____________

3 enlist ____________

4 fix ____________

B 5~8 다음 뜻에 맞는 영어 단어와 영어 동의어, 영어 설명을 쓰시오.

5 고치다, 고정시키다, (시간, 장소 등을) 정하다

____________ ____________

____

6 숨기다, 감추다, 가리다, 숨다

____________ ____________

____

7 입대하다, 참가하다, 협력을 약속하다

____________ ____________

____

8 예고하다, 예측하다, 예언하다

____________ ____________

____

C 9~12 다음 영어 문장을 의미가 떠오를 때까지 소리 내어 읽어보시오. 3초 이내

9 An astrologer is a person who foretells the future from the stars.

____

10 He enlisted as a soldier for the army in the Korean War.

____

11 After fixing a broken machine, I fixed the mirror to the wall.

____

12 After hiding the bicycle in the bushes, we hid behind a tree.

____

Test 3 Imaging Exercise

➢ 다음 단어에 맞는 나만의 짧은 영어 설명을 써보자. (또는 그림을 그려보자.)

enlist
[inlíst]

fix
[fiks]

foretell
[fɔrte'l]

hide, hid, hidden
[haid, hid, hídn]

➢ Month 06-DAY 19 영어 문장과 우리말

He enlisted as a soldier for the army in the Korean War.
그는 한국전쟁에서 육군 병사로 입대하였습니다.

After fixing a broken machine, I fixed the mirror to the wall.
고장 난 기계를 수리한 후 나는 거울을 벽에 걸었습니다.

An astrologer is a person who foretells the future from the stars.
점성가란 별을 보고 미래를 예언하는 사람입니다.

After hiding the bicycle in the bushes, we hid behind a tree.
수풀 속에 자전거를 숨기고 나서, 우리는 나무 뒤에 숨었습니다.

Vocabulary

➢ 음원을 들으면서 소리를 무조건 따라해 보시오. (빠르기&정확도/브레인+마우스 운동)

immigrate

to immigrate is to settle in a new country, but to emigrate is to leave a native country

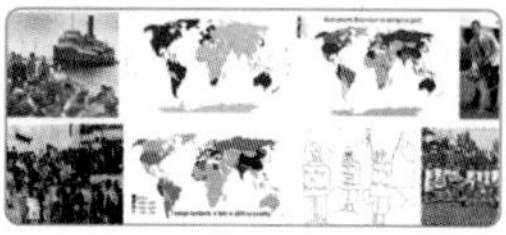

migrate, emigrate, transmigrate

이주해오다

My grandparents emigrated from Russia and they immigrated to the United States.

leap

to move quickly or suddenly upward

spring, jump, bound, bounce

뛰다, 도약하다, 도약

You have to leap over the hurdle of english listening by VOCAPOD.

load

to put on or take on a load, as of passengers or goods

burden, charge, fill, heap

(물건, 짐을) 싣다, 태우다,
힘이 걸리게 하다, 짐

We had loaded all our equipment into the back of the truck.

murder

to kill (someone) unlawfully

kill, assassinate

죽이다, 살인하다, 살해, 살인

Thousands of civilians were murdered in the attacks of September 11, 2001.

* 이미지는 구글에서 찾은 것으로, 단어와 이미지가 다를 수 있습니다. 'Test 3'에서 나만의 이미지를 그려볼 수 있습니다.

Test 1 Connecting Exercise

Score(/16)
Self-Evaluation

➢ 서로 맞는 것을 연결하시오.

Ⓐ 1~4 영어 단어와 우리말 뜻 연결하기

1	leap	● ●	이주해오다
2	immigrate	● ●	죽이다, 살인하다, 살해, 살인
3	murder	● ●	뛰다, 도약하다, 도약
4	load	● ●	(물건, 짐을) 싣다, 태우다, 힘이 걸리게 하다, 짐

Ⓑ 5~8 영어 단어와 영어 설명 연결하기

5	load	● ●	to put on or take on a load, as of passengers or goods
6	murder	● ●	to move quickly or suddenly upward
7	immigrate	● ●	to immigrate is to settle in a new country, but to emigrate is to leave a native country
8	leap	● ●	to kill (someone) unlawfully

Ⓒ 9~12 영어 단어와 동의어 연결하기

9	immigrate	● ●	burden, charge, fill, heap
10	load	● ●	spring, jump, bound, bounce
11	murder	● ●	kill, assassinate
12	leap	● ●	migrate, emigrate, transmigrate

Ⓓ 13~16 우리말 뜻과 영어 단어 연결하기

13	이주해오다	● ●	immigrate
14	죽이다, 살인하다, 살해, 살인	● ●	leap
15	(물건, 짐을) 싣다, 태우다, 힘이 걸리게 하다, 짐	● ●	murder
16	뛰다, 도약하다, 도약	● ●	load

Test 2 Writing Exercise

Score(/12)
Self-Evaluation

Ⓐ 1~4 다음 단어에 맞는 뜻을 쓰시오.

1 murder ____________________

2 leap ____________________

3 load ____________________

4 immigrate ____________________

Ⓑ 5~8 다음 뜻에 맞는 영어 단어와 영어 동의어, 영어 설명을 쓰시오.

5 뛰다, 도약하다, 도약

__________ ____________________

____

6 (물건, 짐을) 싣다, 태우다, 힘이 걸리게 하다, 짐

__________ ____________________

____

7 죽이다, 살인하다, 살해, 살인

__________ ____________________

____

8 이주해오다

__________ ____________________

____

Ⓒ 9~12 다음 영어 문장을 의미가 떠오를 때까지 소리 내어 읽어보시오. 3초 이내

9 You have to leap over the hurdle of english listening by VOCAPOD.

____

10 Thousands of civilians were murdered in the attacks of September 11, 2001.

____

11 We had loaded all our equipment into the back of the truck.

____

12 My grandparents emigrated from Russia and they immigrated to the United States.

____

Test 3 Imaging Exercise

➢ 다음 단어에 맞는 나만의 짧은 영어 설명을 써보자. (또는 그림을 그려보자.)

immigrate
[íməgrèit]

leap
[liːp]

load
[loud]

murder
[mə́ːrdər]

➢ Month 06-DAY 20 영어 문장과 우리말

My grandparents emigrated from Russia and they immigrated to the United States.
우리 조부모들은 러시아에서 이민 오셨고, 미국으로 이민 오셨습니다.

You have to leap over the hurdle of english listening by VOCAPOD.
당신은 보카팟으로 영어듣기의 허들(장애물)을 뛰어넘어야 합니다.

We had loaded all our equipment into the back of the truck.
우리는 우리들의 모든 장비를 트럭 뒤 칸에 실었습니다.

Thousands of civilians were murdered in the attacks of September 11, 2001.
2001년 9월 11일 공격에 수천 명의 시민들이 살해당했습니다.

Month **07** Verbs

Day 01	own, pop, pull, punch
Day 02	reach, realize, relax, roll
Day 03	toss, welcome, whirl, affect
Day 04	divide, donate, export, import
Day 05	mix, prepare, push, rebuild
Day 06	thank, emigrate, heat, produce
Day 07	sail, seal, bump, comb
Day 08	compare, bake, crash, imagine
Day 09	print, rear, reserve, state
Day 10	hire, rent, rise, appreciate

DAY 01 Vocabulary

➢ **음원을 들으면서 소리를 무조건 따라해 보시오.** (빠르기 & 정확도/브레인 + 마우스 운동)

own

to have or possess as property

possess, have, hold, retain

소유하다

I own that car, so I am the owner of that car.

pop

to make a short, sharp, explosive sound

burst, bang, explode

(갑자기 뻥하고) 터지다, 커지다, 나타나다

I popped the balloon, and my friend's eyes popped with astonishment.

pull

to draw or tug at with force

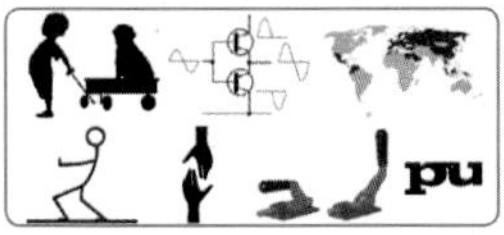

drag, draw, tug, haul

잡아당기다, 끌다

This locomotive of push–pull trains can pull 100 cars at maximum.

punch

to hit with a sharp blow of the fist, or to make a hole

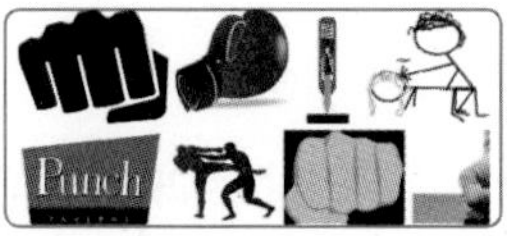

hit, strike, box, smash

(사람, 물건 등을) 세게 치다, 구멍을 뚫다

After punching him on the chin, she hit him over the head.

* 이미지는 구글에서 찾은 것으로, 단어와 이미지가 다를 수 있습니다. 'Test 3'에서 나만의 이미지를 그려볼 수 있습니다.

Test 1 Connecting Exercise

Score(/16)
Self-Evaluation

➢ 서로 맞는 것을 연결하시오.

Ⓐ 1~4 영어 단어와 우리말 뜻 연결하기

1 own	•	•	잡아당기다, 끌다
2 pop	•	•	소유하다
3 punch	•	•	(사람, 물건 등을) 세게 치다, 구멍을 뚫다
4 pull	•	•	(갑자기 뻥하고) 터지다, 커지다, 나타나다

Ⓑ 5~8 영어 단어와 영어 설명 연결하기

5 punch	•	•	to hit with a sharp blow of the fist, or to make a hole
6 pull	•	•	to have or possess as property
7 pop	•	•	to make a short, sharp, explosive sound
8 own	•	•	to draw or tug at with force

Ⓒ 9~12 영어 단어와 동의어 연결하기

9 punch	•	•	possess, have, hold, retain
10 pull	•	•	drag, draw, tug, haul
11 pop	•	•	hit, strike, box, smash
12 own	•	•	burst, bang, explode

Ⓓ 13~16 우리말 뜻과 영어 단어 연결하기

13 소유하다	•	•	own
14 (갑자기 뻥하고) 터지다, 커지다, 나타나다	•	•	pop
15 잡아당기다, 끌다	•	•	pull
16 (사람, 물건 등을) 세게 치다, 구멍을 뚫다	•	•	punch

Test 2 Writing Exercise

Score(/12)
Self-Evaluation

Ⓐ 1~4 다음 단어에 맞는 뜻을 쓰시오.

1 pop

2 own

3 punch

4 pull

Ⓑ 5~8 다음 뜻에 맞는 영어 단어와 영어 동의어, 영어 설명을 쓰시오.

5 잡아당기다, 끌다

6 소유하다

7 (갑자기 뻥하고) 터지다, 커지다, 나타나다

8 (사람, 물건 등을) 세게 치다, 구멍을 뚫다

Ⓒ 9~12 다음 영어 문장을 의미가 떠오를 때까지 소리 내어 읽어보시오. 3초 이내

9 I own that car, so I am the owner of that car.

10 I popped the balloon, and my friend's eyes popped with astonishment.

11 After punching him on the chin, she hit him over the head.

12 This locomotive of push–pull trains can pull 100 cars at maximum.

Test 3 Imaging Exercise

➤ 다음 단어에 맞는 나만의 짧은 영어 설명을 써보자. (또는 그림을 그려보자.)

own
[oun]

pop
[pap]

pull
[pul]

punch
[pʌntʃ]

➤ Month 07-DAY 01 영어 문장과 우리말

I own that car, so I am the owner of that car.
내가 그 차를 소유하고 있습니다, 그래서 내가 그 차의 소유주입니다.

I popped the balloon, and my friend's eyes popped with astonishment.
내가 풍선을 터뜨렸고, 내 친구의 두 눈이 놀라서 휘둥그레졌습니다.

This locomotive of push-pull trains can pull 100 cars at maximum.
이 기관차는 최대 100량의 열차를 끌 수 있습니다.

After punching him on the chin, she hit him over the head.
그의 턱에 펀치를 날린 후 그녀는 그의 머리를 가격했습니다.

Vocabulary

➢ 음원을 들으면서 소리를 무조건 따라해 보시오. (빠르기 & 정확도/브레인 + 마우스 운동)

reach

to stretch out, or to arrive at

extend, attain

쭉 뻗다, 도착하다, 도달하다

I reached out my arm but I could not reach the shelf.

realize

to comprehend completely or correctly

understand, recognize, cognize, know

알다, 깨닫다

I realized my mistake and I apologized to her for my rudeness.

relax

to make lax or loose

ease, let up, loose

쉬다, 긴장을 풀다, 편안하게 하다

I relaxed in the hot tub, because the warm bath relaxed me.

roll

to move forward along a surface by revolving

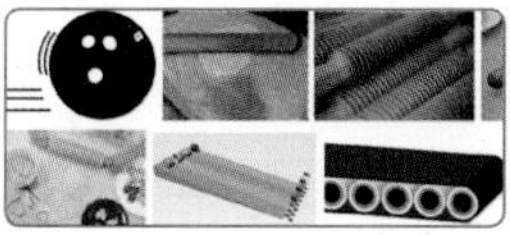

turn, wheel, spin

구르다, 굴리다,
돌돌 말은 것(음식, 과자, 물건 등)

The car went off the road and rolled over into a ditch.

* 이미지는 구글에서 찾은 것으로, 단어와 이미지가 다를 수 있습니다. 'Test 3'에서 나만의 이미지를 그려볼 수 있습니다.

Test 1 Connecting Exercise

Score(/16)
Self-Evaluation

➢ 서로 맞는 것을 연결하시오.

A 1~4 영어 단어와 우리말 뜻 연결하기

1 reach	●	●	알다, 깨닫다
2 roll	●	●	쉬다, 긴장을 풀다, 편안하게 하다
3 relax	●	●	구르다, 굴리다, 돌돌 말은 것(음식, 과자, 물건 등)
4 realize	●	●	쭉 뻗다, 도착하다, 도달하다

B 5~8 영어 단어와 영어 설명 연결하기

5 realize	●	●	to comprehend completely or correctly
6 reach	●	●	to make lax or loose
7 roll	●	●	to stretch out, or to arrive at
8 relax	●	●	to move forward along a surface by revolving

C 9~12 영어 단어와 동의어 연결하기

9 realize	●	●	ease, let up, loose
10 roll	●	●	understand, recognize, cognize, know
11 reach	●	●	turn, wheel, spin
12 relax	●	●	extend, attain

D 13~16 우리말 뜻과 영어 단어 연결하기

13 쉬다, 긴장을 풀다, 편안하게 하다	●	●	reach
14 구르다, 굴리다, 돌돌 말은 것(음식, 과자, 물건 등)	●	●	realize
15 쭉 뻗다, 도착하다, 도달하다	●	●	roll
16 알다, 깨닫다	●	●	relax

Test 2 Writing Exercise

Score(/12)
Self-Evaluation

A 1~4 다음 단어에 맞는 뜻을 쓰시오.

1 relax ______

2 reach ______

3 roll ______

4 realize ______

B 5~8 다음 뜻에 맞는 영어 단어와 영어 동의어, 영어 설명을 쓰시오.

5 구르다, 굴리다, 돌돌 말은 것(음식, 과자, 물건 등)

______ ______

______

6 알다, 깨닫다

______ ______

______

7 쉬다, 긴장을 풀다, 편안하게 하다

______ ______

______

8 쭉 뻗다, 도착하다, 도달하다

______ ______

______

C 9~12 다음 영어 문장을 의미가 떠오를 때까지 소리 내어 읽어보시오. 3초 이내

9 I reached out my arm but I could not reach the shelf.

______

10 I relaxed in the hot tub, because the warm bath relaxed me.

______

11 The car went off the road and rolled over into a ditch.

______

12 I realized my mistake and I apologized to her for my rudeness.

______

Test 3 Imaging Exercise

➢ 다음 단어에 맞는 나만의 짧은 영어 설명을 써보자. (또는 그림을 그려보자.)

reach
[riːʧ]

realize
[ríːəlàiz]

relax
[rilǽks]

roll
[roul]

➢ Month 07-DAY 02 영어 문장과 우리말

I reached out my arm but I could not reach the shelf.
나는 팔을 뻗었지만 선반에 닿을 수 없었습니다.

I realized my mistake and I apologized to her for my rudeness.
나는 나의 실수를 알아챘고, 그녀에게 나의 무례함을 사과했다.

I relaxed in the hot tub, because the warm bath relaxed me.
따뜻한 목욕은 나를 편안하게 하기 때문에 나는 뜨거운 욕조에서 긴장을 풀었습니다.

The car went off the road and rolled over into a ditch.
차가 도로를 벗어나 도랑으로 굴렀습니다.

Vocabulary

➢ 음원을 들으면서 소리를 무조건 따라해 보시오. (빠르기&정확도/브레인+마우스 운동)

toss

to throw lightly

throw, cast, dart, hurl, fling

던지다

We tossed a coin to decide which of us should go first.

welcome

to receive or accept gladly

greet, hail, salute

환영하다, 환영하는, 환영

Several people came out to welcome me and said 'You're welcome!'

whirl

to cause to rotate or turn rapidly

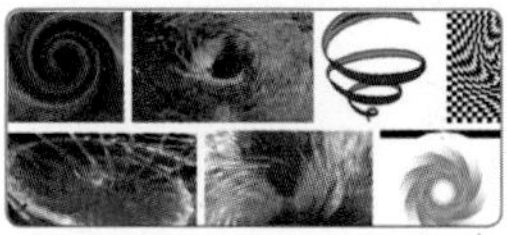

spin, swirl, twiddle, twirl

빠르게 돌리다, 빙빙 돌리다, 돌다, 소용돌이

Figure skate dancers whirl, glide, lift and perform dance movements on ice.

affect

to have an influence on

influence, impact, act on

영향을 미치다

There are many ways in which the climatic change can affect our lives.

* 이미지는 구글에서 찾은 것으로, 단어와 이미지가 다를 수 있습니다. 'Test 3'에서 나만의 이미지를 그려볼 수 있습니다.

Test 1 Connecting Exercise

Score(/16)
Self-Evaluation

➢ 서로 맞는 것을 연결하시오.

Ⓐ 1~4 영어 단어와 우리말 뜻 연결하기

1 affect	•	• 빠르게 돌리다, 빙빙 돌리다, 돌다, 소용돌이
2 welcome	•	• 던지다
3 toss	•	• 환영하다, 환영하는, 환영
4 whirl	•	• 영향을 미치다

Ⓑ 5~8 영어 단어와 영어 설명 연결하기

5 toss	•	• to cause to rotate or turn rapidly
6 welcome	•	• to have an influence on
7 affect	•	• to throw lightly
8 whirl	•	• to receive or accept gladly

Ⓒ 9~12 영어 단어와 동의어 연결하기

9 whirl	•	• throw, cast, dart, hurl, fling
10 affect	•	• greet, hail, salute
11 toss	•	• spin, swirl, twiddle, twirl
12 welcome	•	• influence, impact, act on

Ⓓ 13~16 우리말 뜻과 영어 단어 연결하기

13 빠르게 돌리다, 빙빙 돌리다, 돌다, 소용돌이	•	• toss
14 던지다	•	• affect
15 환영하다, 환영하는, 환영	•	• whirl
16 영향을 미치다	•	• welcome

Test 2 Writing Exercise

Score(/12)
Self-Evaluation

Ⓐ 1~4 다음 단어에 맞는 뜻을 쓰시오.

1 toss ______

2 whirl ______

3 affect ______

4 welcome ______

Ⓑ 5~8 다음 뜻에 맞는 영어 단어와 영어 동의어, 영어 설명을 쓰시오.

5 빠르게 돌리다, 빙빙 돌리다, 돌다, 소용돌이

______ ______

______

6 환영하다, 환영하는, 환영

______ ______

______

7 영향을 미치다

______ ______

______

8 던지다

______ ______

______

Ⓒ 9~12 다음 영어 문장을 의미가 떠오를 때까지 소리 내어 읽어보시오. 3초 이내

9 Figure skate dancers whirl, glide, lift and perform dance movements on ice.

______

10 We tossed a coin to decide which of us should go first.

______

11 There are many ways in which the climatic change can affect our lives.

______

12 Several people came out to welcome me and said 'You're welcome!'

______

Test 3 Imaging Exercise

➢ 다음 단어에 맞는 나만의 짧은 영어 설명을 써보자. (또는 그림을 그려보자.)

toss
[tɔːs]

welcome
[wélkəm]

whirl
[hwəːrl]

affect
[əfékt]

➢ Month 07-DAY 03 영어 문장과 우리말

We tossed a coin to decide which of us should go first.
우리는 우리 중 누가 먼저 가야 할지를 결정하기 위해 동전 던지기를 했습니다.

Several people came out to welcome me and said 'You're welcome!'
여러 사람이 나를 환영하러 나왔고 '당신을 환영합니다'하고 말해 주었습니다.

Figure skate dancers whirl, glide, lift and perform dance movements on ice.
피겨스케이트 댄서들이 얼음 위에서 돌고, 미끄러지고, 도약하고 춤동작을 보입니다.

There are many ways in which the climatic change can affect our lives.
기후 변화가 사람들의 삶에 영향을 미치는 길이 많이 있다.

DAY 04 Vocabulary

➢ 음원을 들으면서 소리를 무조건 따라해 보시오. (빠르기&정확도/브레인+마우스 운동)

divide

to separate into parts, sections, groups, or branches

separate, part, split

나누다, 쪼개다, 분할하다

The World War II divided the Korean Peninsula into South and North Korea.

donate

to present as a gift to a fund

give, present, contribute

기부하다, 기증하다

I donated blood to the Red Cross for the victims of the earthquake.

export

to sell abroad, especially for trade

sell abroad

수출하다, 수출, 수출품

When a country exports more than it imports, it has a trade surplus.

import

to buy (goods or services) from a foreign country

bring in, buy in, ship in

수입하다, 수입, 수입품

When a country imports more than it exports, it has a trade deficit.

* 이미지는 구글에서 찾은 것으로, 단어와 이미지가 다를 수 있습니다. 'Test 3'에서 나만의 이미지를 그려볼 수 있습니다.

Test 1 Connecting Exercise

Score(　　/16)
Self-Evaluation

➢ 서로 맞는 것을 연결하시오.

Ⓐ 1~4 영어 단어와 우리말 뜻 연결하기

1 import	•	• 수출하다, 수출, 수출품
2 export	•	• 나누다, 쪼개다, 분할하다
3 donate	•	• 수입하다, 수입, 수입품
4 divide	•	• 기부하다, 기증하다

Ⓑ 5~8 영어 단어와 영어 설명 연결하기

5 export	•	• to present as a gift to a fund
6 divide	•	• to separate into parts, sections, groups, or branches
7 import	•	• to sell abroad, especially for trade
8 donate	•	• to buy (goods or services) from a foreign country

Ⓒ 9~12 영어 단어와 동의어 연결하기

9 export	•	• separate, part, split
10 donate	•	• bring in, buy in, ship in
11 divide	•	• give, present, contribute
12 import	•	• sell abroad

Ⓓ 13~16 우리말 뜻과 영어 단어 연결하기

13 기부하다, 기증하다	•	• donate
14 수입하다, 수입, 수입품	•	• export
15 나누다, 쪼개다, 분할하다	•	• import
16 수출하다, 수출, 수출품	•	• divide

Test 2 Writing Exercise

Score(　　/12)
Self-Evaluation

Ⓐ 1~4 다음 단어에 맞는 뜻을 쓰시오.

1 export ____________________

2 import ____________________

3 divide ____________________

4 donate ____________________

Ⓑ 5~8 다음 뜻에 맞는 영어 단어와 영어 동의어, 영어 설명을 쓰시오.

5 나누다, 쪼개다, 분할하다

__________ ____________________

____

6 수출하다, 수출, 수출품

__________ ____________________

____

7 기부하다, 기증하다

__________ ____________________

____

8 수입하다, 수입, 수입품

__________ ____________________

____

Ⓒ 9~12 다음 영어 문장을 의미가 떠오를 때까지 소리 내어 읽어보시오. 3.5초 이내

9 When a country imports more than it exports, it has a trade deficit.

____

10 The World War II divided the Korean Peninsula into South and North Korea.

____

11 I donated blood to the Red Cross for the victims of the earthquake.

____

12 When a country exports more than it imports, it has a trade surplus.

____

Test 3 Imaging Exercise

➢ 다음 단어에 맞는 나만의 짧은 영어 설명을 써보자. (또는 그림을 그려보자.)

divide
[diváid]

donate
[dóuneit]

export
[ikspɔ́:rt]

import
[impɔ́:rt]

➢ Month 07-DAY 04 영어 문장과 우리말

The World War II divided the Korean Peninsula into South and North Korea.
2차 세계대전이 한반도를 남한과 북한으로 갈라놓았다.

I donated blood to the Red Cross for the victims of the earthquake.
나는 지진 피해자들을 위하여 적십자사에 헌혈하였다.

When a country exports more than it imports, it has a trade surplus.
한 나라가 수입보다 수출이 많을 때 무역흑자가 됩니다.

When a country imports more than it exports, it has a trade deficit.
한 나라가 수출보다 수입이 많을 때 무역적자가 됩니다.

Vocabulary

➢ 음원을 들으면서 소리를 무조건 따라해 보시오. (빠르기&정확도/브레인+마우스 운동)

mix

to combine or blend into one mass or mixture

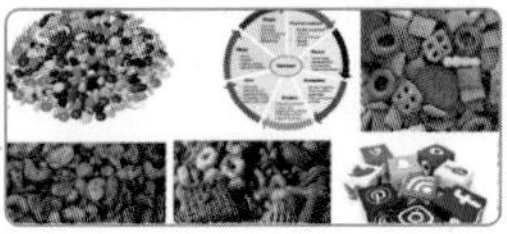

combine, blend, merge, unite

섞다, 섞이다, 섞음, 혼합, 혼합물

I tried to mix oil with water, but oil and water didn't mix.

prepare

to make or get ready

ready, make, arrange

준비하다, 만들다

To prepare for an examination is the best way to pass the exam.

push

to exert pressure or force against something

shove, press, thrust, drive

~을 밀다, 밀어붙이다,
~에 압력이나 힘을 가하다

She pushed him away, and she pushed the door open and ran away.

rebuild, rebuilt, rebuilt

to build again

renovate, remodel, reconstruct, refashion

다시 짓다, 다시 만들다

This building has been rebuilt after it had been destroyed by an earthquake.

* 이미지는 구글에서 찾은 것으로, 단어와 이미지가 다를 수 있습니다. 'Test 3'에서 나만의 이미지를 그려볼 수 있습니다.

Test 1 Connecting Exercise

Score(/16)
Self-Evaluation

➢ 서로 맞는 것을 연결하시오.

Ⓐ 1~4 영어 단어와 우리말 뜻 연결하기

1	push	~을 밀다, 밀어붙이다, ~에 압력이나 힘을 가하다
2	rebuild, rebuilt, rebuilt	섞다, 섞이다, 섞음, 혼합, 혼합물
3	mix	다시 짓다, 다시 만들다
4	prepare	준비하다, 만들다

Ⓑ 5~8 영어 단어와 영어 설명 연결하기

5	rebuild, rebuilt, rebuilt	to make or get ready
6	push	to build again
7	prepare	to combine or blend into one mass or mixture
8	mix	to exert pressure or force against something

Ⓒ 9~12 영어 단어와 동의어 연결하기

9	prepare	renovate, remodel, reconstruct, refashion
10	push	shove, press, thrust, drive
11	mix	combine, blend, merge, unite
12	rebuild, rebuilt, rebuilt	ready, make, arrange

Ⓓ 13~16 우리말 뜻과 영어 단어 연결하기

13	~을 밀다, 밀어붙이다, ~에 압력이나 힘을 가하다	push
14	섞다, 섞이다, 섞음, 혼합, 혼합물	rebuild, rebuilt, rebuilt
15	다시 짓다, 다시 만들다	mix
16	준비하다, 만들다	prepare

Test 2 Writing Exercise

Score(/12)
Self-Evaluation

A 1~4 다음 단어에 맞는 뜻을 쓰시오.

1 mix ______________________

2 push ______________________

3 prepare ______________________

4 rebuild, rebuilt, rebuilt ______________________

B 5~8 다음 뜻에 맞는 영어 단어와 영어 동의어, 영어 설명을 쓰시오.

5 ~을 밀다, 밀어붙이다, ~에 압력이나 힘을 가하다

______________ ______________________

____

6 섞다, 섞이다, 섞음, 혼합, 혼합물

______________ ______________________

____

7 다시 짓다, 다시 만들다

______________ ______________________

____

8 준비하다, 만들다

______________ ______________________

____

C 9~12 다음 영어 문장을 의미가 떠오를 때까지 소리 내어 읽어보시오. 3.5초 이내

9 To prepare for an examination is the best way to pass the exam.

____

10 She pushed him away, and she pushed the door open and ran away.

____

11 This building has been rebuilt after it had been destroyed by an earthquake.

____

12 I tried to mix oil with water, but oil and water didn't mix.

____

Test 3

➢ 다음 단어에 맞는 나만의 짧은 영어 설명을 써보자. (또는 그림을 그려보자.)

mix
[miks]

prepare
[pripέər]

push
[puʃ]

rebuild, rebuilt, rebuilt
[ribi'ld, ribilt, ribilt]

➢ Month 07-DAY 05 영어 문장과 우리말

I tried to mix oil with water, but oil and water didn't mix.
나는 기름을 물에 섞으려고 했지만 기름과 물은 섞이지 않았습니다.

To prepare for an examination is the best way to pass the exam.
시험에서는 준비하는 것이 그 시험에 합격하는 최선의 길이다.

She pushed him away, and she pushed the door open and ran away.
그녀는 그를 밀쳐냈고, 문을 밀어 열고 달아났습니다.

This building has been rebuilt after it had been destroyed by an earthquake.
이 건물은 지진에 무너진 뒤 다시 지어졌습니다.

DAY 06 Vocabulary

➢ 음원을 들으면서 소리를 무조건 따라해 보시오. (빠르기&정확도/브레인+마우스 운동)

thank

to express gratitude or appreciation to

give thanks, acknowledge

~에게 고맙다, 고마워하다

I thanked him for inviting me and he thanked me for the present.

emigrate

to emigrate is to leave a native country, but to immigrate is to settle in a new country

immigrate, migrate, transmigrate

이주해가다

He has emigrated from Vietnam, so we can call him as a Vietnamese immigrant.

heat

to make or become hot or warm, or heat up

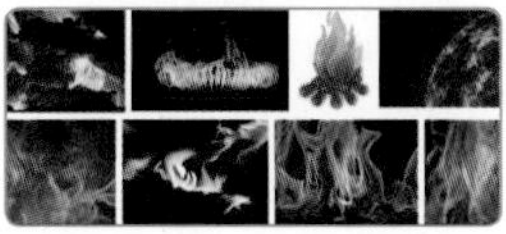

warm, make hot

뜨겁게 하다, 가열하다, 뜨거워지다, 열

The Sun heats up the land and sea while the Earth rotates into sunlight.

produce

to bring forth

make, yield, cause, create

생산하다, 낳다, 만들다

This factory produces goods for export and that factory produces goods for domestic use.

* 이미지는 구글에서 찾은 것으로, 단어와 이미지가 다를 수 있습니다. 'Test 3'에서 나만의 이미지를 그려볼 수 있습니다.

Test 1 Connecting Exercise

Score(/16)
Self-Evaluation

➢ 서로 맞는 것을 연결하시오.

Ⓐ 1~4 영어 단어와 우리말 뜻 연결하기

1	emigrate	뜨겁게 하다, 가열하다, 뜨거워지다, 열
2	thank	~에게 고맙다, 고마워하다
3	heat	이주해가다
4	produce	생산하다, 낳다, 만들다

Ⓑ 5~8 영어 단어와 영어 설명 연결하기

5	thank	to bring forth
6	emigrate	to make or become hot or warm, or heat up
7	heat	to emigrate is to leave a native country, but to immigrate is to settle in a new country
8	produce	to express gratitude or appreciation to

Ⓒ 9~12 영어 단어와 동의어 연결하기

9	heat	give thanks, acknowledge
10	produce	immigrate, migrate, transmigrate
11	emigrate	make, yield, cause, create
12	thank	warm, make hot

Ⓓ 13~16 우리말 뜻과 영어 단어 연결하기

13	이주해가다	produce
14	생산하다, 낳다, 만들다	thank
15	뜨겁게 하다, 가열하다, 뜨거워지다, 열	emigrate
16	~에게 고맙다, 고마워하다	heat

Test 2 Writing Exercise

Score(/12)
Self-Evaluation

A 1~4 다음 단어에 맞는 뜻을 쓰시오.

1 produce ______
2 emigrate ______
3 thank ______
4 heat ______

B 5~8 다음 뜻에 맞는 영어 단어와 영어 동의어, 영어 설명을 쓰시오.

5 생산하다, 낳다, 만들다

______ ______

______

6 이주해가다

______ ______

______

7 뜨겁게 하다, 가열하다, 뜨거워지다, 열

______ ______

______

8 ~에게 고맙다, 고마워하다

______ ______

______

C 9~12 다음 영어 문장을 의미가 떠오를 때까지 소리 내어 읽어보시오. 3.5초 이내

9 The Sun heats up the land and sea while the Earth rotates into sunlight.

______

10 He has emigrated from Vietnam, so we can call him as a Vietnamese immigrant.

______

11 I thanked him for inviting me and he thanked me for the present.

______

12 This factory produces goods for export and that factory produces goods for domestic use.

______

Test 3 Imaging Exercise

➢ 다음 단어에 맞는 나만의 짧은 영어 설명을 써보자. (또는 그림을 그려보자.)

thank
[θæŋk]

emigrate
[émigrèit]

heat
[hiːt]

produce
[prədjúːs]

➢ Month 07-DAY 06 영어 문장과 우리말

I thanked him for inviting me and he thanked me for the present.
나는 그에게 나를 초대해 준 것에 감사했고, 그는 내가 준 선물에 감사했다.

He has emigrated from Vietnam, so we can call him as a Vietnamese immigrant.
그는 베트남에서 이민왔기 때문에 그를 베트남 이민자라 부를 수 있습니다.

The Sun heats up the land and sea while the Earth rotates into sunlight.
지구가 햇빛을 받으며 회전하는 동안 태양은 바다와 육지를 가열합니다.

This factory produces goods for export and that factory produces goods for domestic use.
이 공장은 수출용 상품을 생산하고, 저 공장은 내수용 상품을 생산합니다.

Vocabulary

➢ 음원을 들으면서 소리를 무조건 따라해 보시오. (빠르기&정확도/브레인+마우스 운동)

sail

to travel by water in a vessel

cruise, voyage

항해하다

The Voyager 1 probe is sailing until now after launching on September 5, 1977.

seal

to close or fasten with a seal

close, secure, shut

봉하다, 날인하다

He sealed the box and put down the address and put on a stamp.

bump

to strike or collide with

knock, hit, strike, crash, collide

부딪치다, 충돌하다

I bumped the chair with a knee. Or I bumped a knee against the chair.

comb

to smooth, arrange, or adorn (the hair) with a comb

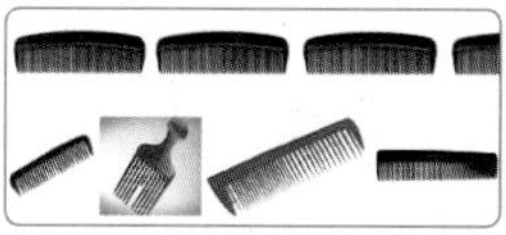

untangle, arrange

빗, 빗질하다

She combed her hair with a comb, but he combed his hair with his fingers.

* 이미지는 구글에서 찾은 것으로, 단어와 이미지가 다를 수 있습니다. 'Test 3'에서 나만의 이미지를 그려볼 수 있습니다.

Test 1 Connecting Exercise

Score(/16)
Self-Evaluation

➢ 서로 맞는 것을 연결하시오.

Ⓐ 1~4 영어 단어와 우리말 뜻 연결하기

1 bump	•	• 빗, 빗질하다
2 comb	•	• 봉하다, 날인하다
3 seal	•	• 부딪치다, 충돌하다
4 sail	•	• 항해하다

Ⓑ 5~8 영어 단어와 영어 설명 연결하기

5 bump	•	• to travel by water in a vessel
6 seal	•	• to strike or collide with
7 comb	•	• to close or fasten with a seal
8 sail	•	• to smooth, arrange, or adorn (the hair) with a comb

Ⓒ 9~12 영어 단어와 동의어 연결하기

9 bump	•	• cruise, voyage
10 seal	•	• untangle, arrange
11 sail	•	• close, secure, shut
12 comb	•	• knock, hit, strike, crash, collide

Ⓓ 13~16 우리말 뜻과 영어 단어 연결하기

13 빗, 빗질하다	•	• comb
14 봉하다, 날인하다	•	• sail
15 항해하다	•	• bump
16 부딪치다, 충돌하다	•	• seal

Test 2 Writing Exercise

Score(/12)
Self-Evaluation

Ⓐ 1~4 다음 단어에 맞는 뜻을 쓰시오.

1 comb ______

2 sail ______

3 seal ______

4 bump ______

Ⓑ 5~8 다음 뜻에 맞는 영어 단어와 영어 동의어, 영어 설명을 쓰시오.

5 봉하다, 날인하다

______ ______

______

6 빗, 빗질하다

______ ______

______

7 항해하다

______ ______

______

8 부딪치다, 충돌하다

______ ______

______

Ⓒ 9~12 다음 영어 문장을 의미가 떠오를 때까지 소리 내어 읽어보시오. 3.5초 이내

9 He sealed the box and put down the address and put on a stamp.

______

10 The Voyager 1 probe is sailing until now after launching on September 5, 1977.

______

11 She combed her hair with a comb, but he combed his hair with his fingers.

______

12 I bumped the chair with a knee. Or I bumped a knee against the chair.

______

Test 3 Imaging Exercise

➢ 다음 단어에 맞는 나만의 짧은 영어 설명을 써보자. (또는 그림을 그려보자.)

sail
[seil]

seal
[siːl]

bump
[bʌmp]

comb
[koum]

➢ Month 07-DAY 07 영어 문장과 우리말

The Voyager 1 probe is sailing until now after launching on September 5, 1977.
보이저 1호 탐사선은 1977년 9월 5일 발사된 이후 지금까지 항해하고 있습니다.

He sealed the box and put down the address and put on a stamp.
그는 박스를 봉인하고 주소를 기입하고 우표를 붙였습니다.

I bumped the chair with a knee. Or I bumped a knee against the chair.
나는 의자에 무릎이 부딪쳤다.

She combed her hair with a comb, but he combed his hair with his fingers.
그녀는 빗으로 그녀의 머리를 빗었으나, 그는 손가락으로 그의 머리를 빗었다.

DAY 08 Vocabulary

➢ 음원을 들으면서 소리를 무조건 따라해 보시오. (빠르기&정확도/브레인+마우스 운동)

compare

to examine in order to observe similarities and differences

contrast, collate, set against

비교하다, 비유하다

When you compare things, you consider how they are different and how they are similar.

bake

to cook food with dry heat

cook, roast, warm up

굽다

A baker is a person who bakes, a bakery is a place where baking is done.

crash

(of moving objects) to collide, esp. violently and noisily

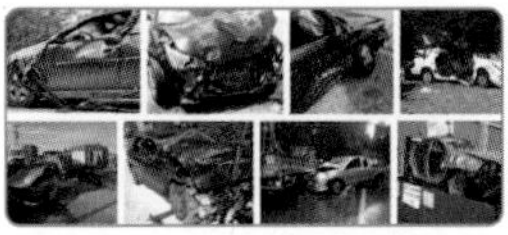

clash, smash, collide, collision

충돌하다, 박살나다, 큰 소리로 부서지다

The car crashed into a tree and the window glass crashed to pieces on the floor.

imagine

to form a mental picture or image of

think, suppose, conjecture

상상하다

You can use an -ing form after imagine, but don't use a to-infinitive after imagine.

* 이미지는 구글에서 찾은 것으로, 단어와 이미지가 다를 수 있습니다. 'Test 3'에서 나만의 이미지를 그려볼 수 있습니다.

Test 1 Connecting Exercise

Score(/16)
Self-Evaluation

➢ 서로 맞는 것을 연결하시오.

Ⓐ 1~4 영어 단어와 우리말 뜻 연결하기

1 compare	•	• 굽다
2 bake	•	• 충돌하다, 박살나다, 큰 소리로 부서지다
3 imagine	•	• 상상하다
4 crash	•	• 비교하다, 비유하다

Ⓑ 5~8 영어 단어와 영어 설명 연결하기

5 crash	•	• to cook food with dry heat
6 bake	•	• (of moving objects) to collide, esp. violently and noisily
7 compare	•	• to form a mental picture or image of
8 imagine	•	• to examine in order to observe similarities and differences

Ⓒ 9~12 영어 단어와 동의어 연결하기

9 bake	•	• cook, roast, warm up
10 imagine	•	• think, suppose, conjecture
11 compare	•	• contrast, collate, set against
12 crash	•	• clash, smash, collide, collision

Ⓓ 13~16 우리말 뜻과 영어 단어 연결하기

13 상상하다	•	• crash
14 충돌하다, 박살나다, 큰 소리로 부서지다	•	• bake
15 굽다	•	• imagine
16 비교하다, 비유하다	•	• compare

Test 2 Writing Exercise

Score(/12)
Self-Evaluation

A 1~4 다음 단어에 맞는 뜻을 쓰시오.

1 crash ______________________

2 bake ______________________

3 compare ______________________

4 imagine ______________________

B 5~8 다음 뜻에 맞는 영어 단어와 영어 동의어, 영어 설명을 쓰시오.

5 상상하다

______________ ______________________

____

6 충돌하다, 박살나다, 큰 소리로 부서지다

______________ ______________________

____

7 굽다

______________ ______________________

____

8 비교하다, 비유하다

______________ ______________________

____

C 9~12 다음 영어 문장을 의미가 떠오를 때까지 소리 내어 읽어보시오. 4초 이내

9 A baker is a person who bakes, a bakery is a place where baking is done.

____

10 You can use an -ing form after imagine, but don't use a to-infinitive after imagine.

____

11 The car crashed into a tree and the window glass crashed to pieces on the floor.

____

12 When you compare things, you consider how they are different and how they are similar.

____

Test 3 Imaging Exercise

➢ 다음 단어에 맞는 나만의 짧은 영어 설명을 써보자. (또는 그림을 그려보자.)

compare
[kəmpέər]

bake
[beik]

crash
[kræʃ]

imagine
[imǽdʒin]

➢ Month 07-DAY 08 영어 문장과 우리말

When you compare things, you consider how they are different and how they are similar.
비교를 할 때, 얼마나 다른지 얼마나 비슷한지를 생각합니다.

A baker is a person who bakes, a bakery is a place where baking is done.
베이커는 굽는 사람을 말하고, 베이커리는 굽는 일이 일어나는 곳을 말한다.

The car crashed into a tree and the window glass crashed to pieces on the floor.
차가 나무에 충돌하였고, 유리창이 바닥에 박살나 흩어졌습니다.

You can use an -ing form after imagine, but don't use a to-infinitive after imagine.
'imagine' 다음에 –ing 형태는 사용합니다만 to–부정사는 사용하지 않습니다.

Vocabulary

➢ 음원을 들으면서 소리를 무조건 따라해 보시오. (빠르기&정확도/브레인+마우스 운동)

print

to reproduce on a paper surface or a digital surface

publish, copy, reproduce, issue

인쇄하다, 발행하다, 프린트하다, 인쇄

You can print a document to PDF files and you can print it on a paper.

rear

to care for and educate (children) until maturity

bring up, raise, breed, build

(성숙할 때까지) 기르다, 교육하다, 세우다, 뒤쪽, 뒤쪽의

She has reared six children and also reared six cows in the rear of the house.

reserve

to keep back, or to arrange in advance

withhold, save, book, make a reservation for

(예비로) 보유하다, (미리) 예약하다

I'd like to reserve a table for four people for tonight at eight o'clock.

state

to set forth in words

declare, phase, province

(말로 상황을) 설명하다, 진술하다, (현상의) 상태, 미국의 주

He stated that The United States of America is a federal republic consisting of 50 states.

* 이미지는 구글에서 찾은 것으로, 단어와 이미지가 다를 수 있습니다. 'Test 3'에서 나만의 이미지를 그려볼 수 있습니다.

Test 1 Connecting Exercise

Score(　　/16)
Self-Evaluation

➢ 서로 맞는 것을 연결하시오.

Ⓐ 1~4 영어 단어와 우리말 뜻 연결하기

1 state	●	● 인쇄하다, 발행하다, 프린트하다, 인쇄
2 rear	●	● (말로 상황을) 설명하다, 진술하다, (현상의) 상태, 미국의 주
3 print	●	● (성숙할 때까지) 기르다, 교육하다, 세우다, 뒤쪽, 뒤쪽의
4 reserve	●	● (예비로) 보유하다, (미리) 예약하다

Ⓑ 5~8 영어 단어와 영어 설명 연결하기

5 rear	●	● to care for and educate (children) until maturity
6 print	●	● to reproduce on a paper surface or a digital surface
7 state	●	● to keep back, or to arrange in advance
8 reserve	●	● to set forth in words

Ⓒ 9~12 영어 단어와 동의어 연결하기

9 reserve	●	● withhold, save, book, make a reservation for
10 state	●	● declare, phase, province
11 print	●	● publish, copy, reproduce, issue
12 rear	●	● bring up, raise, breed, build

Ⓓ 13~16 우리말 뜻과 영어 단어 연결하기

13 인쇄하다, 발행하다, 프린트하다, 인쇄	●	● print
14 (예비로) 보유하다, (미리) 예약하다	●	● state
15 (성숙할 때까지) 기르다, 교육하다, 세우다, 뒤쪽, 뒤쪽의	●	● rear
16 (말로 상황을) 설명하다, 진술하다, (현상의) 상태, 미국의 주	●	● reserve

Test 2 Writing Exercise

Score(/12)
Self-Evaluation

A 1~4 다음 단어에 맞는 뜻을 쓰시오.

1 print ______

2 state ______

3 rear ______

4 reserve ______

B 5~8 다음 뜻에 맞는 영어 단어와 영어 동의어, 영어 설명을 쓰시오.

5 (성숙할 때까지) 기르다, 교육하다, 세우다, 뒤쪽, 뒤쪽의

______ ______

______

6 (말로 상황을) 설명하다, 진술하다, (현상의) 상태, 미국의 주

______ ______

______

7 (예비로) 보유하다, (미리) 예약하다

______ ______

______

8 인쇄하다, 발행하다, 프린트하다, 인쇄

______ ______

______

C 9~12 다음 영어 문장을 의미가 떠오를 때까지 소리 내어 읽어보시오. 1.5초 이내

9 You can print a document to PDF files and you can print it on a paper.

______

10 I'd like to reserve a table for four people for tonight at eight o'clock.

______

11 He stated that The United States of America is a federal republic consisting of 50 states.

______

12 She has reared six children and also reared six cows in the rear of the house.

______

Test 3 Imaging Exercise

➢ 다음 단어에 맞는 나만의 짧은 영어 설명을 써보자. (또는 그림을 그려보자.)

print
[print]

rear
[riər]

reserve
[rizə́ːrv]

state
[steit]

➢ Month 07-DAY 09 영어 문장과 우리말

You can print a document to PDF files and you can print it on a paper.
당신은 문서를 PDF 파일로 프린트할 수 있고, 그것을 종이에 프린트할 수 있습니다.

She has reared six children and also reared six cows in the rear of the house.
그녀는 6명의 아이들을 키웠고, 집 뒤쪽에 6마리의 암소도 키웠습니다.

I'd like to reserve a table for four people for tonight at eight o'clock.
오늘 저녁 8시 네 명의 테이블을 예약하고 싶습니다.

He stated that The United States of America is a federal republic consisting of 50 states.
미국은 50개 주로 구성된 연방공화국이라고 그는 설명했습니다.

Vocabulary

➢ 음원을 들으면서 소리를 무조건 따라해 보시오. (빠르기&정확도/브레인+마우스 운동)

hire

to engage the services of (a person) for a fee

employ, engage, rent

고용하다, 채용하다,
돈을 주고 부리다, 채용, 고용

An employee is a worker who is hired, and an employer is someone who hires an employee.

rent

to use (another's property) in return for regular payments

hire, lease

(임대로) 빌리다, 빌려주다, 임대료가
얼마에 나와 있다, 돈을 주고 부리다

I rent my apartment to my friend for $100 a month, but the other apartments rent for $1,200.

rise, rose, risen

to get up from a lying, sitting, kneeling, or prone position

ascend, climb, soar, mount

일어나다, 뜨다

The Sun, the Moon, the planets, and the stars all rise in the east and set in the west.

appreciate

to feel thankful or grateful for

value, regard, respect, admire

감사하다, 가치를 인정하다,
가치를 알다

Thanks. I really appreciate your help. I'd like to invite you. I would really appreciate it if you could come.

* 이미지는 구글에서 찾은 것으로, 단어와 이미지가 다를 수 있습니다. 'Test 3'에서 나만의 이미지를 그려볼 수 있습니다.

Test 1 Connecting Exercise

Score(/16)
Self-Evaluation

➢ 서로 맞는 것을 연결하시오.

Ⓐ 1~4 영어 단어와 우리말 뜻 연결하기

1 hire	●	● 일어나다, 뜨다
2 rise, rose, risen	●	● 감사하다, 가치를 인정하다, 가치를 알다
3 rent	●	● (임대로) 빌리다, 빌려주다, 임대료가 얼마에 나와 있다, 돈을 주고 부리다
4 appreciate	●	● 고용하다, 채용하다, 돈을 주고 부리다, 채용, 고용

Ⓑ 5~8 영어 단어와 영어 설명 연결하기

5 hire	●	● to feel thankful or grateful for
6 rent	●	● to use (another's property) in return for regular payments
7 rise, rose, risen	●	● to engage the services of (a person) for a fee
8 appreciate	●	● to get up from a lying, sitting, kneeling, or prone position

Ⓒ 9~12 영어 단어와 동의어 연결하기

9 rent	●	● employ, engage, rent
10 appreciate	●	● ascend, climb, soar, mount
11 rise, rose, risen	●	● hire, lease
12 hire	●	● value, regard, respect, admire

Ⓓ 13~16 우리말 뜻과 영어 단어 연결하기

13 일어나다, 뜨다	●	● rent
14 감사하다, 가치를 인정하다, 가치를 알다	●	● appreciate
15 고용하다, 채용하다, 돈을 주고 부리다, 채용, 고용	●	● rise, rose, risen
16 (임대로) 빌리다, 빌려주다, 임대료가 얼마에 나와 있다, 돈을 주고 부리다	●	● hire

Test 2 Writing Exercise

Score(/12)
Self-Evaluation

A 1~4 다음 단어에 맞는 뜻을 쓰시오.

1 rise, rose, risen ______

2 hire ______

3 rent ______

4 appreciate ______

B 5~8 다음 뜻에 맞는 영어 단어와 영어 동의어, 영어 설명을 쓰시오.

5 일어나다, 뜨다

______ ______

______

6 감사하다, 가치를 인정하다, 가치를 알다

______ ______

______

7 고용하다, 채용하다, 돈을 주고 부리다, 채용, 고용

______ ______

______

8 (임대로) 빌리다, 빌려주다, 임대료가 얼마에 나와 있다, 돈을 주고 부리다

______ ______

______

C 9~12 다음 영어 문장을 의미가 떠오를 때까지 소리 내어 읽어보시오. 4초 이내

9 I rent my apartment to my friend for $100 a month, but the other apartments rent for $1,200.

______

10 The Sun, the Moon, the planets, and the stars all rise in the east and set in the west.

______

11 An employee is a worker who is hired, and an employer is someone who hires an employee.

______

12 Thanks. I really appreciate your help. I'd like to invite you. I would really appreciate it if you could come.

______

Test 3 Imaging Exercise

➤ 다음 단어에 맞는 나만의 짧은 영어 설명을 써보자. (또는 그림을 그려보자.)

hire
[haiər]

rent
[rent]

rise, rose, risen
[raiz, rouz, rízn]

appreciate
[əpríːʃièit]

➤ Month 07-DAY 10 영어 문장과 우리말

An employee is a worker who is hired, and an employer is someone who hires an employee.
고용자는 고용되어지는 근로자이고, 고용주는 고용자를 고용하는 사람입니다.

I rent my apartment to my friend for $100 a month, but the other apartments rent for $1,200.
나는 친구에게 월 100달러에 아파트를 임대합니다만 다른 아파트는 임대료가 천달러입니다.

The Sun, the Moon, the planets, and the stars all rise in the east and set in the west.
태양과 달과 행성, 그리고 별들은 모두 동쪽에서 뜨고 서쪽으로 집니다.

Thanks. I really appreciate your help. I'd like to invite you. I would really appreciate it if you could come.
감사합니다. 도와주셔서 정말로 감사드립니다. 당신을 초대하고 싶습니다. 와 주신다면 정말로 고맙겠습니다.

찾아보기

S

귀가 트이는
보카팟 ABC 단어장 BASIC 동사편

지은이 최종근
펴낸이 조승식
펴낸곳 (주) 도서출판 북스힐
등 록 제22-457호(1998년 7월 28일)
주 소 서울시 강북구 한천로 153길 17
인스타그램 @bookshill_official
블로그 blog.naver.com/booksgogo
이메일 bookshill@bookshill.com
전 화 (02) 994-0071
팩 스 (02) 994-0073

2024년 5월 1일 2판 1쇄 인쇄
2024년 5월 5일 2판 1쇄 발행

값 18,000원

ISBN 979-11-5971-573-0